THE TREE

CEDRIC GROLET

MY INSPIRATION

FRUITS

CEDRIC GROLET

FRUIT

THE ART OF PASTRY

DUCASSE
EDITION

FOREWORD

I could sing Cédric Grolet's praises here. There would certainly be enough accolades for this thirtysomething who has spent half his life accumulating awards and distinctions. But because Cédric is the pastry chef at l'Hôtel Le Meurice in Paris, I would doubtless be suspected of bias. I could also tell the food lover reading this book that the recipes presented here are as good to eat as they are beautiful to look at. I would know: I've tasted them all, and they have all seduced me with their absolute precision. But I prefer to leave this delicious surprise to each reader.

So I must discuss the only topic left: Cédric Grolet's extraordinary vision.

Cédric is guided by two requirements. First, simplicity — and everyone knows that this is a complex goal to reach, because it means giving up on ease, pruning away unnecessary things, and keeping only the essential. Second, to be inspired by nature. In the world of confectionery, this ambition opens up new and promising fields. You have only to see Cédric choosing the lemon that has the acidity and texture that will best suit his project, or weighing up the merits of cream matured by one producer or another. Placing the product at the center of his work is a radical perspective shift that leads him to redefine the work of his profession. No pastry chef before him has ever borrowed the techniques of cooking, such as reduction, concentration, and even roasting, with such intelligence.

This book will have a place in history.

Alain Ducasse

PREFACE

When my customers ask me "Why fruit?," I tell them that this focus comes, above all, from the simple way my parents raised me. When I went to school, I took fruit plucked from the tree as a snack. I could tell a long tale of snacking on fruit like this.

For me, the key goal of this book is emphasizing the importance of fruit and the fundamental role it plays in confectionery, whether it comes from our own gardens or the other side of the world. I'm constantly asking myself how to pay homage to it in the best possible way. For this reason, I never forget that every fruit is unique, and that its flavor should be underlined in a specific way. Citrus fruit, for example, shows off all its strength in fresh preparations, while the taste of strawberries is best distinguished when they are cooked simply, warm with a little sugar and a drizzle of olive oil.

This book isn't written for any reader in particular. I would love it if everyone — professionals, seasoned pastry chefs, and everyday home cooks — could make one or another of my recipes. There are many fruit tarts, cookies, and plated desserts that can be easily done at home and are relatively quick to make. Others, such as fruit sculptures — which I do without using a mold and which, in my view, require highly developed skills — are more specialized and difficult to do at home. All kinds of readers can find their level here.

Generally speaking, I love to do and talk about simple things. For this reason, fruit is a perfect subject for me, because everyone loves it. The important thing is that people understand that fruit is for eating. Let's turn, therefore, to the selection of the best possible fruit: Is it good as it is, without any further preparation? Is it ripe enough? Is it in season? Respecting the unique nature of a fruit is the first step toward making an excellent dessert. Next, one must think of a seasoning that will highlight its character and elevate it, generating real emotion and evoking memories. Certain fruit is naturally good as it is, but it can be even better when its flavor is concentrated, reducing it to its essence. I'm not really satisfied until a dessert I've prepared surpasses the goodness of the original fruit.

I could spend hours talking to you about a fruit and telling you its story!

— Cédric Grolet

All Cédric Grolet creations can be found on his Instagram account @cedricgrolet. And you can share your photos with us using #cedricgrolet and #CGfruits.

I began making confectionery when I was thirteen years old, working alongside my grandfather, who had a big hotel where he did the cooking. What attracted me, really, were the sweet things. Therefore, I began my first training course in confectionery at the age of fourteen, as well as a professional two-year confectionery course. I remember that as a student, I couldn't sit still. Making confectionery helped me mature and really let me thrive. And it's let me continue to grow and thrive ever since. Driven by my participation in a number of competitions, I signed up for another two years of study at a technical school in Yssingeaux. Then came the great leap. I plucked up my courage and went to try my luck in Paris. The idea was to take a step toward meeting the greats. The first stop on this initial voyage: Fauchon. I built my range at the heart of this iconic establishment alongside three extraordinary chefs, each of whom, in his way, influenced the philosophy I have today. Christophe Adam taught me creativity, Benoît Couvrand provided me with structure, and Christophe Appert led me to caprice and dynamism. They really thought of me as their little pastry-chef-to-be, and I threw myself into all the different jobs I took. This gave me the opportunity to experiment with a lot of things, to see the whole world and expand my horizons considerably. However, after five years, I felt that I'd gotten all I could, and told myself that it was time to move on to new pastures. At twenty-five, I joined Yannick Alléno and Camille Lesecq at Meurice. It was a slap in the face. The level of performance demanded was like nothing I'd ever seen, and I was uneasy, lost. I realized that I desperately needed to understand flavor, and I was supported in this quest by Alléno and Lesecq. When they left in 2012, I took over the role of pastry chef. It was at this moment that Alain Ducasse arrived, with Christophe Saintagne at his side, and it would be a turning point in my career. Even if there were some bumps at the beginning, Alain Ducasse, with his distinctive identity, held the keys to my success. He was hard, firm, and fair. "Stop making pretty things, work on taste," he told me. With Saintagne in the kitchen, I spent an entire year questioning myself; this was the most important driving force in my journey. Every day, he told me about taste, seasoning, boldness, association, texture, and so on, never letting me catch a breath until I had begun to understand. I was sad to see him leave Meurice, because we'd become a good pair. Fortunately, I recaptured the same balance with Jocelyn Herland, who took up the reins in the kitchen.

Now, I'm working directly with Alain Ducasse. He knows who I am, respects me, and gives me my freedom. Not a day passes when he's not interested in what I'm doing, what drives me to search for boldness and perfection. I'm a great admirer of this visionary chef, and I'm very lucky to have this relationship with him. It is important to me to have reached this point, but I could never have done it without my collaborators. I have always been taught that you must know how to choose those around you. I have a formidable team behind me, working day in and day out to help me push toward perfection. My two sous chefs, Yohann Caron and Thibault Hauchard, have an important role. I give them more and more freedom; they are very good pastry chefs and, thanks to them, I can give myself over completely to creation. These days, my process is simple: I step back, I sketch broadly, and I reflect. I think in terms of season, form, and boldness, associating between them to come up with my desserts. Then my chefs take the baton and, following my directions, propose different trial versions. I taste any number of things, but always with a fresh palate — when I'm not hungry. If a dessert doesn't completely satisfy me, I send it to be remade. It is not until I've begun to find the right flavor that the construction of the dessert in its final form can begin. Then, when everything is perfect, and not a moment before, we put it on the menu. At that point, I gather the impressions of the customers. Thanks to their feedback, my palate expands even more. My current goal is to enrich my confectionery through travel, as I see Alain Ducasse doing. I go all over the world to share my knowledge, and it's fascinating. In every country, people ask me different questions, derived from their cultures and their tastes, and their reactions are never the same. This makes me grow.

This book, which is my first — and which is a dream come true for me — is very important in this way. It lets me examine things from all angles, to step back and gain perspective and to see what I can still improve. I see this as a new way to grow; it makes me question myself. Indeed, what is confectionery but a perpetual process of questioning? If a dessert is pleasing today, it must also be pleasing tomorrow.

CEDRIC GROLET
A FEW DATES

2000
began his professional training as a pastry chef

2006
began working at Fauchon

2011
became sous chef at Meurice

2013
became pastry chef at Meurice

2015
named Pastry Chef of the Year by *Le Chef* magazine

2016
received the Pastry Chef of the Year Excellence Award from Relais Desserts

2016
received the Pastry Chef of the Year trophy from Les Toques Blanches

2017
named Pastry Chef of the Year by Omnivore

Cédric Grolet

CONTENTS

CIT
FRU

CITRUS FRUIT

BERGAMOT

In season

January and February

Choosing fruit

the fruit should have a smooth skin without any brown blemishes

Average weight

between 3¼ and 6¼ ounces (90 and 180 g)

Storage

at room temperature for 1 week, in the refrigerator vegetable drawer for 2 weeks

Flavor pairings

Mirabelle plums, cream cheese, raspberry

LEMON

In season

year-round, according to the location of origin

Choosing fruit

ideally organic or pesticide-free; the fruit should be bright yellow, heavy, and firm

Average weight

4¼ ounces (120 g)

Storage

at room temperature for 8 days, in the refrigerator vegetable drawer for 10 days

Flavor pairings

pepper, honey, verbena

DRIED LIME

Fruit source
lime dried until it blackens

Storage
in a dry place in an airtight container

Flavor pairings
peach, Timut pepper (Sichuan peppercorn), strawberry

LIME

In season
year-round, according to the location of origin

Choosing fruit
the fruit should be firm and a bright, brilliant green

Average weight
3½ ounces (100 g)

Storage
in the refrigerator vegetable drawer for 15 days

Flavor pairings
tarragon, shiso, mint

CLEMENTINE

In season

November to January

Choosing fruit

the firmness of the fruit is more important than its color, as is its aroma

Average weight

2½ ounces (70 g)

Storage

at room temperature for 6 days, in the refrigerator vegetable drawer for 10 days

Flavor pairings

chocolate, quince, walnut

KUMQUAT

In season

November and December

Choosing fruit

the fruit should be a bright, unblemished yellow, and give when squeezed gently

Average weight

½ ounce (15 g)

Storage

at room temperature for 4 days, in the refrigerator vegetable drawer for 2 to 3 weeks

Flavor pairings

lime, cinnamon, pepper

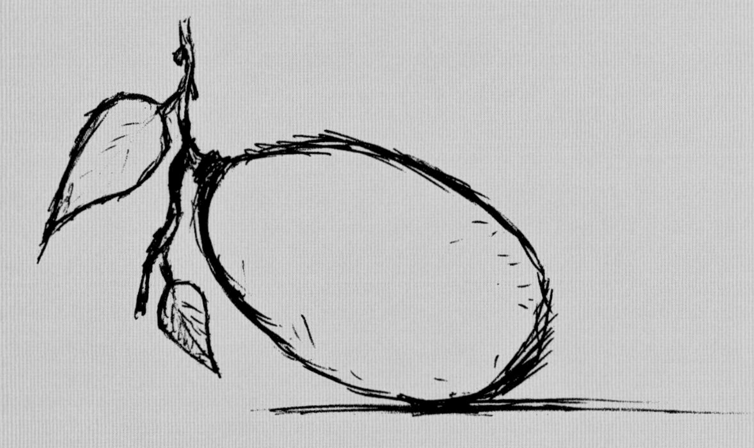

ORANGE

In season

November to April

Choosing fruit

the firmness of the fruit is more important than its color

Average weight

7 ounces (200 g)

Storage

at room temperature for 1 week, in the refrigerator vegetable drawer for 10 days

Flavor pairings

chocolate, anise flower, kirsch

POMELO

In season

year-round, according to the location of origin

Choosing fruit

the fruit should be heavy, firm, smooth, and bright

Average weight

14 ounces (400 g)

Storage

at room temperature for 10 days, in the refrigerator vegetable drawer for 8 days

Flavor pairings

rum, vodka, pear, fromage blanc

PREPARATION TIME: 2 HOURS 30 MINUTES

MAKES 10 PEBBLES

COOKING TIME: 10 MINUTES

RESTING TIME: 1 HOUR 50 MINUTES

BERGAMOT

FOR THE JOCONDE CAKE

4½ large (225 g) eggs (1 cup)
1¾ cups (170 g) confectioners' sugar
1¾ cups (170 g) ground almonds
⅓ cup (45 g) all-purpose flour
2½ tablespoons (35 g) unsalted butter
4½ large (150 g) egg whites (⅔ cup)
2 tablespoons (25 g) superfine sugar

FOR THE BERGAMOT GELATIN CENTER

1 cup (230 g) bergamot juice
1½ tablespoons (15 g) superfine sugar
1 teaspoon (8 g) agar powder
1 fresh bergamot (6 ounces/170 g)
3½ tablespoons (15 g) Earl Grey tea leaves

FOR THE LEMON CHEESECAKE

⅔ cup (160 g) Philadelphia cream cheese
½ cup (120 g) fromage blanc or Greek yogurt
¼ cup (40 g) superfine sugar
5 teaspoons (25 g) lemon juice
Zest of 4 lemons
¼ cup (50 g) olive oil

FOR THE SHINY GOLD GLOSS

2 tablespoons (25 g) glucose
1½ teaspoons (2.5 g) edible gold luster dust
⅓ cup (75 g) superfine sugar
1 teaspoon (2.5 g) kappa carrageenan

FOR THE YELLOW COATING

7 ounces (200 g) white couverture chocolate
¾ cup plus 2 tablespoons (200 g) cocoa butter
1 teaspoon (4 g) yellow fat-soluble food coloring

TIP

Wear gloves when molding the pebbles.

FOR THE JOCONDE CAKE

Preheat the oven to 360°F (180°C). In an electric stand mixer fitted with a whisk attachment, beat together the whole eggs, confectioners' sugar, and almonds. Add the flour, then the butter. Set aside. Use the mixer with the whisk attachment to beat the egg whites, then add the superfine sugar and beat until firm. Fold the beaten whites into the almond mixture and spread on a baking sheet. Bake for 6 minutes. Remove from the sheet and place the cake in a 12 by 16-inch (30 by 40-cm) baking dish.

FOR THE BERGAMOT GELATIN CENTER

In a saucepan, heat ⅓ cup (80 g) water and the bergamot juice, then add the sugar mixed with the agar. Boil for 2 minutes and cool rapidly by placing the pan in the freezer for 20 minutes. When the gelatin is cold, mix with an immersion blender, being careful not to beat in any air. Separate the fresh bergamot into suprêmes and add them to the gelatin. Chop the Earl Grey tea and add to the gelatin. Pour the resulting mixture over the joconde cake and freeze for 30 minutes.

FOR THE LEMON CHEESECAKE

Mix the cream cheese with the fromage blanc, superfine sugar, lemon juice and zest, and oil. Pour over the bergamot gelatin and spread using a spatula. Freeze for 1 hour, then use a cookie cutter to cut out ten 4-inch (10-cm)-diameter disks and ten 1½-inch (4-cm)-diameter disks. Shape them into pebbles, using a knife to trim off the sharp corners, then molding them into a natural shape using your hands.

FOR THE SHINY GOLD GLOSS

Heat 1 cup (250 g) water with the glucose and gold luster dust. Mix the superfine sugar and carrageenan and add to the warm liquid. Bring to a boil, then remove from the heat and let cool, about 20 minutes. Put into a bowl set over a saucepan of simmering water to remelt the cold, gelled kappa, stirring constantly to remove any flakes that form on the surface.

FOR COATING, ASSEMBLY, AND FINISHING

Make the yellow coating as described on page 317. Heat it to 80°F (25°C) and coat the pebbles completely. Wait 1 minute, then glaze them by dipping them in the gold gloss heated to 130 to 140°F (55 to 60°C).

BERGAMOT

½ cup (1 stick/125 g) unsalted butter
1 tablespoon (18 g) Béton honey
1¾ large (87 g) eggs (⅓ cup), at room temperature
2½ tablespoons (37 g) milk, warmed
⅓ cup (80 g) superfine sugar
Zest of 2 bergamots, grated with a Microplane
1½ teaspoons (2.5 g) Earl Grey tea leaves, chopped
1 cup (125 g) cake flour
1½ teaspoons (6 g) baking powder

Preheat the oven to 390°F (200°C). In a saucepan, heat the butter until it browns. Remove from the heat and mix in the honey to melt it.

In a large bowl, beat the room-temperature eggs with the warm milk, the superfine sugar, bergamot zest, and tea leaves. Sift together the flour and baking powder and stir them into the egg mixture. Add the warm brown butter mixture. Pour into a pastry bag and pipe to fill the indentations of a stainless steel 3-inch (8-cm) madeleine pan, using a little less than 1 ounce (25 g) batter for each madeleine. Bake for 20 minutes.

PREPARATION TIME: 30 MINUTES

MAKES 20 MADELEINES

COOKING TIME: 6 MINUTES

PREPARATION TIME: 2 HOURS 30 MINUTES

SERVES 10

COOKING TIME: 5 MINUTES

RESTING TIME: 12 HOURS PLUS 3 HOURS 20 MINUTES

LEMONS

FOR THE WHIPPED YUZU GANACHE

1 teaspoon (3 g) gelatin powder
2¼ cups (530 g) whipping cream
5 ounces (140 g) white couverture chocolate, chopped
½ cup (120 g) yuzu juice

FOR THE LEMON GEL CENTERS

¾ cup (180 g) lemon juice
2½ tablespoons (30 g) superfine sugar
¾ teaspoon (5 g) agar powder
⅓ cup (15 g) chopped fresh mint
4 to 5 finger limes (2 ounces/55 g)
1 cup (170 g) poached Meyer lemons (see page 315), finely chopped
¼ cup (40 g) lemon suprêmes (about 3 lemons)

FOR THE LEMON YELLOW COATING

2 cups (500 g) coating mixture (see page 317)
1 teaspoon (4 g) yellow fat-soluble food coloring

FOR THE GOLD AIRBRUSHING SOLUTION

4 teaspoons (20 g) kirsch
1 tablespoon (5 g) edible gold luster dust

FOR ASSEMBLY AND FINISHING

1½ tablespoons (20 g) neutral glaze (see page 317)
10 Menton lemon leaves

TIP

Be careful to avoid trapping any condensation or frost between the dipped and airbrushed layers of the coating.

FOR THE WHIPPED YUZU GANACHE

The previous day, soak the gelatin in 4 teaspoons (21 g) cold water for 20 minutes. Bring half the cream to a boil, then add the gelatin. Gradually pour the cream over the chopped chocolate and blend together. Add the remaining cream, which should be cold, then add the yuzu juice. Use an immersion blender to emulsify the mixture. Pour into a pan and seal by covering the surface of the ganache with plastic wrap. Refrigerate for 12 hours.

FOR THE LEMON GEL CENTERS

The next day, heat ½ cup (120 g) water with the lemon juice, then add the superfine sugar mixed with the agar. Boil for 2 minutes, then pour into a shallow pan and refrigerate until chilled. Mix with an immersion blender, being careful not to beat in any air. Add the mint, finger limes, Meyer lemons, and lemon suprêmes. Pour into 1⅓-inch (3.5-cm)-diameter silicone half-dome molds and freeze for 2 hours.

FOR COATING, ASSEMBLY, AND FINISHING

Whip the cold yuzu ganache and divide among 1¾-inch (4.5-cm) molds. Insert a lemon gel center into the middle of the ganache in each mold, then freeze for 1 hour. Sculpt it into a lemon shape. Make the yellow coating as described on page 317; heat to 80°F (25°C), then dip in the sculpted lemons to coat. Secure them to a baking sheet with a little almond paste. Airbrush them with the same coating to create a stippled surface, being careful to leave a few areas smooth to create an irregular effect. Use a brush to lightly coat the entire surface with the neutral glaze. Mix the kirsch and gold luster dust, straining them through a conical sieve. Pour into the airbrush and use to gild the lemons. Top each dessert with a lemon leaf.

FOR THE LEMON GANACHE

1 teaspoon (3.5 g) gelatin powder
2¼ cups (525 g) whipping cream
4¾ ounces (135 g) white couverture chocolate, chopped
½ cup (135 g) lemon juice
Zest of 5 lemons

FOR THE PUFF PASTRY

Kneaded butter (beurre manié)

1¾ cups (14¾ ounces/420 g) unsalted dry butter (84% fat content)
1⅓ cups (165 g) pastry flour

Water dough (détrempe)

⅔ cup (160 g) water
1 tablespoon (15 g) salt
1 teaspoon (4 g) distilled white vinegar
½ cup (1 stick/125 g) unsalted butter, softened
3¼ cups (395 g) pastry flour
4 teaspoons (10 g) confectioners' sugar

FOR THE LEMON GEL

¾ cup (180 g) lemon juice
2½ tablespoons (30 g) superfine sugar
½ teaspoon (4 g) agar powder

FOR THE LEMON GANACHE

The previous day, soak the gelatin in 4 teaspoons (21 g) cold water until it swells. Bring half the cream to a boil, then add the gelatin. Gradually pour the cream over the chocolate and blend together. Add the remaining cream, which should be cold, then add the lemon juice and zest. Mix well using an immersion blender until perfectly smooth, then refrigerate for 12 hours.

FOR THE PUFF PASTRY

The next day, make the puff pastry dough, turning it six times as described on page 313.

Preheat the oven to 360°F (180°C). Use a rolling pin to roll the puff pastry to a thickness of 1/16 inch (2 mm), then bake on two baking sheets for 30 minutes. Cut out eighteen 4 by 1½-inch (10 by 4-cm) rectangles. Sprinkle with the confectioners' sugar, then return to the oven for 5 minutes. Finally, sprinkle with the sugar and let cook until shiny, about 10 minutes on the normal setting at 500°F (250°C).

FOR THE LEMON GEL

Heat ½ cup (120 g) water with the lemon juice, then add the sugar mixed with the agar. Boil for 2 minutes, then cool rapidly by pouring the mixture into a pan and refrigerating. When the gel is cold, mix with an immersion blender, being careful not to beat in any air.

FOR ASSEMBLY AND FINISHING

Use a pastry bag fitted with a no. 14 plain tip to pipe two lines of ganache over two of the puff pastry rectangles, caramelized side down. Use a pastry bag without a tip to pipe a line of lemon gel between the two lines of ganache. Smooth the edges with a hot knife. Stack the two rectangles, then top with a third, caramelized size up. Use this method to make another five millefeuilles.

PREPARATION TIME: 2 HOURS

SERVES 8

COOKING TIME: 45 MINUTES

RESTING TIME: 12 HOURS

FOR THE BABA DOUGH
3¼ cups (400 g) all-purpose flour
2 teaspoons (12 g) salt
2 tablespoons (40 g) honey
⅓ (20 g) cake yeast or 2¼ teaspoons active dry yeast (dissolved in water or milk)
5 large (260 g) eggs
½ cup (1 stick/120 g) unsalted butter, at room temperature

FOR THE LEMON SYRUP
3 teaspoons (9 g) gelatin powder
1½ cups (300 g) superfine sugar
Zest of 3 lemons

FOR THE LEMON COMPOTE
2 cups (400 g) lemon suprêmes
3½ tablespoons (40 g) superfine sugar
2 teaspoons (6 g) pectin NH

FOR THE ASSEMBLY AND FINISHING
4 cups (500 g) vanilla whipped cream (see page 314)
Fresh mint leaves

FOR THE BABA DOUGH

In an electric stand mixer fitted with the dough hook, combine the flour, salt, honey, yeast, and eggs and knead until the dough begins to come away from the sides of the bowl. Add the butter in several stages, kneading until the dough again begins to come away from the sides of the bowl. Let stand in a cool place for 1 hour. Butter two muffin tins generously, then divide the dough into 1¼-ounce (35-g) balls, placing each in the cup of a muffin pan. Cover with a damp cloth and let rise for 40 minutes in a warm place. Preheat the oven to 360°F (180°C). Cover each muffin pan with a sheet of parchment paper, then place a baking sheet on top. Bake for 20 to 30 minutes, until the babas are just beginning to brown. Remove from the muffin pan, place on the oven rack, and dry for 1 hour at 210°F (100°C).

FOR THE LEMON SYRUP

Soak the gelatin in 3 tablespoons (63 g) cold water until it swells. In a saucepan, bring 2 cups plus 10 tablespoons (600 g) water, the superfine sugar, and lemon zest to a boil. Remove from heat and let cool to 160°F (70°C), then add the gelatin. Let cool to 120°F (50°C), then saturate the babas on both sides using a brush. Drain on a wire rack.

FOR THE LEMON COMPOTE

Put the lemon sections and half of the superfine sugar in a vacuum-sealing bag and cook for 20 minutes in a steam oven at 210°F (100°C) or in a pot of boiling water. Pour the contents of the bag into a saucepan, then add the remaining sugar mixed with the pectin. Boil for 2 minutes, then cool rapidly in the refrigerator.

FOR THE ASSEMBLY AND FINISHING

Cut the babas horizontally into four layers, spreading the compote between them. Make the vanilla whipped cream as described on page 314 and serve with the babas. Add a few mint leaves.

PREPARATION TIME: 2 HOURS

SERVES 8

COOKING TIME: 1 HOUR 40 MINUTES

RESTING TIME: 1 HOUR 40 MINUTES

LEMON TARTLETS

FOR THE LEMON HALF TOPPING

10 sculpted lemon halves
(see recipe for Lemons on page 23)

FOR THE TARTLET SHELLS

1 quantity (1¼ pounds/590 g)
sweet dough (see page 312)

FOR THE ALMOND-LEMON CREAM

⅓ quantity (3½ ounces/100 g)
almond cream (see page 314)
Zest of 2 lemons

FOR THE YELLOW CRUMB DOUGH

¼ quantity (3½ ounces/100 g)
crumb dough (see page 312)
⅜ teaspoon (1.7 g) yellow fat-soluble
food coloring
Zest of 1 lemon

FOR THE LEMON HALF TOPPING

Make the sculpted lemon halves as described in the recipe for Lemons (page 23), but making only half of the shape to create 10 lemon halves.

FOR THE TARTLET SHELLS

Make the sweet dough as described on page 312 and refrigerate for 24 hours.

The next day, preheat the oven to 320°F (160°C). Bake the tartlet shells for 20 minutes. Leave the oven on.

FOR THE ALMOND-LEMON CREAM

Make the almond cream as described on page 314, then mix in the lemon zest.

Fill the prebaked tartlet shells with the almond-lemon cream and bake for 5 minutes at 320°F (160°C).

FOR THE YELLOW CRUMB DOUGH

Preheat the oven to 340°F (170°C). Mix the crumb dough as described on page 312, incorporating the food coloring and lemon zest, then use a rolling pin to roll a 1⁄32-inch (1 mm)-thick layer of dough between two sheets of parchment paper. Bake for 7 minutes, then sift the crumbs, keeping any chunks and discarding any powder.

FOR ASSEMBLY AND FINISHING

Place a lemon half over each tartlet shell, then place the crumbs around the edge.

PREPARATION TIME: 3 HOURS 30 MINUTES

SERVES 10

COOKING TIME: 30 MINUTES

RESTING TIME: 24 HOURS

PREPARATION TIME: 2 HOURS

SERVES 8

COOKING TIME: 50 MINUTES

RESTING TIME: 12 HOURS PLUS 10 MINUTES

LEMON-PEPPER

FOR THE SARAWAK PEPPER GANACHE
½ teaspoon (1.7 g) gelatin powder
¾ cup (201 g) whipping cream
2 ounces (54 g) white couverture chocolate, chopped
3 tablespoons (45 g) lemon juice
1¼ teaspoons (2.5 g) Sarawak pepper

FOR THE ÉCLAIRS (SEE PAGE 318)
1 quantity (14 ounces/400 g) choux paste

Yellow crumb dough
1 quantity (12¼ ounces/350 g) crumb dough
1 teaspoon (5 g) yellow fat-soluble food coloring
¹⁄₃₂ ounce (1 g) food-grade titanium dioxide

White glaze
1¼ cups (300 g) white starch glaze (see page 319)

FOR THE CRISPY WAFER COOKIES (SEE PAGE 313)
½ quantity (1 pound 2 ounces/500 g) wafer cookie dough
Pepper

FOR THE LEMON GEL
¾ cup (180 g) lemon juice
2½ tablespoons (30 g) superfine sugar
2 teaspoons (5 g) agar powder
4 to 5 finger limes (2 ounces/55 g), finely chopped
¼ cup (40 g) lemon suprêmes, cut into pieces
1 cup (170 g) candied lemons, finely chopped

FOR THE SARAWAK PEPPER GANACHE
The previous day, soak the gelatin in ½ tablespoon (8.7 g) water to soften. Bring half the cream to a boil, then add the gelatin. Gradually pour the cream over the chocolate and blend together. Add the remaining cream, then the lemon juice and pepper. Use an immersion blender to blend until perfectly smooth, then refrigerate for 12 hours.

FOR THE ÉCLAIRS, CRUMB DOUGH, AND WHITE GLAZE
The next day, make the éclairs as described on page 318 with the yellow crumb dough and bake for 20 minutes at 360°F (180°C). Dry for 5 minutes at 320°F (160°C). Make the glaze as described on page 319.

FOR THE CRISPY WAFER COOKIES
Make crispy wafer cookie dough balls as described on page 319, then sprinkle with pepper.

FOR THE LEMON GEL
Heat ½ cup (120 g) water with the lemon juice, then add the sugar mixed with the agar. Boil for 2 minutes, then cool rapidly in the refrigerator. When the gel is cold, mix with an immersion blender, being careful not to beat in any air. Add the finger limes, the lemon suprêmes, and the candied lemons. Mix everything together gently.

FOR ASSEMBLY AND FINISHING
Use an electric stand mixer fitted with a whisk attachment to whip the cold pepper ganache, then transfer to a pastry bag without a tip. Make four holes in the bottom of each éclair with the point of a knife or another tool, then pipe in ⅜ ounce (10 g) of ganache, and gel to fill. Reheat the white glaze to 80°F (27°C) in a microwave, then give the éclairs a first coat of glaze. Put in the freezer for 5 minutes, then add another coat of glaze. Refrigerate for a few minutes. Just before serving, top the éclairs with the crispy pepper balls.

LIME AND OLIVE OIL

FOR THE TARTLET SHELLS

1 quantity (1¼ pounds/590 g) sweet dough (see page 312)
6 large (100 g) egg yolks
2 tablespoons (25 g) whipping cream
1 quantity (10½ ounces/300 g) almond cream (see page 314)

FOR THE LIME GEL CENTERS

1 cup (200 g) poached limes (see page 315)
1 cup (230 g) lime juice
4 teaspoons (15 g) superfine sugar
2 teaspoons (6 g) agar powder
⅓ cup (20 g) chopped fresh tarragon
4 to 5 finger limes (2 ounces / 55 g), finely chopped

FOR THE LIME-OLIVE OIL CREAM

2 sheets (5 g) powdered gelatin
Zest of 3 limes
½ cup (142 g) lime juice
3¼ large (162 g) eggs (⅔ cup)
2 teaspoons (15 g) lavender honey
6 tablespoons (3 ounces/85 g) unsalted dry butter (84% fat)
⅓ cup (85 g) Casanova olive oil

FOR THE LEMON MERINGUE

4½ large (150 g) egg whites (⅔ cup)
1 cup plus 2 tablespoons (225 g) superfine sugar
¾ teaspoon (1.5 g) egg white powder
Zest of 1 lemon

FOR THE LEMON GEL

⅓ cup (76 g) fresh unstrained lemon juice
1 teaspoon (5 g) superfine sugar
¾ teaspoon (2 g) agar powder

FOR THE LEMON VINAIGRETTE

2 tablespoons (30 g) olive oil
2 tablespoons (35 g) lemon juice
1 finger lime (⅜ ounce/10 g)

FOR THE TARTLET SHELLS

The previous day, make the sweet dough for the tartlet shells as described on page 312. Let dry in the refrigerator for 1 day.

The next day, preheat the oven to 320°F (160°C) and blind bake the tartlet shells for 20 minutes. Beat the egg yolks with the cream and brush the shells with the mixture. Bake for 5 minutes. Make the almond cream as described on page 314 and divide among the shells. Bake for 5 minutes.

FOR THE LIME GEL CENTERS

Make the poached limes as described on page 315. Finely chop them. Heat ⅓ cup (80 g) water with the lime juice, then add the superfine sugar mixed with the agar. Boil for 2 minutes, then cool rapidly by pouring into a pan and refrigerating. When the gelatin is cold, mix with an immersion blender without beating in any air. Add the tarragon, finger lime, and poached limes. Spread this mixture over the tartlets.

FOR THE LIME-OLIVE OIL CREAM

Soak the gelatin in cold water for 20 minutes. In a saucepan, combine the lime zest, lime juice, eggs, and honey. Heat; when the mixture begins to boil, remove from the heat, strain through a conical sieve, and add the gelatin. Mix using an immersion blender, gradually adding the butter and olive oil. Refrigerate for 1 hour. Top the tartlets with the cream.

FOR THE LEMON MERINGUE

In a bain-marie, heat the egg whites, superfine sugar, and egg white powder to 160°F (70°C). Whip the mixture in an electric stand mixer fitted with a whisk attachment until it has cooled completely, then add the zest. Use a pastry bag fitted with a no. 20 Saint-Honoré tip to pipe the meringue onto the tartlets.

FOR THE LEMON GEL

Heat 2 tablespoons (25 g) water with the lemon juice, then add the superfine sugar mixed with the agar. Boil for 2 minutes, then cool rapidly by pouring into a pan and refrigerating. When the gelatin is cold, mix with an immersion blender without beating in any air.

FOR THE LEMON VINAIGRETTE

Mix 2½ tablespoons (40 g) of the lemon gel with the oil, lemon juice, and finger lime. Put the vinaigrette into the center of the meringue with a spoon.

PREPARATION TIME: 3 HOURS 30 MINUTES

MAKES 10 TARTLETS

COOKING TIME: 35 MINUTES

RESTING TIME: 24 HOURS PLUS 1 HOUR

FOR THE CITRUS SORBET

2⅓ cups (450 g) superfine sugar
½ cup (100 g) glucose powder
3½ tablespoons (40 g) inverted sugar
2 teaspoons (10 g) super neutrose
2 cups (500 g) lime juice
Zest of 2 limes

FOR THE LIME-OLIVE OIL CREAM

2 sheets (5 g) powdered gelatin
⅔ cup (150 g) lime juice
Zest of 3 limes
3 large (160 g) eggs
¾ cup (150 g) superfine sugar
6 tablespoons (3 ounces/85 g) cold unsalted dry butter (84% fat content)
⅓ cup (85 g) Casanova olive oil

FOR THE SHISO PESTO

4 cups (100 g) whole shiso leaves, plus more for garnish
3 tablespoons (50 g) almond paste
Zest of 2 lemons
2 tablespoons (40 g) honey
3 tablespoons (40 g) lemon juice
1 cup (200 g) olive oil

FOR THE LIME-OLIVE OIL DRESSING

¾ cup (200 g) lime juice
2 teaspoons (6 g) gelatin powder
4 teaspoons (48 g) Béton honey
¼ teaspoon (1 g) fleur de sel
¾ cup (180 g) Casanova olive oil

FOR ASSEMBLY AND FINISHING

Fresh shiso leaves
Lime suprêmes

FOR THE CITRUS SORBET

Mix the superfine sugar, glucose, inverted sugar, and super neutrose. Bring 3¾ cups (900 g) water to a boil, add the sugar mixture, and return to a boil. Refrigerate for 3 hours. Add the lime juice and zest and mix using an immersion blender. Store in the freezer.

FOR THE LIME-OLIVE OIL CREAM

Soak the gelatin in cold water for 20 minutes. Heat the lime juice, lime zest, eggs, and sugar. When the mixture begins to boil, remove from the heat, strain through a conical sieve, and add the gelatin. Mix using an immersion blender, then gradually add the butter and oil. Cool rapidly by pouring the mixture into a pan and refrigerating.

FOR THE SHISO PESTO

In a powerful blender, combine the shiso with the almond paste, lemon zest, lemon juice, and honey, then add a little ice. Blend, adding the oil slowly as if making a vinaigrette.

FOR THE LIME-OLIVE OIL DRESSING

Mix the lime juice with the gelatin, honey, and fleur de sel. Whisk together with the oil.

FOR ASSEMBLY AND FINISHING

Place a spoonful of lime-olive oil cream on a plate, then dot a little shiso pesto in the middle. Add the sorbet and top with a few shiso leaves. Garnish with a few fresh lime suprêmes. Serve with the warm lime-olive oil dressing.

PREPARATION TIME: 1 HOUR

SERVES 8

COOKING TIME: 10 MINUTES

RESTING TIME: 3 HOURS

FOR THE TARTLET SHELLS

1 quantity (1¼ pounds/590 g) sweet dough (see page 312)

FOR THE LIME GANACHE

1¼ teaspoons (4 g) gelatin
1¾ cups (410 g) whipping cream
4¼ ounces (120 g) white couverture chocolate
⅓ cup (90 g) lime juice
Zest of 3 limes

FOR THE LIME GEL CENTERS

1 cup (230 g) lime juice
2½ tablespoons (30 g) superfine sugar
2 teaspoons (5 g) agar powder
¼ cup (10 g) fresh tarragon, chopped
1 cup (170 g) poached limes (see page 315), finely chopped
¼ cup (50 g) fresh lime suprêmes

FOR THE EGG WASH

6 large (100 g) egg yolks
1½ tablespoons (25 g) whipping cream

FOR THE ALMOND-TARRAGON CREAM

½ quantity (5¼ ounces/150 g) almond cream (see page 314)
½ cup (20 g) fresh tarragon
1 cup (200 g) lime suprêmes

FOR THE LIME PASTE

6 limes (3½ ounces/400 g)
1 cup (200 g) poached limes (see page 315)
1⅔ cups (400 g) lime juice

FOR THE ASSEMBLY AND FINISHING

1½ tablespoons (20 g) neutral glaze

Lime green coating

1¼ cups (300 g) coating mixture (see page 317)
1¾ teaspoons (8 g) green fat-soluble food coloring

Green airbrushing solution

3½ tablespoons (50 g) kirsch
3 tablespoons (5 g) edible green luster dust

Green crumb dough

¼ quantity (3½ ounces/100 g) crumb dough (see page 312)
¼ teaspoon (1 g) green fat-soluble food coloring
⅛ teaspoon (0.07 g) red fat-soluble food coloring
Zest of 1 lime

FOR THE TARTLET SHELLS

The previous day, make the sweet dough for the tartlet shells as described on page 312 and let dry in the refrigerator for 1 day.

FOR THE LIME GANACHE

Soak the gelatin in 2 tablespoons (28 g) cold water for 20 minutes. Bring half the cream to a boil, then add the gelatin. Gradually pour the cream over the chopped chocolate and blend together. Add the remaining cream, then the lime juice and zest. Use an immersion blender to emulsify the mixture. Pour into a pan and seal by covering the surface of the ganache with plastic wrap. Refrigerate for 12 hours.

Continued

PREPARATION TIME: 3 HOURS 30 MINUTES

SERVES 10

COOKING TIME: 30 MINUTES

RESTING TIME: 24 HOURS PLUS 5 HOURS

FOR THE LIME GEL CENTERS

The next day, heat ½ cup (135 g) water with the lime juice, then add the superfine sugar mixed with the agar. Let simmer for a moment, then pour into a shallow pan and refrigerate until chilled. Mix with an immersion blender, being careful not to beat in any air. Add the tarragon, poached limes, and lime suprêmes. Pour into 1½-inch (3.5-cm)-diameter silicone half-dome molds and freeze for 1 hour.

FOR THE EGG WASH

Preheat the oven to 320°F (160°C). Blind bake the tartlet shells for 20 minutes. Beat the egg yolks with the cream and brush the shells with the mixture. Bake for 5 minutes.

FOR THE ALMOND-TARRAGON CREAM

Meanwhile, make the almond cream as described on page 314. Fill the prebaked tartlet shells and add a few lime suprêmes to each. Bake for 10 minutes.

FOR THE LIME PASTE (YOU'LL END UP WITH EXTRA)

Use a blender to combine the limes, poached limes, and lime juice. Spread the paste over the layer of almond cream in the tartlet shells.

FOR ASSEMBLY AND FINISHING

Whip the cold lime ganache, then transfer to 1¾-inch (4.5-cm)-diameter silicone half-dome molds. Insert a lime gel center into the middle, then freeze for 1 hour. Add a little ganache and sculpt into a lime shape. Return to the freezer for 3 hours.

Prepare the green coating as described on page 317, heating it to 80°F (25°C). Dip in the lime halves, then place them on a baking sheet, securing them with a little almond paste. Thaw in the refrigerator. Using an empty airbrush, blow any condensation off the lime halves. Fill the airbrush with the same green coating and stipple the surfaces of the limes.

Use a brush to lightly coat the entire surface with the neutral glaze, creating the look of a citrus peel. Combine the kirsch and luster dust and airbrush the solution onto the limes. Top each tartlet with a lime half. Finish by preparing the crumb dough as described on page 312 and placing the crumbs around the edge.

PREPARATION TIME: 3 HOURS 30 MINUTES

SERVES 10

COOKING TIME: 30 MINUTES

RESTING TIME: 24 HOURS PLUS 5 HOURS

DRIED LIME—TIMUT PEPPER TARTLETS

FOR THE TARTLET SHELLS

1 quantity (1¼ pounds/590 g) sweet dough (see page 312)

FOR THE WHIPPED DRIED LIME-TIMUT PEPPER GANACHE

2 sheets (5 g) gelatin
½ cup (120 g) milk
2¼ cups (530 g) whipping cream
1 teaspoon (2 g) Timut pepper
1¼ Iranian dried limes (⅜ ounce/10 g)
Zest of 3 lemons
5 ounces (140 g) white couverture chocolate, chopped

FOR THE LEMON GEL CENTERS

1¾ cups (450 g) lemon juice
⅓ cup (75 g) superfine sugar
1½ tablespoons (12 g) agar powder
2½ cups (425 g) poached lemons (see page 315), finely chopped
½ cup (100 g) fresh lemon suprêmes
3¾ teaspoons (7.5 g) Timut pepper

FOR THE EGG WASH

6 large (100 g) egg yolks
1½ tablespoons (25 g) whipping cream

FOR THE ALMOND-TIMUT PEPPER CREAM

½ quantity (5¼ ounces/150 g) almond cream (see page 314)
1 teaspoon (2 g) Timut pepper
1 cup (240 g) fresh lemon suprêmes

FOR THE LEMON PASTE

1 lemon (3½ ounces/100 g)
¼ cup (50 g) candied lemons
⅓ cup (100 g) lemon juice

FOR ASSEMBLY AND FINISHING

Charcoal black coating

1¼ cups (300 g) coating mixture (see page 317)
1 teaspoon (4 g) charcoal black food coloring
1½ tablespoons (20 g) neutral glaze (see page 317)

Charcoal crumb dough

¼ quantity (3½ ounces/100 g) crumb dough (see page 312)
⅜ teaspoon (1.7 g) charcoal food coloring
Zest of 1 lemon

FOR THE TARTLET SHELLS

The previous day, make the sweet dough for the tartlet shells as described on page 312 and let dry in the refrigerator for 1 day.

FOR THE WHIPPED DRIED LIME-TIMUT PEPPER GANACHE

Soak the gelatin in cold water for 20 minutes. Bring half the cream to a boil, then mix in the Timut pepper, dried limes, and lime zest. Drain the gelatin and add. Gradually pour the cream over the chopped chocolate and blend together. Add the other half of the cream. Use an immersion blender to emulsify the mixture. Pour into a pan and seal by covering the surface of the ganache with plastic wrap. Refrigerate for 12 hours.

Continued

DRIED LIME—

FOR THE LEMON GEL CENTERS

The next day, heat 1¼ cups (300 g) water with the lemon juice, then add the superfine sugar mixed with the agar. Boil for 2 minutes, then pour into a shallow pan and refrigerate until chilled. Mix with an immersion blender, being careful not to beat in any air. Add the poached lemons and fresh lemon suprêmes. Pour into 1½-inch (3.5-cm)-diameter silicone half-dome molds and freeze for 1 hour.

FOR THE EGG WASH

Preheat the oven to 320°F (160°C). Blind bake the tartlet shells for 20 minutes. Beat the egg yolks with the cream and brush the shells with the mixture. Bake for 5 minutes.

FOR THE ALMOND-TIMUT PEPPER CREAM

Meanwhile, make the almond cream as described on page 314. Fill the prebaked tartlet shells and add a few lemon suprêmes to each. Bake for another 5 minutes.

FOR THE LEMON PASTE

Use a blender to combine the fresh lemon, candied lemons, and lemon juice. Spread over the baked almond cream.

FOR ASSEMBLY AND FINISHING

In an electric stand mixer fitted with a whisk attachment, whip the cold ganache, then transfer to 1¾-inch (4.5-cm)-diameter silicone half-dome molds. Insert a lemon gel center into the middle, then freeze for 1 hour before sculpting into a half-lemon shape, adding a little ganache to make the tip of the lemon. Freeze for 3 hours. Make the charcoal black coating as described on page 317. Heat to 80°F (25°C), then dip in the molded dried limes. Secure them lightly to a baking sheet and airbrush with the same coating to create a stippled surface, being careful to leave a few areas smooth to create an irregular effect. Use a brush to coat the limes with a thin layer of warm neutral glaze. Top each tartlet with a lime half. Make the charcoal crumb dough as described on page 312 and place around the edge.

TIMUT PEPPER TARTLETS

PREPARATION TIME: 3 HOURS 30 MINUTES

MAKES 10 TARTLETS

COOKING TIME: 30 MINUTES

RESTING TIME: 24 HOURS PLUS 4 HOURS

CLEMENTINE

FOR THE TARTLET SHELLS

1 quantity (1¼ pounds/590 g) sweet dough (see page 312)

FOR THE WHIPPED CLEMENTINE GANACHE

1 teaspoon (3 g) gelatin
2¼ cups (530 g) whipping cream
5 ounces (140 g) white couverture chocolate, chopped
½ cup (120 g) clementine juice

FOR THE CLEMENTINE GEL CENTERS

¾ cup (180 g) clementine juice
2½ tablespoons (30 g) superfine sugar
2 teaspoons (5 g) agar powder
1 cup (170 g) poached clementines (see page 315), finely chopped
¼ cup (40 g) lemon suprêmes, cut into pieces

FOR THE EGG WASH

6 large (100 g) egg yolks
1½ tablespoons (25 g) whipping cream

FOR THE ALMOND CREAM

½ quantity (5¼ ounces/150 g) almond cream (see page 314)

FOR ASSEMBLY AND FINISHING

Orange coating
1¼ cups (300 g) coating mixture (see page 317)
1 teaspoon (4 g) orange fat-soluble food coloring
1½ tablespoons (20 g) neutral glaze (see page 317)
¼ cup (50 g) kirsch
1 tablespoon (5 g) orange luster dust
10 clementine leaves

Orange crumb dough
¼ quantity (100 g) crumb dough (see page 312)
⅜ teaspoon (1.7 g) orange fat-soluble food coloring
Zest of 1 clementine

FOR THE TARTLET SHELLS

The previous day, make the sweet dough for the tartlet shells as described on page 312 and let dry in the refrigerator for 1 day.

FOR THE WHIPPED CLEMENTINE GANACHE

Soak the gelatin in 4 teaspoons (21 g) cold water for 20 minutes. Bring half the cream to a boil, then add the gelatin. Gradually pour the cream over the chocolate and blend together. Add the remaining cream, then the clementine juice. Blend using an immersion blender until perfectly smooth, then refrigerate for 12 hours.

FOR THE CLEMENTINE GEL CENTERS

The next day, heat ½ cup (120 g) water with the clementine juice, then add the superfine sugar mixed with the agar. Boil for 2 minutes, then cool rapidly by pouring into a pan and refrigerating. When the gel is cold, mix with an immersion blender without beating in any air. Add the poached clementines and lemon suprêmes. Pour into 1½-inch (3.5-cm)-diameter silicone half-dome molds. Freeze for 1 hour.

FOR THE EGG WASH

Preheat the oven to 320°F (160°C). Blind bake the tartlet shells for 20 minutes. Beat the egg yolks with the cream and brush the shells with the mixture. Bake for 5 minutes.

FOR THE ALMOND CREAM

Make the almond cream as described on page 314. Pour it into the tartlet shells. Bake for another 5 minutes.

FOR ASSEMBLY AND FINISHING

In the chilled bowl of an electric stand mixer fitted with a whisk attachment, whip the ganache, then transfer to 1¾-inch (4.5-cm)-diameter half-dome silicone molds. Insert the frozen clementine gel centers, cover with ganache, and freeze for 3 hours. Once completely frozen, unmold and sculpt into a clementine shape. Make the orange coating as described on page 317, heating it to 80°F (25°C), and dip in the clementine halves to coat. Secure them lightly to a baking sheet with almond paste and airbrush them with the same coating to create a stippled surface, being careful to leave a few areas smooth to create an irregular effect. Coat them with a thin layer of warm neutral glaze. Combine the kirsch and luster dust and airbrush the clementines with the mixture. Top each tartlet with a clementine half, then place a leaf on top. Make the crumb dough as described on page 312 and place around the edge.

CLEMENTINE

FOR THE FROMAGE BLANC MOUSSE

1¾ cups (400 g) fromage blanc or Greek yogurt
2 teaspoons (10 g) clementine juice
1 cup (250 g) whipped cream
2 large (60 g) egg whites
¼ cup (40 g) superfine sugar

FOR THE CLEMENTINE SORBET

2 cups (500 g) clementine juice
2¼ cups (400 g) clementine puree
1¼ cups (250 g) superfine sugar
⅓ cup (70 g) glucose powder
3 tablespoons plus 1 teaspoon (50 g) ice cream stabilizer
Zest of 4 clementines

FOR THE CANDIED CLEMENTINE PEELS

1 cup (100 g) strips of clementine peel made with a vegetable peeler
2 cups (500 g) clementine juice
1¼ cups (250 g) superfine sugar

FOR THE POACHED CLEMENTINES

10 clementines
1¼ cups (250 g) superfine sugar
2 cups (500 g) water

FOR THE CLEMENTINE-OLIVE OIL DRESSING

1½ sheets (3.5 g powdered) gelatin
2 cups (500 g) clementine juice
¼ cup (50 g) olive oil

FOR ASSEMBLY

20 clementine suprêmes
20 Mandarin orange suprêmes
Timut pepper
Zest of 1 clementine

FOR THE FROMAGE BLANC MOUSSE

The previous day, mix the fromage blanc and clementine juice. In an electric stand mixer fitted with a whisk attachment, whip the cream until it forms stiff peaks, then set aside and wash the bowl of the mixer. Return the bowl to the mixer and use the whisk attachment to whip the egg whites and superfine sugar into a meringue. Combine with the fromage blanc, then mix in the whipped cream. Let drain overnight in a sieve in the refrigerator.

FOR THE CLEMENTINE SORBET

Mix the clementine juice and puree with the superfine sugar, 1⅔ cups (380 g) water, the glucose powder, and stabilizer. Bring to a boil, then refrigerate for 6 hours or overnight. The next day, add the clementine zest and churn to make the sorbet.

FOR THE CANDIED CLEMENTINE PEELS

Put the clementine peel in a saucepan. Add the clementine juice and superfine sugar, then simmer for about 30 minutes, until the peels are sufficiently candied.

FOR THE POACHED CLEMENTINES

Make the poached clementines as described in the poached citrus recipe (see page 315), adjusting the amounts to fit this recipe.

FOR THE CLEMENTINE-OLIVE OIL DRESSING

Soak the gelatin in 4 teaspoons (21 g) cold water to soften it. Cook the clementine juice until reduced by half. Mix with the gelatin using an immersion blender, then pour in the oil in a thin stream while continuing to mix.

FOR ASSEMBLY

Place a spoonful of fromage blanc mousse on each plate; do not shape. Add a few clementine and orange suprêmes, a few pieces of poached clementine, and the candied peels. Sprinkle some Timut pepper over the surface of the sorbet, then scoop out a curl of sorbet and place it next to the mousse, and add a little clementine-olive oil dressing. Use a Microplane to grate clementine zest over the dessert.

PREPARATION TIME: 1 HOUR

SERVES 8

COOKING TIME: 30 MINUTES

RESTING TIME: 1 NIGHT PLUS 6 HOURS

FOR THE LIME SUGAR
Zest of 4 limes
1 cup (200 g) superfine sugar

FOR THE POACHED KUMQUATS
3½ cups (500 g) kumquats
5 cups (1 kg) superfine sugar
8 cups (2 quarts/2 kg) water

FOR THE ORANGE PASTRY CREAM
⅔ quantity (14 ounces/400 g) pastry cream (see page 314)
Zest of 1 orange

FOR THE ALMOND-LIME CREAM
⅘ quantity (8½ ounces/240 g) almond cream (see page 314)
Zest of 1 lime

FOR THE BASQUE SHORTBREAD PASTRY DOUGH
1 cup plus 2 tablespoons (2¼ sticks/250 g) unsalted butter
½ teaspoon (3 g) fine salt
1 cup packed (220 g) light brown sugar
¾ teaspoon (3 g) baking powder
2½ cups (310 g) all-purpose flour
1¼ cups (125 g) ground almonds
2 medium (90 g) eggs

FOR ASSEMBLY AND FINISHING
Ground almonds
1 egg yolk

TIP
Be careful to avoid overcooking the kumquats to make sure they preserve their appearance.

FOR THE LIME SUGAR
Grate the lime zest over the sugar using a Microplane and let dry in the open for 3 hours.

FOR THE POACHED KUMQUATS
Make the poached kumquats as described in the poached citrus recipe (see page 315), but cut them into two pieces instead of eight and blanch them only once.

FOR THE ORANGE PASTRY CREAM
Make the pastry cream as described on page 314, adding the orange zest at the end.

FOR THE ALMOND-LIME CREAM
Make the almond cream as described on page 314, then mix in the lime zest.

FOR THE BASQUE SHORTBREAD PASTRY DOUGH
Rub the butter together with the salt, brown sugar, baking powder, flour, and ground almonds. Beat in the eggs, then roll the dough out to a thickness of 3/8 inch (3 mm) using a rolling pin. Cut out eight 3/8 by 8 3/8-inch (1.5 by 21.25-cm) strips of dough, as well as eight 2¾-inch (7-cm)-diameter disks and eight 2½-inch (6.3-cm)-diameter disks.

FOR ASSEMBLY AND FINISHING
Cut out eight ¾ by 8 7/8-inch (2 by 22.5-cm) strips of parchment paper. Join the ends to make 2¼-inch (7-cm) parchment paper circles. Lay a 2½-inch (6.3-cm) dough disk in the bottom of each and line the sides with a 5/8-inch (1.5-cm) band of dough. Grease a Silpat baking mat and sprinkle with lime sugar. Place the lined circles on top. Sprinkle some ground almonds into the bottom of each pastry, then top with almond-lime cream. Add the poached kumquats, then cover with the orange pastry cream. Top the Basque cakes with the 2¼-inch (7-cm) dough disks, then brush with the beaten egg yolk and let dry for 30 minutes. Preheat the oven to 360°F (180°C). Brush the cakes with egg yolk again, then score the tops with a three-tined fork. Bake for 14 minutes, turning the Silpat mat halfway through. Reduce the oven temperature to 300°F (150°C) and bake for another 12 minutes, turning halfway through.

PREPARATION TIME: 1 HOUR

SERVES 8

COOKING TIME: 25 MINUTES

RESTING TIME: 3 HOURS 30 MINUTES

PREPARATION TIME: 2 HOURS 30 MINUTES

SERVES 8 TO 10

COOKING TIME: 45 MINUTES

RESTING TIME: 24 HOURS PLUS 6 HOURS

FOR THE TART SHELL

1 quantity (1¼ pounds/590 g) sweet dough (see page 312)

FOR THE ORANGE SORBET

2 cups (450 g) orange juice
¾ cup plus 2 tablespoons (175 g) superfine sugar
Zest of 2 oranges

FOR THE EGG WASH

6 large (100 g) egg yolks
1½ tablespoons (25 g) whipping cream

FOR THE ALMOND-ORANGE CREAM

1 quantity (10½ ounces/300 g) almond cream (see page 314)
1 teaspoon (6 g) rum
Zest of 1 orange

FOR THE ORANGE-GRAND MARNIER CREAM

½ sheet (1.25 g powdered) gelatin
⅓ cup (75 g) orange juice
3 tablespoons (40 g) Grand Marnier Cordon Rouge
1 tablespoon (15 g) lemon juice
2½ tablespoons (15 g) orange zest
4 large (200 g) eggs
¼ cup (55 g) superfine sugar
½ cup (1 stick/120 g) unsalted butter

FOR THE SEMICANDIED ORANGES

½ medium orange (2 ounces/60 g)
⅔ cup (125 g) superfine sugar

FOR THE CLEMENTINE PRESERVES

5 clementines (13¼ ounces/375 g)
¾ cup plus 2 tablespoons (165 g) superfine sugar
⅓ cup plus 1 tablespoon (100 g) lemon juice
1⅜ teaspoons (4 g) pectin NH

FOR ASSEMBLY AND FINISHING

4 oranges, suprêmed
Timut pepper

FOR THE TART SHELL

The day before, make the sweet dough for the tart shell as described on page 312. Let dry in the refrigerator for 1 day.

FOR THE ORANGE SORBET

The next day, boil the orange juice with the superfine sugar and ¾ cup (190 g) water, then add the orange zest and pour into a pan. Refrigerate for 6 hours. Churn to make the sorbet. Once done, keep the sorbet in the freezer until the dessert is ready for assembly.

FOR THE EGG WASH

Preheat the oven to 320°F (160°C). Blind bake the tart shell for 25 minutes. Mix the egg yolks with the cream and brush the shell with the mixture. Return to the oven for 10 minutes.

FOR THE ALMOND-ORANGE CREAM

Make the almond cream as described on page 314. Pour it into the tart shell and bake for 10 minutes at 320°F (160°C).

FOR THE ORANGE-GRAND MARNIER CREAM

Soak the gelatin in cold water to soften. Boil the orange juice with the Grand Marnier, lemon juice, orange zest, eggs, and superfine sugar. Remove from the heat and add the gelatin and butter, then mix using an immersion blender.

FOR THE SEMICANDIED ORANGES

Remove the stems from the oranges, cut them into eighths, then remove the insides, leaving only ⅛ inch (3 mm) of flesh attached to the peel. Prick with a fork and blanch three times in boiling water, draining and cooling the oranges in cold water after each time. Boil the superfine sugar with 1 cup (250 g) water and drop the orange peels into this syrup. Cover and simmer gently to reduce. Once the oranges are tender, remove and drain. Let the syrup reduce, then heat it to 220°F (105°C) and return the peels to the syrup. Bring to a simmer and remove from the heat.

FOR THE CLEMENTINE PRESERVES

Remove the stems from the clementines, then cook them in boiling water for 5 minutes, transferring them to cold water to cool. Drain and quarter them, then cook them with ⅔ cup (120 g) of the superfine sugar and the lemon juice. Mix the pectin and remaining sugar, blend the clementines with an immersion blender, add the pectin-sugar mixture, and bring to a boil. Let cool, then use a spoon to add a dash of preserves to each serving plate.

FOR ASSEMBLY AND FINISHING

Top the tart with the orange–Grand Marnier cream, then add the orange suprêmes and the semicandied oranges. Just before serving, scoop a few curls of sorbet sprinkled with Timut pepper and arrange them on the tart. Set each slice on top of the dash of clementine preserves.

PREPARATION TIME: 3 HOURS 30 MINUTES

SERVES 10

COOKING TIME: 30 MINUTES

RESTING TIME: 24 HOURS PLUS 4 HOURS

ORANGE

FOR THE TARTLET SHELLS

1 quantity (1¼ pounds/590 g) sweet dough (see page 312)

FOR THE WHIPPED ORANGE GANACHE

2 sheets (5 g powdered) gelatin
2¼ cups (530 g) whipping cream
5 ounces (144 g) white couverture chocolate, chopped
½ cup (120 g) orange juice

FOR THE ORANGE GEL CENTERS

¾ cup (180 g) orange juice
2 tablespoons (30 g) superfine sugar
1½ tablespoons (4 g) agar powder
1 cup (170 g) poached oranges (see page 315), finely chopped
4 finger limes (2 ounces/54 g), finely chopped
⅓ cup (40 g) orange zest

FOR THE EGG WASH

6 large (100 g) egg yolks
1½ tablespoons (25 g) whipping cream

FOR THE ALMOND-ORANGE CREAM

1 quantity (1½ ounces/300 g) almond cream (see page 314)
1 orange, suprêmed

FOR THE ORANGE PASTE

½ medium to large orange (2¾ ounces/80 g)
¼ cup (40 g) candied orange
⅓ cup (80 g) orange juice

FOR ASSEMBLY AND FINISHING

Orange coating
1¼ cups (300 g) coating mixture (see page 317)
1 teaspoon (5 g) orange fat-soluble food coloring
1½ tablespoons (20 g) neutral glaze (see page 317)
¼ cup (50 g) kirsch
1 tablespoon (5 g) edible orange luster dust

Orange crumb dough
¼ quantity (3½ ounces/100 g) crumb dough (see page 312)
⅜ teaspoon (1.7 g) orange fat-soluble food coloring
Zest of 1 orange

FOR THE TARTLET SHELLS

The previous day, make the sweet dough for the tartlet shells as described on page 312 and let dry in the refrigerator for 1 day.

FOR THE WHIPPED ORANGE GANACHE

Soak the gelatin in 5 teaspoons (24 g) cold water for 20 minutes. Bring half the cream to a boil, then add the gelatin. Gradually pour the cream over the chocolate and blend. Add the remaining cream, then the orange juice. Mix with an immersion blender. Pour into a pan, covering the surface of the ganache with plastic wrap. Refrigerate for 12 hours.

FOR THE ORANGE GELATIN CENTERS

The next day, heat ½ cup (120 g) water with the orange juice, then add the superfine sugar mixed with the agar. Boil for 2 minutes, then pour into a pan and refrigerate. When the gel is cold, mix with an immersion blender without mixing in any air. Add the poached oranges, finger limes, and orange zest. Pour into 1½-inch (3.5-cm)-diameter silicone half-dome molds and freeze for 1 hour.

FOR THE EGG WASH

Preheat the oven to 320°F (160°C). Bake the tartlet shells for 20 minutes. Mix the egg yolks with the cream and brush the shells with the mixture. Return to the oven for 5 minutes.

FOR THE ALMOND-ORANGE CREAM

Make the almond cream as described on page 314. Fill the tartlet shells and add a few orange suprêmes to each. Bake for another 5 minutes.

FOR THE ORANGE PASTE

Blend the orange, candied orange, and orange juice in a blender. Spread this mixture over the layer of baked almond cream.

FOR ASSEMBLY AND FINISHING

Whip the ganache and transfer to 1¾-inch (4.5-cm)-diameter silicone half-dome molds. Insert an orange gel center into each. Freeze for 3 hours, then sculpt into an orange shape. Make the orange coating as described on page 317, then dip the molded oranges into the coating. Airbrush them with the same coating to create a stippled surface, being careful to leave a few areas smooth to create an irregular effect. Coat with a thin layer of warm neutral glaze. Combine the kirsch and luster dust and airbrush the oranges with the solution. Place one on top of each tartlet. Make the crumb dough as described on page 312 and place it around the edges.

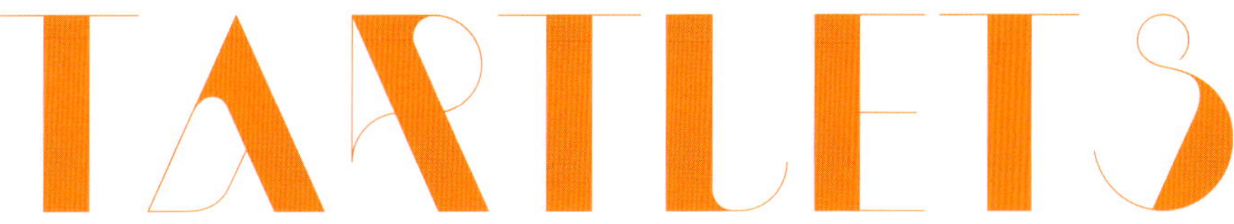

ORANGE–JASMINE ÉCLAIRS

FOR THE ORANGE GANACHE

¾ teaspoon (2 g) gelatin powder
1⅔ cups (400 g) light cream
4 ounces (110 g) white couverture chocolate, chopped
⅓ cup (90 g) orange juice
Zest of 2 oranges

FOR THE ÉCLAIRS (SEE PAGE 318)

1 quantity (14 ounces/400 g) choux paste

Orange crumb dough
1 quantity (12¼ ounces/350 g) crumb dough
1 teaspoon (5 g) orange fat-soluble food coloring
0.04 ounce (1 g) titanium dioxide

Orange glaze
1¼ cups (300 g) starch glaze (see page 319)
2 teaspoons (10 g) orange food coloring

Crispy wafer cookies
⅔ quantity (14 ounces/400 g) crispy wafer cookie dough
Fresh jasmine flowers

FOR THE ORANGE GEL

¾ cup (180 g) orange juice
2 tablespoons (30 g) superfine sugar
1½ teaspoons (4 g) agar powder
1 cup (170 g) poached oranges (see page 315), finely chopped
4 finger limes (2 ounces/54 g), finely chopped
⅓ cup (40 g) orange suprêmes
2 to 3 tablespoons (2 g) fresh jasmine, coarsely chopped

FOR THE ORANGE GANACHE

Soak the gelatin in 1 tablespoon (12 g) water to soften. Bring half the cream to a boil, then add the gelatin. Gradually pour the cream over the chocolate and blend together. Add the remaining cream, then the orange juice and zest. Use an immersion blender to blend until perfectly smooth, then refrigerate for 12 hours in a pastry bag with a plain tip.

FOR THE ÉCLAIRS

The next day, make the éclairs as described on page 318 with the orange crumb dough and bake for 20 minutes at 360°F (180°C). Dry for 15 minutes at 320°F (160°C). Make the orange glaze and crispy wafer cookies as described on page 319.

FOR THE ORANGE GEL

Heat ½ cup (120 g) water with the orange juice, then add the superfine sugar mixed with the agar. Boil for 2 minutes, then cool rapidly in the refrigerator. When the gel is cold, mix with an immersion blender, being careful not to beat in any air. Add the poached oranges, finger limes, and orange suprêmes. Mix together gently. Add the jasmine.

FOR ASSEMBLY AND FINISHING

Make four holes in the bottom of each éclair with the point of a knife or other tool, then pipe in the ganache, then the gelatin to fill. Reheat the glaze to 80°F (27°C) in a microwave, then give the éclairs a first coat of glaze. Put into the freezer for 5 minutes, then give them another coat of glaze. Refrigerate for a few minutes. Just before serving, place a few jasmine petals in each wafer cookie and place three along the top of each éclair.

PREPARATION TIME: 2 HOURS

COOKING TIME: 35 MINUTES

SERVES 8

RESTING TIME: 12 HOURS PLUS 1 HOUR

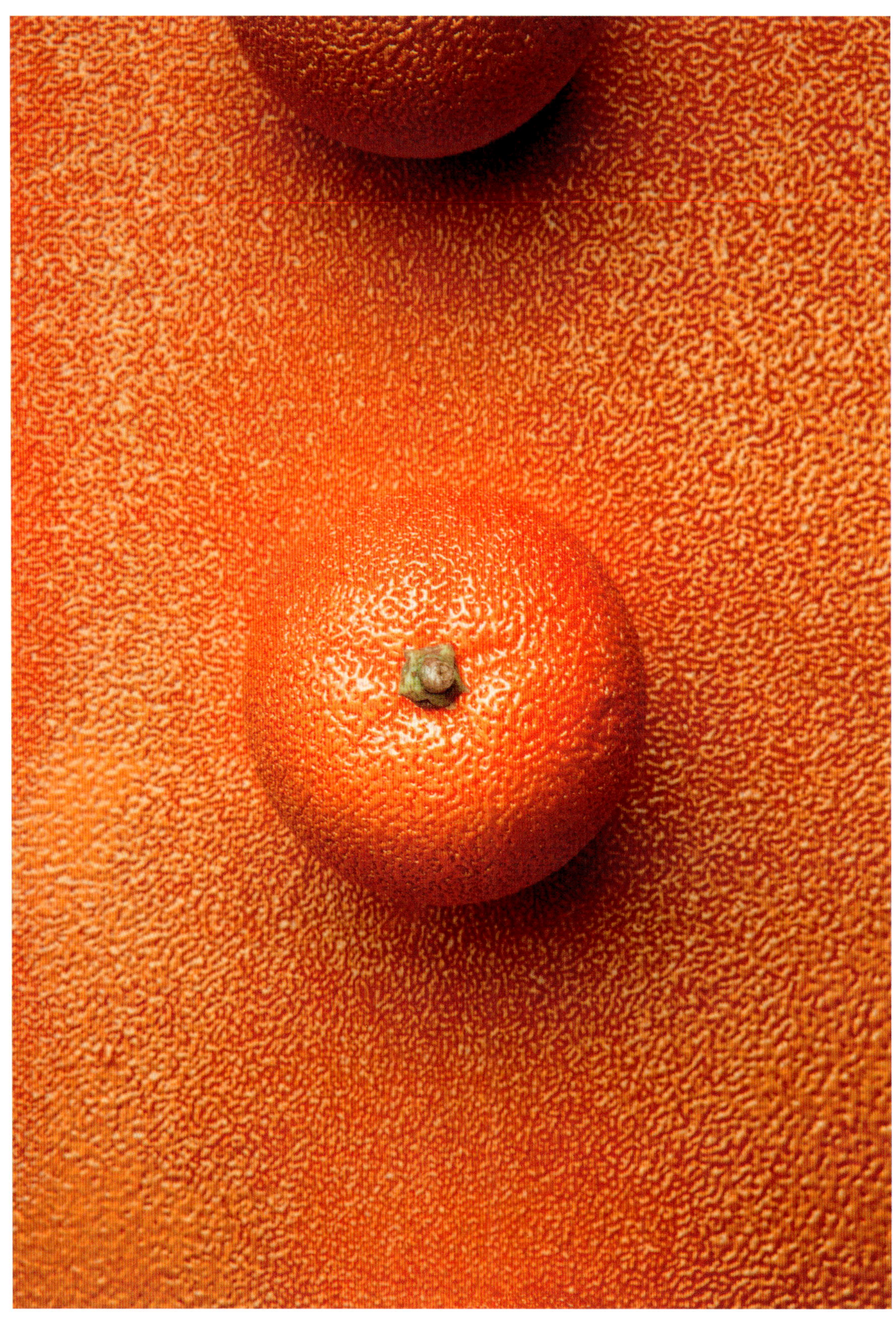

GRAPEFRUIT

FOR THE TARTLET SHELLS
1 quantity (1¼ pounds/590 g) sweet dough (see page 312)

FOR THE WHIPPED GRAPEFRUIT GANACHE
1¼ teaspoons (4 g) gelatin powder
5 teaspoons (24 g) water
2¼ cups (530 g) whipping cream
5 ounces (144 g) white couverture chocolate, chopped
½ cup (120 g) grapefruit juice

FOR THE GRAPEFRUIT GEL CENTERS
½ cup (120 g) water
¾ cup (180 g) grapefruit juice
2 tablespoons (30 g) superfine sugar
1½ teaspoons (4 g) agar powder
1 cup (170 g) poached grapefruit (see page 315)
4 finger limes (2 ounces/54 g), finely chopped
¼ cup (40 g) grapefruit suprêmes

FOR THE EGG WASH
6 large (100 g) egg yolks
1½ tablespoons (25 g) whipping cream

FOR THE ALMOND-GRAPEFRUIT CREAM
1 quantity (10½ ounces/300 g) almond cream (see page 314)
1 grapefruit, suprêmed

FOR THE GRAPEFRUIT PASTE
½ cup (80 g) chopped fresh grapefruit
¼ cup (40 g) candied grapefruit
⅓ cup (80 g) grapefruit juice

FOR ASSEMBLY AND FINISHING

Pink coating
1¼ cups (300 g) coating mixture (see page 317)
1 teaspoon (5 g) titanium fat-soluble food coloring
1/16 teaspoon (0.2 g) red food coloring
1½ tablespoons (20 g) neutral glaze (see page 317)
¼ cup (50 g) kirsch
1 tablespoon (5 g) edible ruby luster dust

Orange crumb dough
¼ quantity (3½ ounces/100 g) crumb dough (see page 312)
⅜ teaspoon (1.7 g) orange fat-soluble food coloring
Zest of 1 orange

The procedure is exactly the same as for the Orange Tartlets. Make the recipe as described on page 55, adapting it to use the ingredients listed here.

PREPARATION TIME: 3 HOURS 30 MINUTES

SERVES 10

COOKING TIME: 35 MINUTES

RESTING TIME: 24 HOURS PLUS 4 HOURS

PREPARATION TIME: 1 HOUR

SERVES 8

COOKING TIME: 15 MINUTES

RESTING TIME: OVERNIGHT

GRAPEFRUIT

FOR THE FROMAGE BLANC MOUSSE

1¾ cups (400 g) fromage blanc or Greek yogurt
2½ tablespoons (40 g) grapefruit juice
2 cups (250 g) whipped cream
2 large (60 g) egg whites
3½ tablespoons (40 g) superfine sugar

FOR THE GRAPEFRUIT SORBET

2 cups (500 g) grapefruit juice
¼ cup (50 g) superfine sugar
1 teaspoon (5 g) glucose powder
Zest of ½ grapefruit

FOR THE CANDIED GRAPEFRUIT PEELS

½ cup (100 g) strips of grapefruit peel made with a vegetable peeler
2 cups (500 g) grapefruit juice
1¼ cups (250 g) superfine sugar

FOR THE POACHED GRAPEFRUIT

5 grapefruits
1¾ cups plus 2 tablespoons (175 g) superfine sugar
1 cup (250 g) water

FOR THE PESTO

2½ cups (100 g) fresh mint
¼ cup (50 g) almond paste
1 cup (200 g) olive oil
2 tablespoons (40 g) honey
¼ cup (50 g) crushed ice

FOR THE GRAPEFRUIT GRANITA

2 cups (500 g) grapefruit juice

FOR ASSEMBLY AND FINISHING

Timut pepper
40 pink grapefruit suprêmes
40 pomelo suprêmes

FOR THE FROMAGE BLANC MOUSSE

The previous day, mix the fromage blanc and grapefruit juice. In an electric stand mixer fitted with a whisk attachment, whip the cream until it forms stiff peaks, then set aside and wash the bowl of the mixer. Return the bowl to the mixer and use the whisk attachment to whip the egg whites and superfine sugar together into a meringue. Combine with the fromage blanc, then mix in the whipped cream. Let drain overnight in a sieve in the refrigerator.

FOR THE GRAPEFRUIT SORBET

Heat some of the grapefruit juice with the superfine sugar and glucose powder to make a syrup. Refrigerate overnight.

The next day, add the rest of the juice and the grapefruit zest and churn to make the sorbet.

FOR THE CANDIED GRAPEFRUIT PEELS

Put the grapefruit peel in a saucepan. Add the grapefruit juice and superfine sugar, then simmer for about 15 minutes, until the peels are sufficiently candied.

FOR THE POACHED GRAPEFRUIT

Make the poached grapefruit as described in the poached citrus recipe (see page 315), adjusting the amounts to fit this recipe.

FOR THE PESTO

In a powerful blender, combine the mint, almond paste, oil, honey, crushed ice, and ¼ cup (50 g) water.

FOR THE GRAPEFRUIT GRANITA

Freeze the grapefruit juice. Grate it with a fork to make a granita.

FOR ASSEMBLY AND FINISHING

Chill the serving plates in the freezer beforehand so that the granita can be placed on it without melting. Put a little pesto on the plate. Sprinkle some Timut pepper over the surface of the sorbet, then scoop up a curl of sorbet and place on top of the pesto. Arrange the fromage blanc mousse, fresh grapefruit and pomelo suprêmes, a few candied grapefruit peels, and some poached grapefruit around the plate.

STONE

APRICOT

<u>In season</u>
June to August

<u>Choosing fruit</u>
the fruit should be aromatic, plump, and give when squeezed gently

<u>Average weight</u>
1½ ounces (45 g)

<u>Storage</u>
at room temperature or in the refrigerator vegetable drawer in hot weather, 2 or 3 days maximum

<u>Flavor pairings</u>
rosemary, rum, lavender, honey, lemon juice

MIRABELLE PLUM

<u>In season</u>
August and September

<u>Choosing fruit</u>
the fruit should be aromatic, with a thin, taut skin covered with reddish blemishes

<u>Average weight</u>
½ ounce (15 g)

<u>Storage</u>
in the refrigerator vegetable drawer up to 5 days; take them out 20 minutes before eating

<u>Flavor pairings</u>
kirsch, tomato, almond, honey

NECTARINE

In season

June to August

Choosing fruit

it should be aromatic and give when squeezed gently

Average weight

5¼ ounces (150 g)

Storage

in a cool place for up to 2 days

Flavor pairings

almond, cardamom, lemon

PEACH

In season

June to August

Choosing fruit

it should be aromatic and give when squeezed gently; the skin should be velvety and between orange and purple

Average weight

5¼ ounces (150 g)

Storage

in a cool place for up to 2 days

Flavor pairings

hazelnut, orange, pear, verbena

APRICOT

FOR THE TARTLET SHELLS

1 quantity (1¼ pounds/590 g) sweet dough (see page 312)

FOR THE WHIPPED APRICOT GANACHE

¾ teaspoon (2.5 g) gelatin powder
2 ounces (60 g) white couverture chocolate, chopped
½ cup (100 g) whipping cream
¼ cup (62 g) cocoa butter
1⅓ cups (330 g) apricot juice
⅓ cup (100 g) mascarpone cheese

FOR THE APRICOT GEL

½ cup (150 g) apricot juice
1 teaspoon (7 g) superfine sugar
2 tablespoons (2.5 g) agar powder
1 teaspoon (5 g) lemon juice

FOR THE APRICOT CENTERS

6 apricots (7 ounces/ 200 g)
Olive oil
1 sprig fresh rosemary
1 quantity (5¾ ounces/160 g) apricot gel (see above)

FOR THE EGG WASH

6 large (100 g) egg yolks
1½ tablespoons (25 g) whipping cream

FOR THE ALMOND-ROSEMARY CREAM

½ quantity (5¼ ounces/150 g) almond cream (see page 314)
0.1 ounces (5 g) fresh rosmary, chopped

FOR THE APRICOT COMPOTE

14 apricots (1 pound 2 ounces/500 g)
2 tablespoons (30 g) lemon juice
2 teaspoons (15 g) honey
1 sprig fresh rosemary

FOR ASSEMBLY AND FINISHING

Orange coating
1¼ cups (300 g) coating mixture (see page 317)
¾ teaspoon (4 g) orange fat-soluble food coloring

Red coating
⅓ cup (100 g) coating mixture (see page 317)
¼ teaspoon (1 g) red food coloring
3 tablespoons (50 g) mirror glaze

Orange crumb dough
¼ quantity (3½ ounces/100 g) crumb dough (see page 312)
¼ teaspoon (1 g) orange fat-soluble food coloring
1 ounce (30 g) chocolate (see page 317)
½ cup (50 g) cocoa powder

Continued

TARTLETS

PREPARATION TIME: 3 HOURS 30 MINUTES

SERVES 10

COOKING TIME: 40 MINUTES

RESTING TIME: 24 HOURS PLUS 6 HOURS 30 MINUTES

APRICOT

FOR THE TARTLET SHELLS

The previous day, make the sweet dough for the tartlet shells as described on page 312. Let dry in the refrigerator for 1 day.

FOR THE WHIPPED APRICOT GANACHE

Soak the gelatin in 1 tablespoon (17.5 g) cold water until it swells. Melt the chocolate and add the gelatin. Heat the cream, then pour it over the chocolate-gelatin mixture. Melt the cocoa butter, add it to the mixture, and use an immersion blender to blend for 2 minutes. Finally, add the apricot juice and mascarpone. Mix well using the immersion blender and refrigerate for 12 hours.

FOR THE APRICOT GEL

The next day, heat the apricot juice and add the superfine sugar mixed with the agar, then the lemon juice. Refrigerate for 30 minutes, then use an immersion blender to blend the cold gelatin for 3 minutes.

FOR THE APRICOT CENTERS

Preheat the oven to 500°F (250°C). Cut the apricots into uneven cubes and sprinkle them over a baking sheet. Drizzle with oil and flash roast for 2 minutes so that they release their juices. Remove from the baking sheet and refrigerate for 1 hour. Chop the rosemary. Mix the apricot cubes and the chopped rosemary into the apricot gel, then transfer to 1⅜-inch (3.5-cm)-diameter silicone half-dome molds and freeze for 1 hour.

FOR THE EGG WASH

Preheat the oven to 320°F (160°C). Blind bake the tartlet shells for 20 minutes. Beat the egg yolks with the cream and brush the shells with the mixture. Return to the oven for 5 minutes.

FOR THE ALMOND-ROSEMARY CREAM

Meanwhile, make the almond cream as described on page 314.
Transfer to a pastry bag and fill the tartlet shells with almond cream. Bake for 5 minutes.

TARTLETS

FOR THE APRICOT COMPOTE

Cut the apricots into cubes and put them in a vacuum-sealing bag. Add the lemon juice, honey, and rosemary and vacuum seal. Cook in a steam oven at 210°F (100°C) for 7 minutes or by placing the bag in a pot of simmering water.

FOR ASSEMBLY

In the chilled bowl of an electric stand mixer fitted with a whisk attachment, whip the apricot ganache, then transfer to 1¾-inch (4.5-cm)-diameter half-dome silicone molds. Insert the frozen apricot centers, cover with ganache, and freeze for 3 hours. Once completely frozen, unmold and sculpt into an apricot shape. Heat the orange coating to 80°F (25°C), then dip each apricot half to coat. Defrost for 1 hour in the refrigerator.

FOR FINISHING

Make the orange and red coatings as described on page 317. Heat the orange coating to 100°F (40°C), then stipple the surface of each apricot by airbrushing the entire surface of the shaped fruit. Heat the red coating to 100°F (40°C) and use a small brush to add little red dots. Heat the mirror glaze to 100°F (40°C) and spray all over the shaped fruit to create a shiny, moist effect. Add apricot compote to each tartlet on top of the almond cream. Top with a shaped apricot, then place the crumb dough around the edge. To finish, shape the chocolate to make uneven pieces. Roll them in the cocoa powder to make your stems. Arrange on top of the shaped apricot.

PREPARATION TIME: 2 HOURS

SERVES 8 TO 10

COOKING TIME: 1 HOUR

RESTING TIME: 24 HOURS PLUS 40 MINUTES

ROSEMARY-

FOR THE TART SHELL

1 quantity (1¼ pounds/590 g) sweet dough (see page 312)

FOR THE EGG WASH

6 large (100 g) egg yolks
1½ tablespoons (25 g) whipping cream

FOR THE ALMOND-ROSEMARY CREAM

1 quantity (10½ ounces/300 g) almond cream (see page 314)
2 apricots
1 sprig fresh rosemary

FOR THE APRICOT COMPOTE

28 apricots (2¼ pounds/1 kg)
¼ cup (½ stick/50 g) unsalted butter
¼ cup (50 g) packed light brown sugar
1 tablespoon (8 g) custard powder

FOR THE CRUMB DOUGH

1 cup (2 sticks/220 g) unsalted butter
¾ cup (150 g) superfine sugar
2 cups plus 2 tablespoons (275 g) cake flour
3 cups (300 g) sliced almonds
Confectioners' sugar

FOR ASSEMBLY AND FINISHING

11 apricots
Butter and sugar for frying
0.04 ounce (1 g) rosemary powder (see page 317)

FOR THE TART SHELL

The previous day, make the dough for the tart shells as described on page 312 and let dry in the refrigerator for 1 day. The next day, blind bake the tart shell for 25 minutes at 320°F (160°C).

FOR THE EGG WASH

Beat the egg yolks with the cream, then use a brush or airbrush gun to apply a thin layer of the mixture to the baked tart shell. Return the tart shell to the oven for 10 minutes to brown.

FOR THE ALMOND-ROSEMARY CREAM

Make the almond cream as described on page 314 and refrigerate for 30 minutes. Pour into the prebaked tart shell. Cut the apricots into wedges, chop the rosemary, and arrange both on top of the cream. Bake for 10 minutes.

FOR THE APRICOT COMPOTE

Cut the apricots into ⅜-inch (1-cm) cubes. In a saucepan, brown the butter, then add the apricot cubes, turning to coat. Cover and let cook for 5 minutes, stirring occasionally, until one-third of the apricots have broken down. Add the brown sugar and let dissolve for 30 seconds. Mix the custard powder with 2 tablespoons (30 g) water, then add to the compote. Boil for 2 minutes, then chill for 10 minutes in the freezer. Use a pastry bag with a plain tip to pipe the compote over the tart, then use an offset spatula to smooth.

FOR THE CRUMB DOUGH

In an electric stand mixer fitted with the flat beater, cream the butter, superfine sugar, and flour to make a shortbread dough. Add the almonds. Sprinkle the crumbs over the tart, dust with confectioners' sugar, and bake the tart for 15 minutes at 320°F (160°C).

FOR ASSEMBLY AND FINISHING

Cut the apricots into wedges. Pan-fry half the apricots with a little butter and sugar. Set aside the remaining uncooked apricots. Arrange all the apricot wedges — both raw and cooked — on top of the tart and add the rosemary powder. Serve warm.

PREPARATION TIME: 1 HOUR

SERVES 6

COOKING TIME: 8 MINUTES

RESTING TIME: 2 HOURS 20 MINUTES

ROASTED APRICOTS WITH LAVENDER

FOR THE MASCARPONE-LAVENDER CREAM

½ cup (125 g) whipping cream
0.1 ounces (5 g) fresh lavender flowers
½ cup (125 g) mascarpone cheese
2 tablespoons (25 g) superfine sugar

FOR THE ROASTED APRICOTS

12 fresh apricots
1½ tablespoons (20 g) unsalted butter, melted
½ teaspoon (2 g) ascorbic acid
3 tablespoons (35 g) superfine sugar
1 tablespoon (10 g) vanilla sugar
1 sprig fresh lavender

FOR THE APRICOT-OLIVE OIL VINAIGRETTE

1 teaspoon (3 g) gelatin powder
1 cup (250 g) apricot juice
1 tablespoon (24 g) Béton honey or lavender honey
2½ tablespoons (36 g) lemon juice
½ cup (120 g) Casanova olive oil

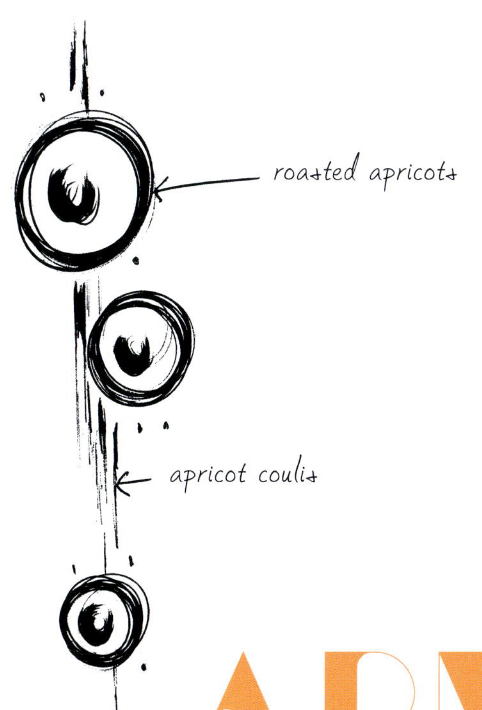

FOR THE MASCARPONE-LAVENDER CREAM

In a saucepan, combine one-third of the whipping cream with the lavender and heat gently, then refrigerate for 20 minutes. Transfer to the bowl of an electric stand mixer fitted with a whisk attachment, add the rest of the whipping cream, the mascarpone, and superfine sugar, and whip. Refrigerate for 2 hours.

FOR THE ROASTED APRICOTS

Preheat the oven to 350°F (175°C). Cut the apricots in half and remove their pits, then mix them with the melted butter and ascorbic acid in a large mixing bowl. Turn onto a baking sheet lined with parchment paper and sprinkle with superfine sugar, vanilla sugar, and lavender. Bake for 8 minutes.

FOR THE APRICOT-OLIVE OIL VINAIGRETTE

Soak the gelatin in 4 teaspoons (21 g) cold water until it swells. In a saucepan, gently heat the apricot juice, then add the gelatin, honey, and lemon juice. Use an immersion blender to emulsify while adding the oil slowly as if making a vinaigrette.

FOR ASSEMBLY AND FINISHING

Lightly whip the mascarpone-lavender cream with a wire whisk and place some in the center of each roasted apricot half. Serve with a drizzle of apricot-olive oil vinaigrette.

TIP

The mascarpone-lavender cream will begin to melt when it comes into contact with the roasted apricots. This is the moment to add the vinaigrette.

MIRABELLE PLUM TART

FOR THE VERJUICE PLUMS
10 Mirabelle plums (3½ ounces/100 g)
½ cup (100 g) verjuice

FOR THE TART SHELL
1 quantity (1¼ pounds/590 g) sweet dough (see page 312)

FOR THE EGG WASH
6 large (100 g) egg yolks
1½ tablespoons (25 g) whipping cream

FOR THE ALMOND-PLUM CREAM
1 quantity (10½ ounces/300 g) almond cream (see page 314)
½ cup (100 g) Mirabelle plums, cut into small pieces

FOR THE PLUM PRESERVES
50 Mirabelle plums (1 pound 2 ounces/500 g)
2½ tablespoons (30 g) superfine sugar
5 teaspoons (25 g) lemon juice
¼ teaspoon (1 g) ascorbic acid
2 teaspoons (10 g) kirsch
1¼ teaspoons (3.5 g) pectin NH

FOR ASSEMBLY AND FINISHING
18 fresh Mirabelle plums (6¼ ounces/180 g)

TIP
The verjuice gives a sour taste to the plums and a twist to the tart.

FOR THE VERJUICE PLUMS
The previous day, put the plums in the verjuice and soak for 1 day.

FOR THE TART SHELL
Make the dough for the tart shells as described on page 312 and let dry in the refrigerator overnight. The next day, preheat the oven to 320°F (160°C) and blind bake the tart shell for 25 minutes.

FOR THE EGG WASH
Beat the egg yolks with the cream, then use a brush or airbrush gun to apply a thin layer of the mixture to the baked tart shell. Return the tart shell to the oven for 10 minutes to brown.

FOR THE ALMOND-PLUM CREAM
Make the almond cream as described on page 314. Wash and pit the plums, then cut into small pieces. Fill the tart shell with the almond cream, then cover with the plum pieces, pressing them down lightly into the cream. Bake for 10 minutes.

FOR THE PLUM PRESERVES
Wash the plums, cut them in half, and remove the pits. Cook over low heat with 1½ tablespoons (20 g) of the superfine sugar, the lemon juice, and ascorbic acid. Flambé with the kirsch, then reduce for 5 minutes, until the preserves reaches the desired consistency. Mix the pectin with the remaining sugar. Add to the preserves, boil for 1 minute, then remove from the pan.

FOR ASSEMBLY AND FINISHING
Once the tart is baked, arrange the verjuice-soaked plums on top, then add the plum preserves. Cut the fresh plums in half and arrange them tastefully.

PREPARATION TIME: 2 HOURS

SERVES 8 TO 10

COOKING TIME: 50 MINUTES

RESTING TIME: 24 HOURS

PREPARATION TIME: 2 HOURS

SERVES 8 TO 10

COOKING TIME: 1 HOUR

RESTING TIME: 24 HOURS

NORMANDY

FOR THE TART SHELL
1 quantity (1¼ pounds/590 g) sweet dough (see page 312)

FOR THE EGG WASH
6 large (100 g) egg yolks
1½ tablespoons (25 g) whipping cream

FOR THE ALMOND-VERBENA CREAM
1 quantity (10½ ounces/300 g) almond cream (see page 314)
2 nectarines
6 verbena leaves

FOR THE NECTARINE COMPOTE
7 nectarines
¼ cup (½ stick/50 g) unsalted butter
¼ cup (50 g) packed light brown sugar
1 tablespoon (8 g) custard powder

FOR THE CRUMB DOUGH
1 cup (2 sticks/220 g) unsalted butter
¾ cup (150 g) superfine sugar
2 cups plus 2 tablespoons (275 g) cake flour
3 cups (300 g) sliced almonds
Confectioners' sugar

FOR ASSEMBLY AND FINISHING
15 nectarines
Butter for frying
Verbena powder (see page 317)
Fresh verbena

FOR THE TART SHELL
Make the sweet dough for the tart shell as described on page 312 and let dry in the refrigerator for 1 day. The next day, blind bake the tart shell for 25 minutes at 320°F (160°C).

FOR THE EGG WASH
Beat the egg yolks with the cream, then use a brush or airbrush gun to apply a thin layer of the mixture to the baked tart shell. Return the tart shell to the oven for 10 minutes to brown.

FOR THE ALMOND-VERBENA CREAM
Make the almond cream as described on page 314. Cut the nectarines into wedges and chop the verbena. Fill the tart shell with almond cream, then cover with the nectarine wedges, pressing them down lightly into the cream. Add the verbena. Bake for 10 minutes.

FOR THE NECTARINE COMPOTE
Peel the nectarines and cut them into ³/₈-inch (1-cm) cubes. In a saucepan, brown the butter, then add the nectarine cubes and turn to coat. Cover and let cook for 5 minutes, stirring occasionally, until the nectarines begin to break down. Add the brown sugar and let dissolve for 30 seconds. Mix the custard powder with 2 tablespoons (30 g) water, then add to the compote. Boil for 2 minutes, then cool rapidly by pouring into a pan and refrigerating. Spread the compote over the baked tart.

FOR THE CRUMB DOUGH
Rub the butter, superfine sugar, and flour together by hand. Add the almonds and sprinkle over the tart. Dust with confectioners' sugar and bake for about 15 minutes at 320°F (160°C).

FOR ASSEMBLY AND FINISHING
Cut the nectarines into neat wedges. Set half aside and pan-fry the other half. Arrange all the nectarine wedges tastefully over the tart. Season with the verbena powder and place the fresh verbena on the tart once it has finished baking. Serve warm.

PEACH VERBENA

FOR THE TARTLET SHELLS

1 quantity (1¼ pounds/590 g) sweet dough (see page 312)

FOR THE WHIPPED PEACH GANACHE

2 teaspoons (7 g) gelatin powder
½ cup (100 g) fresh peach pulp (4 peaches)
¼ teaspoon (1 g) ascorbic acid
1⅔ cups (400 g) whipping cream
4 ounces (110 g) white couverture chocolate, chopped
3½ tablespoons (50 g) crème de pêche liqueur

FOR THE PEACH GEL CENTERS

2 small white peaches (8¾ ounces/ 250 g)
½ teaspoon (2 g) ascorbic acid
2 teaspoons (10 g) lime juice
2½ teaspoons (10 g) superfine sugar
1 teaspoon (3 g) pectin NH
1 tablespoon (5 g) chopped fresh verbena
1⅓ cups (250 g) firm peach cubes (about 7 peaches)
2 teaspoons (10 g) crème de pêche liqueur

FOR THE EGG WASH

6 large (100 g) egg yolks
1½ tablespoons (25 g) whipping cream

FOR THE ALMOND-VERBENA CREAM

½ quantity (5¼ ounces/150 g) almond cream (see page 314)
1 tablespoon (6 g) chopped verbena

FOR THE PEACH PRESERVES

4 white peaches, not too ripe (1¼ pounds/600 g), peeled
½ teaspoon (2 g) ascorbic acid
1½ tablespoons (20 g) crème de pêche liqueur

FOR ASSEMBLY AND FINISHING

Ivory coating

1¼ cups (300 g) coating mixture (see page 317)

Red coating

¾ cup (200 g) coating mixture (see page 317)
2 teaspoons (10 g) red food coloring

White coating

¾ cup (200 g) coating mixture (see page 317)
0.02 ounce (0.5 g) titanium dioxide

SILVER LUSTER DUST

1 cup (100 g) finely chopped toasted almonds (see page 317)
1 ounce (30 g) chocolate
Cocoa powder

Continued

PREPARATION TIME: 3 HOURS 30 MINUTES

SERVES 10

COOKING TIME: 40 MINUTES

RESTING TIME: 24 HOURS PLUS 4 HOURS

FOR THE TARTLET SHELLS

The previous day, make the sweet dough for the tartlet shells as described on page 312 and let dry in the refrigerator for 1 day.

FOR THE WHIPPED PEACH GANACHE

Soak the gelatin in ¼ cup (70 g) cold water until it swells. Mix the peach pulp with the ascorbic acid and strain through a conical sieve. Heat ½ cup (100 g) of the cream without letting it boil, then remove from the heat and add the gelatin. Melt the chocolate, then pour the hot cream over and use an immersion blender to blend together. Add the rest of the cream, which should be cold, and the crème de pêche. Mix and pour into a pan. Refrigerate for 12 hours.

FOR THE PEACH GEL CENTERS

The next day, peel the white peaches and mix their flesh with half of the ascorbic acid. Strain through a conical sieve, then heat in a saucepan with the lime juice. Meanwhile, mix the superfine sugar and pectin, then add to the saucepan. Boil for 2 minutes, then chill by pouring the mixture into a pan and refrigerating. Mix with an immersion blender, then add the verbena, peach cubes, and crème de pêche mixed with the remaining half of the ascorbic acid. Pour into 1³/₈-inch (3.5-cm)-diameter silicone half-dome molds and freeze for 1 hour.

FOR THE EGG WASH

Preheat the oven to 320°F (160°C). Blind bake the tartlet shells for 20 minutes. Beat the egg yolks with the cream and brush the shells with the mixture. Return to the oven for 5 minutes.

FOR THE ALMOND-VERBENA CREAM

Make the almond cream as described on page 314 and use to fill the tartlet shells along with the chopped verbena. Bake for 5 minutes, then let cool.

FOR THE PEACH PRESERVES

Cut the peeled peaches into ¼-inch (5-mm) cubes. Cook 1¼ cups (200 g) of the peaches in a dry skillet for about 5 minutes, stirring gently with a spoon, until the peaches break down and some of their juice boils off. Combine the cooked peaches with the remaining peach cubes, the ascorbic acid, and crème de pèche. Spread this preserve over the almond-verbena cream layer, filling the tartlet shells to the top. Set aside.

FOR ASSEMBLY AND FINISHING

Whip the peach ganache and transfer to 1¾-inch (4.5-cm)-diameter silicone half-dome molds. Insert a peach gelatin center into each. Freeze for 3 hours, then sculpt into a peach shape. Prepare the coatings as described on page 317, using the different food colorings. Heat the ivory coating to 80°F (27°C) and use to coat the ganache peaches, then thaw. Airbrush with the red coating, then spray from a distance with a tiny amount of white coating to make a light veil. To finish, blow the silver luster dust gently over the shaped peaches and place them on top of the tartlets. Apply a little collar of toasted almonds around the edge.

Shape the chocolate to obtain uneven pieces and roll them in the cocoa powder. Place these stems on top of the peaches.

PREPARATION TIME: 1 HOUR

SERVES 6

COOKING TIME: 3 HOURS

RESTING TIME: 3 HOURS

PEACHES WITH

FOR THE MERINGUE BALLS
3¾ large (125 g) egg whites (½ cup)
⅔ cup (125 g) superfine sugar
1 cup (125 g) confectioners' sugar

FOR THE MASCARPONE-ALMOND CREAM
½ cup (125 g) whipping cream
¼ cup (25 g) whole almonds
½ cup (125 g) mascarpone cheese
2 tablespoons (25 g) superfine sugar
1 tablespoon (15 g) almond milk

FOR THE ALMOND PRALINE
1¾ cups (250 g) whole almonds
⅔ cup (132 g) superfine sugar
2½ teaspoons (10 g) fleur de sel
1½ tablespoons (20 g) grapeseed oil

FOR THE PEACH-OLIVE OIL VINAIGRETTE
1 teaspoon (3 g) gelatin powder
1 cup (250 g) peach juice
1 tablespoon (24 g) Béton honey
5 teaspoons (36 g) lemon juice
½ cup (120 g) Casanova olive oil

FOR FINISHING
30 whole fresh almonds
1¼ cups (300 g) milk
12 yellow peaches, at room temperature

FOR THE MERINGUE BALLS

Preheat the oven to 200°F (90°C). In a stand mixer fitted with a whisk attachment, whip the egg whites, then gradually add the superfine sugar. Whip for 2 minutes to set the meringue, then turn off the mixer and use a silicone spatula to gently fold in the confectioners' sugar. Transfer the meringue to a pastry bag fitted with a ¾-inch (20-mm) plain round tip. Pipe six large meringue kisses onto a baking sheet lined with parchment paper. Dust with confectioners' sugar and put in the oven. Bake for 1 hour, then take out the meringues and use a teaspoon to make a hole in the bottom of each. Return to the oven and let dry for 2 hours at the same temperature.

FOR THE MASCARPONE-ALMOND CREAM

Heat one-third of the whipping cream, then add the whole almonds. Blend with an immersion blender, then strain though a conical sieve. Refrigerate for about 20 minutes. Transfer to an electric stand mixer fitted with a whisk attachment, add the rest of the whipping cream, the mascarpone, superfine sugar, and almond milk, then whip. Refrigerate for 2 hours.

FOR THE ALMOND PRALINE

Preheat the oven to 340°F (170°C). Sprinkle the almonds over a baking sheet lined with parchment paper and bake for 10 minutes. In a saucepan, mix the sugar with 3 tablespoons (47.5 g) water and heat to 220°F (110°C), then add the almonds. Stir, then let cook to make a light caramel. Pour onto a Silpat baking mat, sprinkle with the fleur de sel, and let cool. Chop in a food processor to make chunks. Adjust the consistency with the grapeseed oil — it should have the feel of a praline.

FOR THE PEACH-OLIVE OIL VINAIGRETTE

Soak the gelatin in 4 teaspoons (21 g) cold water until it swells. Gently heat the peach juice, then remove from the heat and add the gelatin, honey, and lemon juice. Use an immersion blender to emulsify while adding the oil as if making a vinaigrette.

FOR ASSEMBLY AND FINISHING

Shell the fresh almonds, cut them in half, and soak in the milk for 1 hour. Cut the room-temperature peaches into wedges. Gently whip the cold mascarpone-almond cream and transfer to a pastry bag. Fill the hole in the meringues with mascarpone-almond cream, then with praline.

In the center of each plate, pour out a little peach vinaigrette and arrange the yellow peach wedges around it in a fan shape. Place the filled meringue in the middle, then garnish with the milky almonds.

FRUITÉS

WITH
EDS

QUINCE

In season
October

Choosing fruit
the fruit should be aromatic, and its skin should be yellow, firm, and smooth

Average weight
8¾ ounces (250 g)

Storage
in a cool, well-ventilated place for several weeks

Flavor pairings
cardamom, apple, chocolate

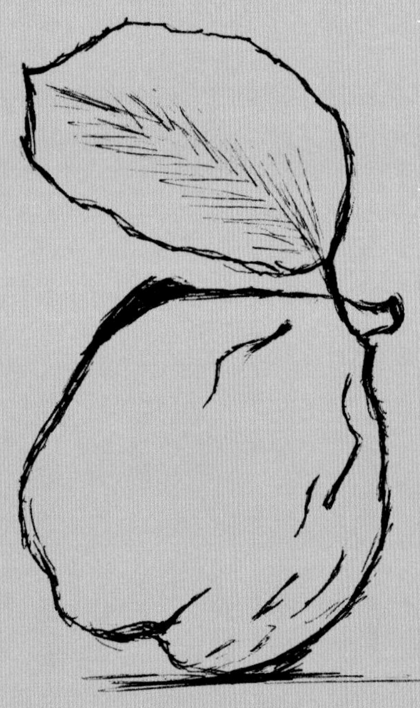

MELON

In season

June to September

Choosing fruit

it should be heavy and aromatic (but not too much so), with a supple rind; the stem should be a little cracked

Average weight

1¼ pounds (600 g)

Storage

in the refrigerator vegetable drawer for up to 6 days

Flavor pairings

pepper, Muscat, mint

TOMATO

In season

May to September

Choosing fruit

the fruit should be somewhat dense, bright, unblemished, and have a little give, but above all, the vine should be aromatic

Average weight

between 2¾ and 7 ounces (75 and 200 g), depending on the variety

Storage

at room temperature for up to 4 days; store on the vine to preserve maximum freshness

Flavor pairings

basil, caramel, hazelnut

PEAR

In season

August to April

Choosing fruit

the fruit should have smooth, taut skin with no bruising, and the stem still attached

Average weight

4¼ ounces (120 g)

Storage

at room temperature for a few weeks for fruit that is still hard, 3 days maximum for ripe fruit

Flavor pairings

chocolate, black truffle, maple syrup

APPLE

In season

September to May

Choosing fruit

the fruit should be aromatic, firm, smooth, and unblemished

Average weight

5¼ ounces (150 g)

Storage

at room temperature for up to 8 days, in the refrigerator for up to 6 weeks

Flavor pairings

basil, dill, lemon, honey

TATIN-STYLE

FOR THE PUFF PASTRY DOUGH

Kneaded butter (beurre manié)
1½ cups plus 2 tablespoons (14¾ ounces/420 g) unsalted dry butter (84% fat content)
1½ cups (180 g) pastry flour

Water dough (détrempe)
⅔ cup (160 g) water
1 tablespoon (15 g) salt
⅝ teaspoon (3 g) distilled white vinegar
½ cup (1 stick 125 g) unsalted butter, softened
3 cups (380 g) pastry flour

FOR THE CARDAMOM SYRUP

2½ cups (500 g) superfine sugar
Zest of 1 orange
Zest of 1 lemon
5 cardamom pods

FOR ASSEMBLY AND FINISHING

10 quinces
Olive oil

TIP

Serve with Normandy crème fraîche and a scoop of vanilla ice cream.

FOR THE PUFF PASTRY DOUGH

Make the puff pastry dough using the amounts listed here, turning it six times as described on page 313. Use a rolling pin to roll the dough to a thickness of 1/16 inch (2 mm), then cut out a rectangle the same size as your cake pan.

FOR THE CARDAMOM SYRUP

Boil the superfine sugar with 2 cups (500 g) water, the orange and lemon zests, and cardamom.

FOR ASSEMBLY AND FINISHING

Preheat the oven to 360°F (180°C). Peel the quinces and use a mandoline to cut them into ribbons. Line the cake pan with parchment paper, then pour the syrup over the bottom. Lay a ribbon of quince on top, then brush the ribbon with the syrup. Repeat this process, layering in all the quince ribbons. Bake between two baking trays (so tha the mold stays closed) for about 1 hour 30 minutes. After baking, place the puff pastry rectangle on top of the quinces and return to the oven for about 30 minutes, until the pastry begins to brown. Let stand for 30 minutes, then remove from the pan. Brush lightly with oil.

PREPARATION TIME: 3 HOURS

SERVES 4

COOKING TIME: 2 HOURS

RESTING TIME: 6 HOURS 30 MINUTES

PEPPERED

FOR THE MELON GRANITA

¼ cup (50 g) superfine sugar
¼ cup (50 g) glucose powder
2½ teaspoons (5 g) long pepper
4¼ cups (1 kg) fresh melon juice

FOR THE MELON BALLS

2 Cavaillon melons
1½ tablespoons (20 g) olive oil
2 teaspoons (4 g) long pepper

FOR THE MELON GRANITA

Heat the superfine sugar, glucose, and pepper with 1¼ cups (300 g) water. Remove from the heat, add the melon juice, and freeze for 2 hours.

FOR THE MELON BALLS

Cut open the Cavaillon melons and remove their seeds. Use a melon baller to scoop out balls of flesh. Gently roll the balls in olive oil, then pepper. Serve with the granita.

PREPARATION TIME: 20 MINUTES

SERVES 4

COOKING TIME: 5 MINUTES

RESTING TIME: 2 HOURS

PREPARATION TIME: 2 HOURS

SERVES 8

COOKING TIME: 5 MINUTES

RESTING TIME: 24 HOURS PLUS 2 HOURS 45 MINUTES

BLACK TRUFFLE PIZZA

FOR THE BLACK TRUFFLE CREAM
¾ ounce (20 g) black truffle
1½ tablespoons (20 g) olive oil
1¾ cups (400 g) crème fraîche

FOR THE BRIOCHE DOUGH
4¼ cups (525 g) all-purpose flour
2½ teaspoons (15 g) salt
3½ tablespoons (40 g) superfine sugar
6¼ large (315 g) eggs (1¼ cups)
⅓ (20 g) cake yeast or 2¼ teaspoons active dry yeast
1½ cups (3 sticks/350 g) unsalted butter, at room temperature

FOR ASSEMBLY AND FINISHING (FOR EACH PIZZA)
1 egg yolk
1½ teaspoon (8 g) Borniambuc cream
⅛ ounce (4 g) truffle shavings
2 tablespoons (15 g) Alain Ducasse 70% cocoa powder
⅜ ounce (11 g) Alain Ducasse Peru chocolate, melted
⅛ ounce (4 g) fresh truffle
A few thin shavings of pear
¼ teaspoon (1 g) fleur de sel
½ teaspoon (2 g) olive oil

FOR THE BLACK TRUFFLE CREAM
The previous day, clean the truffle, then use a mortar and pestle to grind it with the oil. Add half the crème fraîche and mix. Refrigerate for 24 hours.

The next day, add the remaining crème fraîche.

FOR THE BRIOCHE DOUGH
In an electric stand mixer fitted with the dough hook, mix the flour, salt, sugar, and three-quarters of the eggs. Gradually add the yeast and the remaining eggs. Knead for about 5 minutes, then add the butter and run the mixer for another 10 minutes. Remove from the mixer and let rise for 30 minutes in a warm place. Refrigerate for 2 hours.

FOR ASSEMBLY
Cut eight 3¼-ounce (90-g) pieces of brioche dough, form them into balls, and let rest for 5 minutes on the work surface. Flatten them into even disks and place them into eight 5-inch (12-cm) round baking pans. Use a brush to moisten the edges with water and glaze the entire surface of the dough with the beaten egg yolk. Let rise in a warm place for 10 minutes, then prick the pizzas with a fork.

FINISHING
Preheat a deck oven or pizza oven to 540°F (280°C). Spread 1 tablespoon (15 g) truffle cream and 1 teaspoon (5 g) Borniambuc cream evenly over each pizza, add half of the truffle shavings, and bake for 4 minutes. After baking, add the chocolate powder, five dots of melted chocolate, the rest of the truffle shavings, 1 teaspoon (5 g) truffle cream, and ½ teaspoon (3 g) Borniambuc cream. Return to the oven for 1 minute. Shave off a few strips of fresh truffle and unpeeled raw pear and arrange them on the pizza. Finally, add the fleur de sel, oil, and the remaining melted chocolate.

FOR THE TARTLET SHELLS

1 quantity (1¼ pounds/590 g) sweet dough (see page 312)

FOR THE WHIPPED PEAR GANACHE

1½ teaspoons (5 g) gelatin powder
2¾ cups (660 g) Boiron pear pulp
1 teaspoon (2 g) juniper berries
4¼ cups (120 g) white couverture chocolate, chopped
½ cup (125 g) cocoa butter, melted
1½ teaspoons (4 g) xanthan gum
¾ cup (200 g) cold whipping cream
¾ cup (200 g) mascarpone cheese

FOR THE PEAR GEL

1¼ cups (300 g) pear juice
2½ teaspoons (14 g) superfine sugar
2 teaspoons (5 g) agar powder
2 teaspoons (10 g) lemon juice

FOR THE PEAR CENTERS

1 medium-large Bartlett pear (7 ounces/200 g)
Olive oil
Confectioners' sugar
1 medium-large Conference pear (7 ounces/200 g)
1 quantity (10½ ounces/300 g) pear gelatin
¾ cup (205 g) lemon juice
½ teaspoon (1 g) juniper berries, crushed

FOR THE EGG WASH

6 large (100 g) egg yolks
1½ tablespoons (25 g) whipping cream

FOR THE ALMOND-VERBENA CREAM

½ quantity (5¼ ounces/150 g) almond cream (see page 314)
2 tablespoons (6 g) chopped fresh verbena

FOR THE PEAR COMPOTE

3 pears (1 pound 2 ounces/500 g)
¼ cup (60 g) lemon juice

FOR ASSEMBLY AND FINISHING

Yellow coating

1¼ cups (300 g) coating mixture (see page 317)
Yellow food coloring

Chocolate coating

10½ ounces (300 g) chocolate
½ cup (100 g) cocoa butter
1 cup (100 g) finely chopped toasted almonds (see page 317)
10 milk chocolate stems (see page 317)

PREPARATION TIME: 3 HOURS 30 MINUTES

SERVES 10

COOKING TIME: 40 MINUTES

RESTING TIME: 24 HOURS PLUS 4 HOURS

PEAR

FOR THE TARTLET SHELLS

The previous day, make the sweet dough for the tartlet shells as described on page 312. Let dry in the refrigerator for 1 day.

FOR THE WHIPPED PEAR GANACHE

Soak the gelatin in 5 teaspoons (25 g) cold water until it swells. Heat the pear pulp with the juniper berries, then pour over the melted chocolate and gelatin. Add the melted cocoa butter and the xanthan gum, then use an immersion blender to blend for 2 minutes. Add the cream and mascarpone. Refrigerate for 12 hours.

FOR THE PEAR GEL

Heat the pear juice, then add the superfine sugar mixed with the agar. Add the lemon juice, then remove from heat, pour into a pan, and refrigerate until cold. Using an immersion blender, blend for 3 minutes without beating in any air.

FOR THE PEAR CENTERS

Preheat a deck oven to 500°F (250°C) or a normal oven to 360°F (180°C).
Peel the Bartlett pear and cut it into uneven cubes. Put them on a baking sheet, drizzle with oil, sprinkle with confectioners' sugar, and bake in a deck oven for exactly 5 minutes at 500°F (250°C) or in a normal oven for 10 minutes at 360°F (180°C). Transfer to a container and let cool. Peel the Conference pear and cut it into cubes. Mix the raw and cooked pears into the pear gel, then add the lemon juice and juniper berries. Transfer the mixture to 1³/₈-inch (3.5-cm)-diameter silicone half-dome molds. Freeze for 1 hour.

FOR THE EGG WASH

Preheat the oven to 320°F (160°C). Blind bake the tartlet shells for 20 minutes. Beat the egg yolks with the cream and brush the shells with the mixture. Return to the oven for 5 minutes.

FOR THE ALMOND-VERBENA CREAM

Meanwhile, make the almond cream as described on page 314. Transfer to a pastry bag and pipe the cream into the prebaked tartlet shells. Return to the oven at 320°F (160°C) for 5 minutes. Let cool.

TARTLETS

FOR THE PEAR COMPOTE

Peel the pears and cut them into small 1/8-inch (3-mm) dice. Add the lemon juice and transfer to a vacuum-sealing bag. Cook in a steam oven at 210°F (100°C) or in a pot of boiling water for 13 minutes. Spread this compote over the baked almond cream layer, filling the tartlet shells to the top.

TIP

Be careful — this center requires you to pay attention to the ingredients. Not all the fruit may be equally ripe.

FOR ASSEMBLY AND FINISHING

In an electric stand mixer fitted with a whisk attachment, whip the cold ganache, then transfer to 1¾-inch (4.5-cm)-diameter silicone half-dome molds. Insert a frozen center into the middle and freeze for 3 hours. Make the coatings as described on page 317. Once the shapes have been made, place a ball of ganache on top and smooth to form a pear shape. Heat the yellow coating to 95°F (35°C), dip the shapes in it using a toothpick, and let thaw. Airbrush with yellow coating, then with chocolate coating to make a light veil. Use a fine brush to dot the chocolate coating. Top the tartlets with the shaped pears, then apply a little collar of finely chopped toasted almonds around the edge. Place a chocolate stem on top of each pear.

PREPARATION TIME: 2 HOURS

SERVES 8 TO 10

COOKING TIME: 50 MINUTES

RESTING TIME: 24 HOURS

This version of the Bourdaloue tart was dreamed up and created by Andy Jeanson, one of my assistants, for an online challenge. I liked the recipe so much that I wanted to make sure to give him a little recognition!

C. Grolet

FOR THE TART SHELL

1 quantity (1¼ pounds/590 g) sweet dough (see page 312)

FOR THE EGG WASH

6 large (100 g) egg yolks
1½ tablespoons (25 g) whipping cream

FOR THE ALMOND CREAM

1 quantity (10½ ounces/300 g) almond cream (see page 314)
4 teaspoons (18 g) rum

FOR THE CRUMB DOUGH

1 cup (1 stick/220 g) unsalted butter
¾ cup (150 g) superfine sugar
2⅓ cups (300 g) cake flour
2¾ cups (300 g) slivered almonds

FOR ASSEMBLY AND FINISHING

2 Comice pears
Codineige sugar
3 tablespoons (40 g) neutral glaze (see 317)

FOR THE TART SHELL

The previous day, make the sweet dough for the tart shell as described on page 312. Let dry in the refrigerator for 1 day. The next day, blind bake the tart shell for 25 minutes at 320°F (160°C).

FOR THE EGG WASH

Beat the egg yolks with the cream and brush the tart shell with the mixture. Return to the oven for 10 minutes.

FOR THE ALMOND CREAM

Make the almond cream as described on page 314. Transfer to a pastry bag and pipe the cream into the prebaked tart shell.

FOR THE CRUMB DOUGH

In an electric stand mixer fitted with the flat beater, cream the butter, superfine sugar, and flour to make a shortbread dough. Add the almonds.

FOR ASSEMBLY AND FINISHING

Increase the heat to 340°F (170°C). Peel the pears, setting aside the top of one to place in the middle of the tart. Cut the rest into wedges and distribute them over the tart, pressing them lightly into the almond cream. Sprinkle the crumb dough over the almond cream between the pears, then bake for about 25 minutes. Let cool, then sprinkle lightly with Codineige sugar. Brush the pears with the glaze.

CHARBROILED

FOR THE FROMAGE BLANC SHERBET

1¼ cups (300 g) milk
¼ cup (50 g) superfine sugar
¼ teaspoon (1 g) super neutrose
1¼ cups (375 g) fromage blanc or Greek yogurt
¼ cup (50 g) glucose powder
2 teaspoons (10 g) lemon juice

FOR THE PEPPER PASTRY CREAM

1 quantity (10½ ounces/300 g) pastry cream (see page 314)
5 teaspoons (10 g) ground black pepper

FOR THE ALMOND CRUMB DOUGH

½ cup (1 stick/110 g) unsalted butter
⅓ cup (75 g) superfine sugar
1 cup plus 2 tablespoons (150 g) cake flour
1 cup (150 g) fresh almonds, halved

FOR THE PEPPERY WAFER COOKIES

¾ quantity (1 pound/450 g) wafer cookie dough (see page 313)
2½ teaspoons (5 g) ground black pepper
⅓ cup (50 g) pine nuts (pignoli)
½ cup (50 g) walnuts, crushed

FOR THE CHARBROILED PEARS

5 Comice pears

FOR THE HONEY-OLIVE OIL DRESSING

1¼ cups (400 g) honey with propolis
Juice of 2 lemons
⅔ cup (140 g) olive oil

FOR THE FINISHING

⅓ cup (100 g) farmer's cream or crème fraîche
Pepper

FOR THE FROMAGE BLANC SORBET

The previous day, heat the milk to 120°F (50°C), then add the superfine sugar mixed with the super neutrose. Strain the fromage blanc, glucose, and lemon juice through a conical sieve, then heat the milk mixture to 175°F (80°C) and pour over the fromage blanc mixture. Mix with an immersion blender and let ripen overnight in the fridge. Churn to make the sherbet.

FOR THE PEPPER PASTRY CREAM

The next day, make the pastry cream as described on page 314, adding the pepper at the cooking stage. Strain the cream through a conical sieve and refrigerate for 30 minutes.

FOR THE ALMOND CRUMB DOUGH

Preheat the oven to 360°F (180°C). In an electric stand mixer fitted with the flat beater, beat the butter, superfine sugar, flour, and almonds. Pass the mixture through a sieve. Sprinkle the mixture over a baking sheet and bake for 15 minutes.

FOR THE PEPPERY WAFER COOKIES

Make the wafer cookie dough as described on page 313. Transfer to a 24 by 16-inch (60 by 40-cm) baking sheet and sprinkle with the pepper, pine nuts, and walnuts. Bake for 24 minutes, turning the baking sheet halfway through.

FOR THE CHARBROILED PEARS

Quarter and trim the pears, then let stand for 1 hour at room temperature. Use a chef's kitchen torch to char until they begin to blacken.

FOR THE HONEY-OLIVE OIL DRESSING

Combine all the ingredients with 3 tablespoons (40 g) water and heat. Use an immersion blender to emulsify the dressing.

FOR ASSEMBLY AND FINISHING

In an electric stand mixer fitted with a whisk attachment, whip the farmer's cream. Dot the pepper pastry cream and whipped cream onto the serving plates. Lightly sprinkle with pepper, then almond crumbs. Place a curl of fromage blanc sherbet on top of the crumbs. Insert four large pieces of wafer cookie into the side of the sherbet, then arrange the charbroiled pears between them. Serve with hot honey-olive oil dressing in a sauceboat.

PREPARATION TIME: 45 MINUTES

SERVES 10

COOKING TIME: 40 MINUTES

RESTING TIME: 12 HOURS PLUS 1 HOUR 30 MINUTES

APPLE-DILL

FOR THE TARTLET SHELLS

1 quantity (1¼ pounds/590 g) sweet dough (see page 312)

FOR THE APPLE GANACHE

3¾ teaspoons (12 g) gelatin powder
1 cup plus 3 tablespoons (280 g) whipping cream
2¾ ounces (80 g) white couverture chocolate, chopped
¼ cup (60 g) Granny Smith apple juice
2 teaspoons (10 g) Manzana green apple liqueur

FOR THE APPLE-DILL CENTERS

¾ quantity (10 ounces/280 g) apple gelatin (see page 315)
2 teaspoons (10 g) Manzana green apple liqueur
1½ tablespoons (4 g) chopped fresh dill
½ teaspoon (2 g) ascorbic acid
2 Granny Smith apples (10 ounces/280 g)

FOR THE EGG WASH

6 large (100 g) egg yolks
1½ tablespoons (25 g) whipping cream

FOR THE ALMOND-DILL CREAM

½ quantity (5¼ ounces/150 g) almond cream (see page 314)
2 tablespoons (6 g) chopped fresh dill

FOR THE GRANNY SMITH COMPOTE

5 Granny Smith apples (1 pound 10 ounces/750 g)
¼ cup (70 g) lemon juice
1¼ teaspoons (5 g) ascorbic acid

FOR THE APPLE-GREEN GLAZE

2 tablespoons (20 g) fish gelatin
1½ cups (300 g) superfine sugar
1½ cups (300 g) glucose syrup
⅛ teaspoon (0.83 g) water-soluble pistachio green food coloring
1⅛ teaspoons (5.50 g) lemon yellow water-soluble food coloring
½ cup (175 g) sweetened condensed milk
11¼ ounces (320 g) white couverture chocolate, chopped
¾ teaspoon (2 g) vanilla powder
⅛ ounce (0.5 g) silver flakes

FOR THE ASSEMBLY AND FINISHING

<u>Apple-green coating</u>
1¼ cups (300 g) coating mixture (see page 317)
⅜ teaspoon (2 g) yellow food coloring
½ teaspoon (2.5 g) green food coloring
1 teaspoon (3 g) vanilla powder
1 cup (100 g) finely chopped toasted almonds (see page 317)
10 chocolate stems (see page 317)

Continued

PREPARATION TIME: 3 HOURS 30 MINUTES

SERVES 10

COOKING TIME: 40 MINUTES

RESTING TIME: 24 HOURS PLUS 4 HOURS

APPLE-DILL

FOR THE TARTLET SHELLS

The previous day, make the sweet dough for the tartlet shells as described on page 312. Let dry in the refrigerator for 1 day.

FOR THE APPLE GANACHE

Soak the gelatin in ¼ cup (58 g) cold water until it swells. Heat 1/3 cup (80 g) of the cream, pour over the couverture chocolate and blend, then add the gelatin. Blend with an immersion blender, add the remaining cream, which should be cold, the apple juice, and Manzana liqueur, and blend again. Refrigerate for 12 hours.

FOR THE APPLE-DILL CENTERS

The next day, make the apple gelatin (see page 315) and use an immersion blender to blend, beating in as little air as possible. Add the Manzana liqueur, dill, and ascorbic acid. Peel the apples, cut into 1/8-inch (3-mm) dice, and add to the mixture. Pour into 1 3/8-inch (3.5-cm)-diameter silicone half-dome molds and freeze for 1 hour.

FOR THE EGG WASH

Preheat the oven to 320°F (160°C). Blind bake the tartlet shells for 20 minutes. Beat the egg yolks with the cream and brush the shells with the mixture. Return to the oven for 5 minutes.

FOR THE ALMOND-DILL CREAM

Make the almond cream as described on page 314. Transfer to a pastry bag and pipe the cream into the prebaked tartlet shells. Return to the oven at 320°F (160°C) for 5 minutes. Let cool.

FOR THE GRANNY SMITH COMPOTE

Peel the apples and cut them into 1/8-inch (3-mm) dice. Set aside 2 cups (250 g), then put the rest into a vacuum-sealing bag with the lemon juice. Cook for 13 minutes in a steam oven at 210°F (100°C) or in a pot of boiling water. Mix the compote with the ascorbic acid and reserved apple cubes. Transfer to a pastry bag and pipe over the baked almond cream layer, filling the tartlet shells to the top.

FOR THE APPLE-GREEN GLAZE

Soak the gelatin in ½ cup (120 g) cold water until it swells. Heat ²/₃ cup (150 g) water, the superfine sugar, glucose syrup, and food colorings to 250°F (120°C). Add the sweetened condensed milk and let cool to 110°F (45°C). Melt the chocolate and add along with the gelatin. Finally, add the vanilla powder, mix with an immersion blender, and strain the mixture through a conical sieve.

FOR ASSEMBLY AND FINISHING

In an electric stand mixer fitted with a whisk attachment, whip the cold apple ganache, then transfer to 1¾-inch (4.5-cm)-diameter silicone half-dome molds. Insert a frozen apple-dill center into each and freeze for 3 hours, then sculpt into an apple shape, using a vegetable peeler to make a gentle indentation in each. Make the coating as described on page 317, adding the vanilla powder along with the food colorings. Heat the apple green coating to 100°F (40°C) and the glaze to 85°F (30°C), then use a toothpick to dip the shapes first into the coating, then the glaze. Top each tartlet with a shaped apple, then add the toasted almonds around the edge. Add a chocolate stem.

PREPARATION TIME: 3 HOURS 30 MINUTES

SERVES 10

COOKING TIME: 40 MINUTES

RESTING TIME: 24 HOURS PLUS 4 HOURS

FOR THE TARTLET SHELLS

1 quantity (1¼ pounds/590 g) sweet dough (see page 312)

FOR THE PINK APPLE GANACHE

3¾ teaspoons (12 g) gelatin powder
¼ cup (58 g) soaking water
1¼ cups (280 g) whipping cream
2¾ ounces (80 g) white couverture chocolate
¼ cup (60 g) apple juice
2 drops rose extract

FOR THE APPLE-ROSE CENTERS

¾ quantity (10 ounces/280 g) apple gelatin (see page 315)
2 tablespoons (28 g) crystallized rose petals
2½ cups (280 g) apple cubes

FOR THE EGG WASH

6 large (100 g) egg yolks
1½ tablespoons (25 g) whipping cream

FOR THE ALMOND-APPLE CREAM

½ quantity (4¼ ounces/150 g) almond cream (see page 314)
1 Royal Gala apple

FOR THE GALA APPLE COMPOTE

1 large Royal Gala apple (8¾ ounces/250 g)
2½ tablespoons (70 g) lemon juice
1¼ teaspoons (5 g) ascorbic acid
2 tablespoons (20 g) crystallized rose petals

FOR THE BLOOD-RED GLAZE

2 tablespoons (20 g) fish gelatin
½ cup (120 g) soaking water
⅔ cup (150 g) water
1½ cups (300 g) superfine sugar
1½ cups (300 g) glucose syrup
1½ teaspoons (8 g) strawberry red food coloring
½ cup (175 g) sweetened condensed milk
11¼ ounces (320 g) white couverture chocolate, chopped
¾ teaspoon (2 g) vanilla powder
0.02 ounce (0.5 g) gold flakes

FOR ASSEMBLY AND FINISHING

Red coating

1¼ cups (300 g) coating mixture (see page 317)
½ teaspoon (2 g) PCB red food coloring
1 teaspoon (3 g) vanilla powder
1 cup (100 g) finely chopped toasted almonds (see page 317)
10 chocolate stems (see page 317)

Make the candy apple tartlets following the same procedure as for the Apple-Dill Tartlets (page 116), adapting it to use the ingredients listed here.

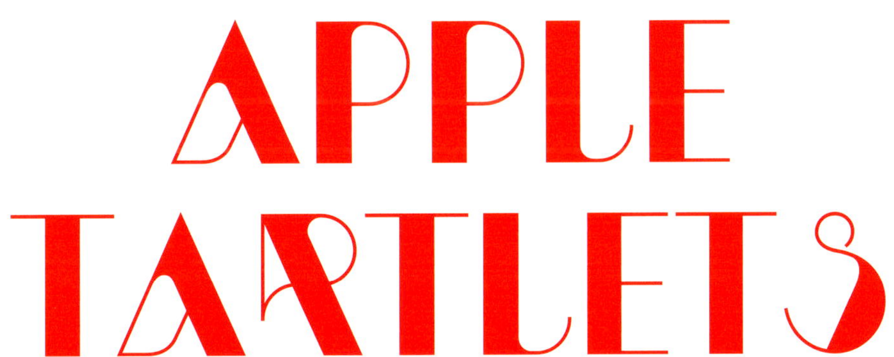

FOR THE TART SHELL

1 quantity (1¼ pounds/590 g) sweet dough (see page 312)

FOR THE EGG WASH

6 large (100 g) egg yolks
1½ tablespoons (25 g) whipping cream

FOR THE ALMOND CREAM

1 quantity (10½ ounces/300 g) almond cream (see page 314)

FOR THE APPLE COMPOTE

7 Granny Smith apples (2¼ pounds/1 kg)
½ cup (125 g) lemon juice

FOR ASSEMBLY AND FINISHING

8 Royal Gala apples, unpeeled
7 tablespoons (100 g) unsalted butter

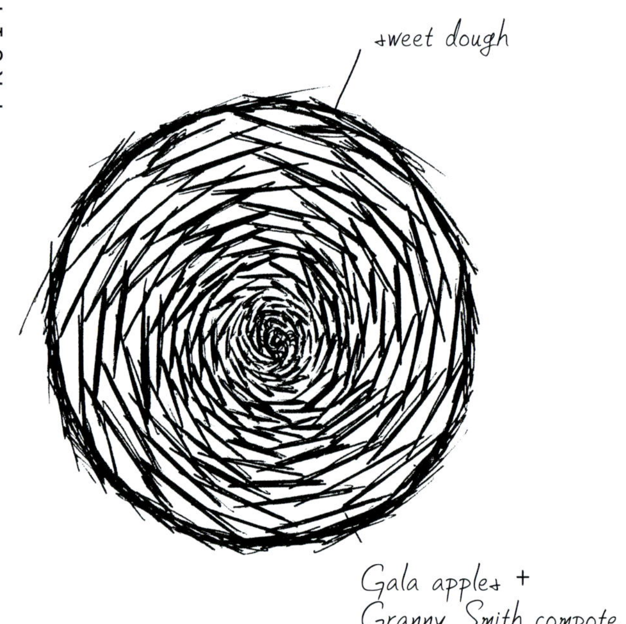

FOR THE TART SHELL

The day before, make the sweet dough for the tart shell as described on page 312. Let dry in the refrigerator for 1 day. The next day, blind bake the tart shell for 25 minutes at 320°F (160°C).

FOR THE EGG WASH

Beat the egg yolks with the cream and brush the shell with the mixture. Return to the oven for 10 minutes.

FOR THE ALMOND CREAM

Make the almond cream as described on page 314. Transfer to a pastry bag and pipe a layer of cream into the tart shell. Bake for 10 minutes.

FOR THE APPLE COMPOTE

Peel the apples and cut them into small 1/8-inch (3-mm) dice. Add the lemon juice and transfer to a vacuum-sealing bag. Cook for 13 minutes in a steam oven at 210°F (100°C) or in a pot of boiling water. Spread a thin layer of this compote over the baked almond cream layer.

FOR ASSEMBLY AND FINISHING

Quarter and core the apples, keeping 3/4 inch (2 cm) on each side, then use an adjustable-blade slicer or mandoline to cut thin slices 1/32 inch (1 mm) thick, all the same shape and size. Arrange them flat into a spiral on the tart, like a snail shell, beginning from the outside and spiraling toward the center. Melt the butter and brush it over the tart. Bake for 6 minutes at 350°F (175°C).

PREPARATION TIME: 2 HOURS

SERVES 10

COOKING TIME: 1 HOUR

RESTING TIME: 24 HOURS

TROP
FRU

ICAL
IT

TROPICAL

PINEAPPLE

In season

October to April

Choosing fruit

the pineapple's leaves should be very green and firm and come off easily; the fruit should be aromatic and heavy

Average weight

4 pounds (1.8 kg)

Storage

at room temperature for up to 6 days

Flavor pairings

coconut, avocado, lemon balm

AVOCADO

In season

October to April

Choosing fruit

the flesh should have a little give around the stem

Average weight

10½ ounces (300 g)

Storage

at room temperature for up to 5 days if the avocado is still hard; if it is ripe, in the refrigerator for 3 days

Flavor pairings

Espelette pepper, wild strawberries, apple

BANANA

In season

year-round

Choosing fruit

green going on yellow to let it ripen gradually, without light brown blemishes

Average weight

5¼ ounces (150 g)

Storage

at room temperature for up to 5 days

Flavor pairings

rum, verbena, lemon balm

PASSION FRUIT

In season

year-round

Choosing fruit

not too light, with wrinkled skin, which is a sign of ripeness

Average weight

2¾ ounces (75 g)

Storage

1 week at room temperature for fruit that is still hard; 2 days maximum in the refrigerator vegetable drawer for ripe fruit

Flavor pairings

ginger, coffee, fromage blanc or Greek yogurt

LYCHEE

In season

November to January

Choosing fruit

the fruit should be fairly hard, with an unbroken, very pink rind

Average weight

¾ ounce (20 g)

Storage

at room temperature for 2 days, or in the refrigerator vegetable drawer for 15 days

Flavor pairings

rose, mint, raspberry

KIWI

In season

November to May

Choosing fruit

according to taste and the planned time of consumption, it may be hard (unripe) or softer (ripe)

Average weight

3½ ounces (100 g)

Storage

in the refrigerator vegetable drawer for several weeks if the kiwi is still hard, or 1 week once it is ripe

Flavor pairings

pine nuts (pignoli), black sesame, chocolate

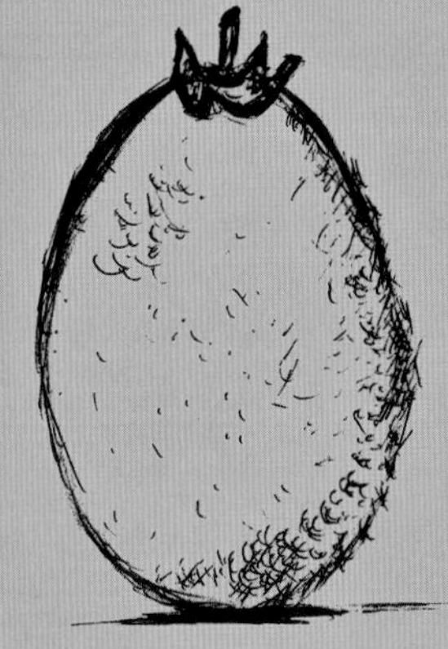

MANGO

In season

April to July, December

Choosing fruit

more than the color, it is important to make sure that the mango gives a little when squeezed gently

Average weight

14 ounces (400 g)

Storage

eat immediately if the fruit is ripe, or store in a cool place (at 43°F/6°C) for a few days

Flavor pairings

coriander, passion fruit, ginger

PREPARATION TIME: 2 HOURS

SERVES 10

COOKING TIME: 5 MINUTES

RESTING TIME: 2 HOURS

PINEAPPLE,

FOR THE PINEAPPLE-LIME SORBET

⅔ pineapple (1¼ pounds/600 g)
¼ cup (55 g) lime juice
⅓ cup (70 g) glucose powder
¾ cup (140 g) superfine sugar
¾ teaspoon (4 g) super neutrose

FOR THE PINEAPPLE-AVOCADO PRESERVES

About ½ Victoria pineapple (1 pound 2 ounces/500 g)
2½ organic avocados (1 pound 2 ounces/500 g)
¼ cup (50 g) pineapple juice

FOR THE PINEAPPLE-OLIVE OIL DRESSING

3 sheets (6.4 g powdered) gelatin
2¼ cups (540 g) pineapple juice
2¼ tablespoons (48 g) Béton honey or lavender honey
2½ tablespoons (36 g) lemon juice
1 cup (240 g) olive oil

FOR THE SMASHED AVOCADO

2½ organic avocados (1 pound 2 ounces/500 g)
Juice of 1 lemon
Fleur de sel
1 pinch Espelette pepper
3 fresh mint leaves, torn

FOR ASSEMBLY AND FINISHING

Pineapple chips (see page 316)
Espelette pepper
A few fresh mint leaves

FOR THE PINEAPPLE-LIME SORBET

Use a juicer to extract 2½ cups (600 g) juice from the pineapple. In a saucepan, heat ½ cup (100 g) of the juice, ⅔ cup (140 g) water, the lime juice, and glucose powder. Once the mixture reaches 100°F (40°C), add the superfine sugar and super neutrose. Continue to heat to 185°F (85°C). Refrigerate for about 2 hours. Add the rest of the fresh pineapple juice and mix. Churn to make the sorbet, transfer to a cold pan, and freeze.

FOR THE PINEAPPLE-AVOCADO PRESERVES

Cut the pineapple and avocado into small cubes. Mix with the pineapple juice and refrigerate until serving.

FOR THE PINEAPPLE-OLIVE OIL DRESSING

Soak the gelatin in 4 teaspoons (21 g) cold water until it swells. Gently heat the pineapple juice. Add the gelatin, honey, and lemon juice and use an immersion blender to emulsify with the oil as if making a vinaigrette. Serve the dressing hot.

FOR THE SMASHED AVOCADO

Mash the avocado just before serving to prevent it from darkening, adding the lemon juice, a little fleur de sel, Espelette pepper, and mint.

FOR ASSEMBLY AND FINISHING

Place a scoop of pineapple-lime sorbet on top of the crushed avocado. Arrange the pineapple-avocado preserves alongside and poke in a few pineapple chips. Sprinkle with Espelette pepper. Tear the mint and sprinkle large pieces of it over the pineapple-avocado preserves. Pour the hot dressing over the dessert just before serving

AVOCADO-COCONUT ÉCLAIRS

FOR THE CRISPY COCONUT WAFER COOKIES

⅔ quantity (14 ounces/400 g) wafer cookie dough (see page 319)
⅔ cup (50 g) shredded coconut

FOR THE AVOCADO-COCONUT CREAM

1 (2 by 3-inch/5 by 7.5-cm) piece fresh coconut (2 ounces/60 g)
1⅓ cups (280 g) coconut puree
½ cup (120 g) coconut milk
½ cup (80 g) chopped avocado
1½ teaspoons (4 g) xanthan gum
½ cup (120 g) whipping cream
½ cup (100 g) mascarpone cheese

FOR THE ÉCLAIRS (SEE PAGE 318)

1 quantity (14 ounces/400 g) choux paste

White crumb dough
1 quantity (12.35 ounces/350 g) crumb dough
⅜ ounce (9 g) titanium dioxide

White glaze
1¼ cups (300 g) white starch glaze (see page 319)

FOR THE CRISPY COCONUT WAFER COOKIES

Make the cookies as described on page 319, sprinkling with shredded coconut just before tearing into pieces and crumpling them into balls.

AVOCADO-COCONUT CREAM

Smash the coconut open with a rolling pin, then remove the flesh needed. Mix the coconut puree, coconut milk, fresh coconut, and avocado, then use an immersion blender to blend, incorporating the xanthan gum. Make sure the fresh coconut is well blended. In an electric stand mixer fitted with a whisk attachment, gently whip the cream with the mascarpone, then fold into the coconut mixture. Refrigerate for 20 minutes.

FOR THE ÉCLAIRS

Make the éclairs as described on page 318 with the white crumb dough and bake for 20 minutes at 360°F (180°C). Dry for 15 minutes at 320°F (160°C). Make the glaze as described on page 319.

FOR ASSEMBLY AND FINISHING

Make four holes in the bottom of each éclair with the point of a knife or other tool, then fill with the avocado-coconut cream. Reheat the white glaze to 80°F (27°C) in a microwave, then give the éclairs a first coat of glaze. Freeze for 5 minutes, then give them another coat of glaze. Refrigerate for a few minutes. Just before serving, top the éclairs with the coconut wafer balls.

PREPARATION TIME: 2 HOURS

SERVES 8

COOKING TIME: 35 MINUTES

RESTING TIME: 1 HOUR 20 MINUTES

PREPARATION TIME: 2 HOURS

SERVES 8

COOKING TIME: 20 MINUTES

RESTING TIME: 4 DAYS PLUS 7 HOURS 30 MINUTES

BANANA

FOR THE PUFF PASTRY DOUGH

Kneaded butter (beurre manié)
2 cups (14¾ ounces/420 g) unsalted dry butter (84% fat content)
1⅓ cups (165 g) pastry flour

Water dough (détrempe)
⅔ cup (160 g) water
1 tablespoon (15 g) salt
1 teaspoon (4 g) distilled white vinegar
½ cup (1 stick/130 g) unsalted butter, softened
3¼ cups (395 g) pastry flour

FOR THE ALMOND-BANANA PASTE

2 small bananas (7 ounces/200 g)
1⅓ cups (300 g) almond paste

FOR THE ALMOND-BANANA CREAM

1¼ cups (160 g) toasted almonds, ground
1¼ cups (150 g) confectioners' sugar
½ cup (1 stick/120 g) unsalted butter
3½ teaspoons (20 g) custard powder
2¼ large (120 g) eggs (½ cup), at room temperature
⅔ cup (150 g) banana juice
4 teaspoons (20 g) rum

FOR ASSEMBLY AND FINISHING

4 egg yolks, beaten
4 bananas, diced
Softened butter for the baking mat
Light brown sugar for sprinkling

FOR THE PUFF PASTRY

Four days in advance, make the puff pastry dough using the amounts listed here, turning six times as described on page 313. Do two turns per day, leaving the dough to rest until the next day after each pair of turns. On the final day, use a rolling pin to roll out the dough to a thickness of ⅛ inch (3 mm). Use a cookie cutter to cut out eight 4¾-inch (12-cm)-diameter disks and eight 5½-inch (14-cm)-diameter disks. Refrigerate overnight.

FOR THE ALMOND-BANANA PASTE

The next day, mash the bananas and mix them with the almond paste. Transfer to a pastry bag without a tip.

FOR THE ALMOND-BANANA CREAM

In an electric stand mixer fitted with the flat beater, cream together the toasted ground almonds, confectioners' sugar, and butter for at least 10 minutes. Add the custard powder, then the eggs, one by one. Finally, add the banana juice and rum. Transfer to a pastry bag without a tip.

FOR ASSEMBLY AND FINISHING

Place the 4¾-inch (12-cm) dough disks on a baking sheet and use a brush to apply the beaten egg yolk around the edge. Pipe a 3¼-ounce (90-g) circle of almond-banana paste onto each, remaining cleanly within the egg border; next, pipe 3½ ounces (100 g) of almond-banana cream on top. Top with diced raw banana, about ¼ inch (5 mm) in size. Cover with the 5½-inch (14-cm) dough disks, pressing them down gently to push out any extra air. Firmly seal the edges of the two dough disks, sealing up to the edge of the filling. Refrigerate for 1 hour, then press down on the edges again. Freeze for 30 minutes to harden the dough, then cut a 4-inch (10-cm) steam hole in the top of each using a cookie cutter. Crimp the edges with the back of a paring knife, then refrigerate for 3 hours. Remove from the refrigerator and brush again with the egg yolk. Let dry in the refrigerator for 3 hours, then brush a second time. Score lines from the middle to the edge.

TO BAKE

Preheat the oven to 360°F (180°C). Butter a Silpat baking mat with softened butter, then sprinkle with brown sugar. Place the pies on the mat and bake for 10 minutes at 360°F (180°C). Place four rings, 1½ inches (4 cm) high and 1¼ inches (3 cm) in diameter, around the edge of the pan, then set a baking sheet and a rack over the pies. Finish baking at 340°F (170°C) for 10 minutes.

PREPARATION TIME: 2 HOURS

SERVES 8 TO 10

COOKING TIME: 1 HOUR

RESTING TIME: 24 HOURS PLUS 10 MINUTES

FLUFFY BANANA–

FOR THE TART SHELL
1 quantity (1¼ pounds/590 g) sweet dough (see page 312)

FOR THE EGG WASH
6 large (100 g) egg yolks
1½ tablespoons (25 g) whipping cream

FOR THE ALMOND-VERBENA CREAM
¼ quantity (3½ ounces/100 g) almond cream (see page 314)
1½ tablespoons (3 g) fresh verbena

FOR THE LIME-VERBENA-LEMONGRASS PRESERVES
3¾ limes (8¾ ounces/250 g)
½ cup (100 g) superfine sugar
1 teaspoon (3 g) pectin NH
2 tablespoons (5 g) fresh verbena
⅓ stalk (20 g) lemongrass

FOR THE LIME MERINGUE
6 large (200 g) egg whites
1 cup (200 g) superfine sugar
Zest of 2 limes

FOR ASSEMBLY AND FINISHING
3 bananas
Confectioners' sugar

FOR THE TART SHELL
The previous day, make the dough for the tart shell as described on page 312 and let dry in the refrigerator for 1 day.
The next day, blind bake the tart shell for 25 minutes at 320°F (160°C).

FOR THE EGG WASH
Mix the egg yolks with the cream and brush the shell with the mixture. Return to the oven for 10 minutes.

FOR THE ALMOND-VERBENA CREAM
Make the almond cream as described on page 314. Wash and chop the verbena, then mix into the cream. Transfer to a pastry bag and pipe into the tart shell. Bake for 10 minutes.

FOR THE LIME-VERBENA-LEMONGRASS PERSERVES
Peel the limes with a knife and blanch the peels five successive times, boiling them in a large saucepan and then immersing in cold water. Use a knife to cut into small ¼-inch (5-mm) dice. Separate the lime into suprêmes, then squeeze the membranes to produce 4 teaspoons (20 g) juice. Boil the peels with the suprêmes, juice, and 4 teaspoons (20 g) water. Mix the superfine sugar with the pectin, verbena, and lemongrass, then pour over the lime mixture. Boil for 1 minute, then refrigerate.

FOR THE LIME MERINGUE
In an electric stand mixer fitted with a whisk attachment, beat the egg whites, then add the superfine sugar and beat until stiff. Finely grate the lime zest and use a silicone spatula to fold it into the meringue.

FOR ASSEMBLY AND FINISHING
Peel the bananas and cut them lengthwise into two 3/8-inch- (1-cm)-thick slices. Lay the banana halves next to each other and cut out a 4¾-inch (12-cm) disk using a cookie cutter. Bake for 10 minutes at 320°F (160°C), then let cool. Sand down the edges of the tart shell with a Microplane. Fill with preserves, then top with the banana disk. Flatten the top with a spatula, then freeze for 10 minutes. Pipe lime meringue kisses over the entire surface of the tart, then sprinkle with confectioners' sugar. Toast in a deck oven at 500°F (250°C) for 2 minutes.

PURE PASSION

FOR THE TARTLET SHELLS

1 quantity (1¼ pounds/590 g) sweet dough (see page 312)

FOR THE WHIPPED PASSION FRUIT GANACHE

1¼ teaspoons (4 g) gelatin powder
2¼ cups (530 g) whipping cream
5 ounces (144 g) white couverture chocolate, chopped
1½ passion fruits (4¼ ounces/120 g)

FOR THE PASSION FRUIT GEL CENTERS

½ cup (120 g) lemon juice
¾ cup (180 g) passion fruit pulp
2½ tablespoons (30 g) superfine sugar
1½ teaspoons (4 g) agar powder
2 passion fruits (6 ounces/170 g)

FOR THE EGG WASH

6 large (100 g) egg yolks
1½ tablespoons (25 g) whipping cream

FOR THE ALMOND-PASSION FRUIT CREAM

½ quantity (5¼ ounces/150 g) almond cream (see page 314)
⅓ passion fruit (1 oz/30 g)

FOR ASSEMBLY AND FINISHING

Black coating

1¼ cups (300 g) coating mixture (see page 317)
1 teaspoon (5 g) charcoal fat-soluble food coloring

Charcoal crumb dough

¼ quantity (3½ ounces/100 g) crumb dough (see page 312)
⅜ teaspoon (1.7 g) charcoal food coloring

FOR THE TARTLET SHELLS

The previous day, make the dough for the tartlet shells as described on page 312 and let dry in the refrigerator for 1 day.

FOR THE WHIPPED PASSION FRUIT GANACHE

Soak the gelatin in 1½ tablespoons (24 g) cold water for 20 minutes. Bring half the cream to a boil, then add the gelatin. Gradually pour the cream over the chocolate and blend together. Add the remaining cream, then the passion fruit. Pour into a pan and seal by covering the surface of the ganache with plastic wrap. Refrigerate for 12 hours.

FOR THE PASSION FRUIT GEL CENTERS

The next day, heat the lemon juice and passion fruit pulp, then add the superfine sugar mixed with the agar. Boil for 2 minutes, then cool rapidly by pouring the mixture into a shallow pan. When the gelatin is cold, use an immersion blender to blend without mixing in any air. Add the passion fruit, then transfer the mixture to 1⅜-inch (3.5-cm)-diameter silicone half-dome molds. Freeze for 1 hour.

FOR THE EGG WASH

Preheat the oven to 320°F (160°C). Blind bake the tartlet shells for 20 minutes. Mix the egg yolks with the cream and brush the shells with the mixture. Return to the oven for 5 minutes.

FOR THE ALMOND-PASSION FRUIT CREAM

Make the almond cream as described on page 314, add the passion fruit, and use to fill the tartlet shells. Bake for 5 minutes.

FOR ASSEMBLY AND FINISHING

In an electric stand mixer fitted with a whisk attachment, whip the cold ganache, then transfer to a pastry bag. Pipe into 1¾-inch (4.5-cm)-diameter silicone half-dome molds, then insert the passion fruit gel centers. Freeze for 3 hours. Make the black coating as described on page 317, then dip the hard ganache domes in the coating. To give them a wrinkled look, use an airbrush to stipple them with the same coating. Add a few red and white blemishes by holding the airbrush longer in certain places, creating an irregular effect. Top each tartlet shell with a passion fruit half, then finish by adding the charcoal crumb dough around the edge.

PREPARATION TIME: 3 HOURS 30 MINUTES

SERVES 10

COOKING TIME: 35 MINUTES

RESTING TIME: 24 HOURS PLUS 4 HOURS

PREPARATION TIME: 2 HOURS

SERVES 8

COOKING TIME: 1 HOUR 10 MINUTES

RESTING TIME: 12 HOURS PLUS 1 HOUR

PASSION FRUIT–

FOR THE PASSION FRUIT-GINGER GANACHE

1 teaspoon (3 g) gelatin powder
1⅔ cups (400 g) whipping cream
4 ounces (110 g) white couverture chocolate, chopped
⅓ cup (90 g) passion fruit pulp
2½ tablespoons (15 g) grated fresh ginger

FOR THE ÉCLAIRS (SEE PAGE 318)

1 quantity (14 ounces/400 g) choux paste

Yellow crumb dough
1 quantity (12¼ ounces/350 g) crumb dough
1 teaspoon (5 g) fat-soluble food coloring
0.04 ounce (1 g) titanium dioxide

Yellow glaze
1¼ cups (300 g) starch glaze (see page 319)
2 teaspoons (10 g) yellow food coloring

Crispy wafer cookies (see page 319)
⅔ quantity (14 ounces/400 g) wafer cookie dough
1 quantity (1¾ ounces/50 g) crystallized ginger (see below)

FOR THE CRYSTALLIZED GINGER

1½-inch (4-cm) piece fresh ginger (1¾ ounces/50 g)
2½ cups (500 g) superfine sugar

FOR THE PASSION FRUIT-GINGER PRESERVES

¾ cup (180 g) lemon juice
2½ tablespoons (30 g) superfine sugar
1½ teaspoons (4 g) agar powder
1 cup (170 g) passion fruit pulp
1 quantity (1¾ ounces/ 50 g) crystallized ginger (see above)

FOR THE PASSION FRUIT-GINGER GANACHE

The previous day, soak the gelatin in 4 teaspoons (18 g) water to hydrate. Bring half the cream to a boil, then add the gelatin. Gradually pour the cream over the chocolate and blend together. Add the remaining cream, then the passion fruit pulp and ginger. Use an immersion blender to blend until perfectly smooth, then refrigerate for 12 hours in a pastry bag with a plain tip.

FOR THE ÉCLAIRS

The next day, make the éclairs as described on page 318 with the yellow crumb dough and bake for 20 minutes at 360°F (180°C). Dry for 15 minutes at 320°F (160°C). Also make the yellow starch glaze and cookie balls as described on page 319.

FOR THE CRYSTALLIZED GINGER

Peel the ginger and cut it into large chunks. Blanch them three times by boiling them in a large saucepan and then immersing in cold water. Boil half the superfine sugar with ½ cup (125 g) water to make a syrup. Drop in the ginger pieces and let simmer, covered, for 30 minutes, keeping the temperature below 160°F (70°C). Concentrate the syrup by incorporating the other half of the sugar in several additions. Once the ginger is tender, drain, then heat the syrup to 217°F (103°C). Let cool, then add the ginger pieces back to the syrup. Refrigerate.

FOR THE PASSION FRUIT-GINGER PRESERVES

Heat ½ cup (120 g) water with the lemon juice, then add the sugar mixed with the agar. Boil for 2 minutes, then cool in a pan in the refrigerator. Once cold, use an immersion blender to blend without mixing in any air. Add the passion fruit seeds and crystallized ginger.

FOR ASSEMBLY AND FINISHING

Make four small holes in the bottom of each éclair; fill with ganache and preserves. Reheat the white glaze to 80°F (27°C) in a microwave, then glaze the éclairs. Refrigerate for 5 minutes. Apply another coat of glaze and refrigerate for another few minutes. Place a few little pieces of crystallized ginger in each wafer cookie ball and place three along the top of each éclair.

FOR THE WHIPPED KIWI GANACHE

3 sheets (6 g powdered) gelatin powder
2½ cups (600 g) whipping cream
3¾ ounces (108 g) white couverture chocolate, melted
Pulp from 1 large kiwi (3½ ounces/100 g)

FOR THE ALMOND CAKE

1⅓ cups (130 g) ground almonds
1 cup (225 g) packed light brown sugar
10 large (330 g) egg whites
3 large (50 g) egg yolks
2 tablespoons (30 g) whipping cream
1½ tablespoons (20 g) superfine sugar
⅛ teaspoon (1 g) salt
½ cup (1 stick/105 g) unsalted butter
⅓ cup plus 1 tablespoon (50 g) all-purpose flour
¾ teaspoon (3 g) baking powder
A few fresh almonds

FOR THE KIWI GEL

1 cup (180 g) diced kiwi
½ teaspoon (2 g) ascorbic acid
2¾ cups (500 g) kiwi puree
2 tablespoons (30 g) lime juice
2 tablespoons (30 g) superfine sugar
1⅜ teaspoons (4 g) pectin NH

FOR THE TUILE BATTER

3 eggs
1 cup plus 2 tablespoons (215 g) superfine sugar
3 large (105 g) egg whites

FOR THE SEED CRUNCH

⅓ cup (40 g) pine nuts (pignoli)
1½ tablespoons (15 g) white sesame seeds
1½ tablespoons (15 g) black sesame seeds
1¾ tablespoons (15 g) sunflower seeds
2 tablespoons (20 g) pumpkin seeds
1½ tablespoons (15 g) black quinoa
2 tablespoons (20 g) red quinoa

FOR ASSEMBLY AND FINISHING

Shiny green glaze
1¼ cups (300 g) neutral glaze (see page 317)
2 tablespoons (10 g) green luster dust
A few slices fresh kiwi

Continued

PREPARATION TIME: 2 HOURS

SERVES 8

COOKING TIME: 1 HOUR

RESTING TIME: 12 HOURS PLUS 6 HOURS

FOR THE WHIPPED KIWI GANACHE

The previous day, soak the gelatin in ¾ cup plus 2 tablespoons (210 g) water to hydrate it. Heat ½ cup (100 g) cream without letting it boil, then add the gelatin. Pour over the melted chocolate and blend together. Use an immersion blender to blend and add the remaining cream, which should be cold, along with the kiwi pulp. Refrigerate for 12 hours.

FOR THE ALMOND CAKE

The next day, preheat the oven to 340°F (170°C). Combine the ground almonds with the brown sugar, ¼ cup (60 g) of the egg whites, and the egg yolks, cream, superfine sugar, and salt. Brown the butter, then let it cool. In an electric stand mixer fitted with a whisk attachment, whip the remaining egg whites, then add the remaining brown sugar and beat until stiff. Add the cooled brown butter to the almond mixture, then incorporate the beaten whites. Sprinkle the flour and baking powder on top. Spread the batter ¼-inch thick onto a Silpat baking mat, grate a few fresh almonds over the top, and bake for 15 minutes. Use a circle as a guide to cut out a 5½-inch (14-cm)-diameter disk.

FOR THE KIWI GEL

Cook half the diced kiwi for 5 minutes. Use an immersion blender to blend them with the remaining raw diced kiwi and the ascorbic acid. Heat the kiwi puree with the lime juice, then add the superfine sugar mixed with the pectin. Boil for 2 minutes, then cool in a pan in the refrigerator. Mix again once the gel is thoroughly chilled, then use a silicone spatula to combine with the kiwi-ascorbic acid mixture.

Mold a disk of gelatin 5½ inches (14 cm) in diameter and ¾ inch (2 cm) thick on top of the almond cake. Freeze for 2 hours.

FOR THE TUILE BATTER

Mix the whole eggs with the superfine sugar and egg whites. Refrigerate for 2 hours.

FOR THE SEED CRUNCH

Place the pine nuts and all the seeds on a baking sheet and bake for about 15 minutes at 360°F (180°C). Let cool, then combine all the seeds with 1/3 quantity (5¼ ounces/150 g) of the tuile batter, mixing well. Pour onto a Silpat baking mat into a 6¼-inch (16-cm)-diameter circle and bake for 10 minutes, still at 360°F (180°C).

FOR ASSEMBLY AND FINISHING

In the chilled bowl of an electric stand mixer fitted with a whisk attachment, whip the kiwi ganache, then transfer it to a 6-inch (15-cm) PCB plastic pebble mold. Place the kiwi–almond cake center into the mold, then top with the seedy crunch. Freeze for 2 hours. Make the shiny green glaze as described on page 317, replacing the food coloring with the green luster dust. Remove the dessert from the freezer, unmold it, and apply the glaze. Decorate with slices of fresh kiwi.

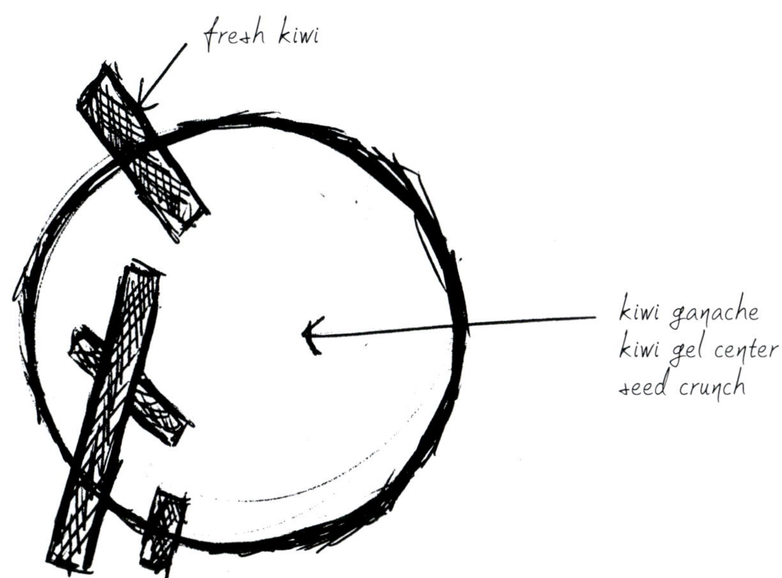

SILVER LYCHEE

FOR THE PUFF PASTRY DOUGH

Kneaded butter (beurre manié)
3 cups (1½ pounds/670 g) dry unsalted butter (84% fat content)
2¼ cups (270 g) pastry flour

Water dough (détrempe)
1 cup plus 2 tablespoons (260 g) water
4 teaspoons (25 g) salt
1 teaspoon (6 g) distilled white vinegar
¾ cup plus 2 tablespoons (1¾ sticks/200 g) unsalted butter, softened
5¼ cups (630 g) pastry flour

FOR THE LYCHEE CREAM

2 cups (500 g) whipping cream
3½ tablespoons (50 g) mascarpone cheese
1½ tablespoons (17 g) superfine sugar
1 drop lychee extract

FOR THE ALMOND CREAM

¾ quantity (8½ ounces/240 g) almond cream (see page 314)
1 teaspoon (8 g) rum

FOR THE WHITE CRUMB DOUGH

7 tablespoons (100 g) unsalted butter
1 cup (125 g) all-purpose flour
⅔ cup (125 g) packed light brown sugar
0.18 ounce (5 g) titanium dioxide

FOR THE SMALL CREAM PUFFS

1 quantity (14 ounces/400 g) choux paste (see page 312)

FOR THE LYCHEE PASTRY CREAM

2 teaspoons (6 g) gelatin powder
5¼ large (90 g) egg yolks (⅓ cup)
½ cup (90 g) superfine sugar
1½ tablespoons (25 g) custard powder
3½ tablespoons (25 g) all-purpose flour
3 cups (500 g) lychee pulp
2 tablespoons (30 g) cocoa butter
½ cup (90 g) Casanova olive oil

FOR THE SILVER SUGAR

2½ cups (500 g) isomalt
0.76 ounces (50 g) silver flakes

FOR ASSEMBLY AND FINISHING

24 fresh lychees (7 ounces/200 g)

Continued

SAINT-HONORÉ CAKE

PREPARATION TIME: 3 HOURS

SERVES 8

COOKING TIME: 1 HOUR

RESTING TIME: 24 HOURS PLUS 2 HOURS 30 MINUTES

SILVER LYCHEE

FOR THE PUFF PASTRY DOUGH

The previous day, make a Saint-Honoré puff pastry dough as described on page 313 with the ingredient quantities listed, then let rest for 24 hours. The next day, cut and bake as described on page 313.

FOR THE LYCHEE CREAM

Combine the cream with the mascarpone, superfine sugar, and lychee extract. Use an immersion blender to blend. Refrigerate for 1 hour.

FOR THE ALMOND CREAM

Preheat the oven to 340°F (170°C). Make the almond cream as described on page 314, adding the rum. Transfer to a pastry bag and refrigerate for 30 minutes. Fill the puff pastry shells with a thin layer of almond cream, then bake for 5 minutes.

FOR THE WHITE CRUMB DOUGH

In an electric stand mixer fitted with the flat beater, beat the butter with the flour, brown sugar, and titanium dioxide to make a dough, being careful not to overbeat. Using a rolling pin or pasta machine, roll it out to a thickness of ¼ inch (5 mm) between two sheets of parchment paper. Freeze for 15 minutes, then cut out ¾-inch (2-cm)-diameter disks with a cookie cutter.

FOR THE SMALL CREAM PUFFS

Make the choux paste as described on page 312. Preheat the oven to 360°F (180°C). Top each choux with a ¾-inch (2-cm) disk of white crumb dough, then bake for 15 minutes. Reduce the oven temperature to 320°F (160°C) and bake for another 5 minutes.

SAINT-HONORÉ CAKE

FOR THE LYCHEE PASTRY CREAM

Soak the gelatin in 2½ tablespoons (41 g) cold water until it swells. Whisk the egg yolks with the superfine sugar, custard powder, and flour until pale. Bring the lychee pulp to a boil, then pour over the egg mixture. Boil for 2 minutes, then remove from the heat and add the cocoa butter and gelatin. Use an immersion blender to blend, then cool rapidly by pouring into a shallow pan. Refrigerate for 30 minutes. In an electric stand mixer fitted with the flat beater, beat the cream until it has cooled, then add the oil.

FOR THE SILVER SUGAR

In a saucepan, heat the isomalt. Once it has reached 340°F (170°C), add the silver flakes. Remove from the heat and dip the cream puffs in the mixture to glaze them. Place them in 1-inch (2.5-cm)-diameter silicone half-dome molds for a few minutes to let the sugar harden, then remove from the molds.

FOR ASSEMBLY AND FINISHING

Working from the top, fill the cream puffs with lychee cream, then lychee pastry cream, until they are completely filled. Fill the center of the puff pastry bottom with lychee pastry cream, adding it on top of the baked almond cream layer. Arrange the cream puffs around the cream. Cut disks of fresh lychee and arrange so that they completely cover the lychee pastry cream. In an electric stand mixer fitted with a whisk attachment, whip the rest of the lychee cream to make whipped cream, then transfer to a pastry bag fitted with a no. 20 Saint-Honoré tip. Pipe over the Saint-Honoré cakes, topping it off with a little puff in the middle.

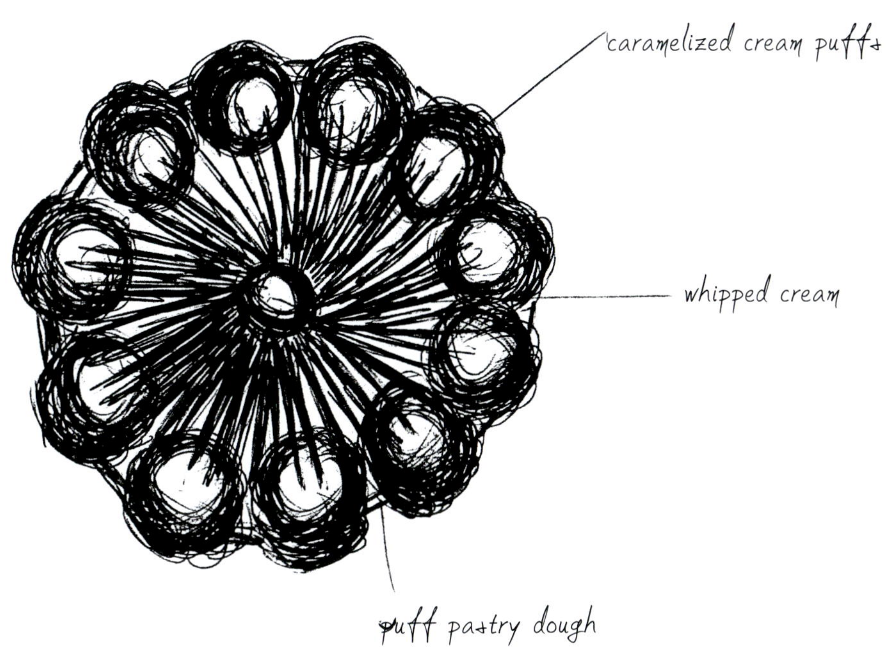

PREPARATION TIME: 3 HOURS

SERVES 15

COOKING TIME: 35 MINUTES

RESTING TIME: 12 HOURS PLUS 6 HOURS

LYCHEE-

FOR THE GERANIUM GANACHE

2 teaspoons (6 g) gelatin powder
6¼ ounces (172 g) white couverture chocolate, chopped
3¼ cups (775 g) whipping cream
1 drop Baume des Anges geranium extract (no. 43)

FOR THE LYCHEE GEL

1¾ cups (300 g) lychee pulp
⅓ cup (80 g) lemon juice
2 tablespoons (25 g) superfine sugar
3¾ teaspoons (10 g) agar powder

FOR THE LEMON CAKE

2½ cups (255 g) ground almonds
1 cup (225 g) packed light brown sugar
10 large (330 g) egg whites
6 large (105 g) egg yolks
¼ cup (60 g) whipping cream
¼ cup (45 g) superfine sugar
¼ teaspoon (1 g) salt
1 cup (2 sticks/210 g) unsalted butter
¾ cup plus 2 tablespoons (105 g) all-purpose flour
1½ teaspoons (6 g) baking powder
Zest of 2 lemons

FOR THE LYCHEE CENTERS

10 fresh lychees (3¼ ounces/90 g), coarsely chopped
¼ cup (40 g) crystallized geranium petals
1 drop Baume des Anges geranium extract (no. 43)

FOR THE SHORTBREAD PASTRY

1 extra-large (20 g) egg yolk
1 extra-large (55 g) egg
1 teaspoon (5 g) vanilla paste
1½ cups plus 2 tablespoons (3¼ sticks/375 g) unsalted butter, at room temperature
2⅓ cups (280 g) pastry flour
1 cup plus 2 tablespoons (140 g) confectioners' sugar, sifted
1 cup (100 g) ground almonds
¾ cup plus 2 tablespoons (200 g) cocoa butter
Zest of 5 lemons
1½ tablespoons (25 g) citric acid

FOR THE COATING

1¼ cups (300 g) coating (see page 317)
Titanium dioxide food coloring or red food coloring

FOR THE GERANIUM GANACHE

The previous day, soak the gelatin in 3 tablespoons (42 g) cold water until it swells. Heat half the cream, add the gelatin, then pour over the chocolate, blending them. Add the remaining cream, which should be cold, and blend with an immersion blender, adding the geranium extract. Pour into a shallow pan and refrigerate for 12 hours.

FOR THE LYCHEE GEL

The next day, heat the lychee pulp and lemon juice with ½ cup (127 g) water, then add the superfine sugar mixed with the agar. Bring to a boil and cook for 2 minutes. Refrigerate for 30 minutes, then use an immersion blender to blend.

FOR THE LEMON CAKE

Preheat the oven to 360°F (180°C). Mix the ground almonds with ¾ cup plus 2 tablespoons (195 g) of the packed brown sugar, 2 (60 g) egg whites, the egg yolks, cream, superfine sugar, and salt. Melt the butter and keep it warm. In an electric stand mixer fitted with a whisk attachment, whip the egg whites until they hold soft peaks, then add the remaining brown sugar and whip until firm. Mix the warm butter into the almond mixture, then add the flour and baking powder. Add the beaten egg whites, then finally the lemon zest. Spread the batter into a layer ¼ inch (5 mm) thick and bake for 10 minutes, turning halfway through. Cut out ¾-inch (2-cm)-diameter disks and place them in the bottom of 1¾-inch (3.5-cm)-diameter silicone half-dome molds.

FOR THE LYCHEE CENTERS

Mix ½ quantity (7 ounces/200 g) of the lychee gelatin with the lychees, crystallized geranium petals, and geranium extract. Fill the half-dome molds with this mixture, adding it on top of the lemon cake disks. Freeze for 2 hours.

FOR THE SHORTBREAD PASTRY

Beat the egg yolk and whole egg together until pale, then add the vanilla paste. Beat the butter with the flour, confectioners' sugar, and ground almonds, then add the egg mixture. Refrigerate for 2 hours, then roll out between two acetate sheets to a thickness of 3/8 inch (9 mm). Freeze for at least 30 minutes.

Preheat the oven to 340°F (170°C). Transfer the shortbread dough to a baking sheet and bake for 15 minutes, then let cool. Once cool, grind into a powder, then mix with the cocoa butter, lemon zest, and citric acid.

FOR ASSEMBLY AND COATING

In the chilled bowl of an electric stand mixer fitted with a whisk attachment, whip the ganache, then transfer to a pastry bag fitted with a Saint-Honoré tip. Pipe a rose around each unmolded lychee center by piping petals, using a toothpick to hold it. Freeze for about 1 hour. Make the coating as described on page 317 and use it to airbrush the roses. Select the color of your roses by playing with food colorings and airbrush them accordingly. Cut the shortbread mixture into 2¼-inch (5.5-cm)-diameter disks, then place each rose on a shortbread stand.

PREPARATION TIME: 2 HOURS

SERVES 10

COOKING TIME: 15 MINUTES

RESTING TIME: 12 HOURS PLUS 9 HOURS

MANGO, VANILLA,

FOR THE WHIPPED VANILLA GANACHE

4 teaspoons (12 g) gelatin powder
3 cups plus 2 tablespoons (750 g) whipping cream
5 vanilla beans
¾ teaspoon (4 g) vanilla extract
12 ounces (344 g) white couverture chocolate, melted

FOR THE MANGO-GINGER CENTERS

1 tablespoon (10 g) gelatin powder
2 cups (575 g) mango puree
¼ cup (63 g) ginger vinegar
2½ cups (413 g) diced mango

FOR THE ALMOND DACQUOISE

7 large (225 g) egg whites
⅓ cup (74 g) superfine sugar
2 cups (200 g) ground almonds
2¾ cups (225 g) confectioners' sugar

FOR ASSEMBLY AND FINISHING

Cocoa powder

Titanium silver triangles

10½ ounces (300 g) white couverture chocolate
¼ ounce (8 g) titanium dioxide
Silver luster dust

Titanium white spray

¾ cup (7 ounces/200 g) spray mixture (see page 317)
0.18 ounce (5 g) titanium dioxide

FOR THE WHIPPED VANILLA GANACHE

The previous day, soak the gelatin in ⅓ cup (84 g) cold water. Heat the gelatin and one-third of the cream. Cut the vanilla beans in half lengthwise and scrape out the seeds, and add to the cream to let the vanilla flavor infuse for 30 minutes. Strain through a conical sieve, then add the vanilla extract. Pour over the melted chocolate and blend together. Add the rest of the cream, which should be cold, then use an immersion blender to blend. Pour into a pan and refrigerate for 12 hours.

FOR THE MANGO-GINGER CENTERS

The next day, soak the gelatin in ¼ cup (70 g) cold water. In a saucepan, heat the mango puree, then remove from the heat and add the gelatin. Finally, add the ginger vinegar and diced mango. Pour into 1¾-inch (4.5-cm)-diameter silicone half-dome molds and freeze for 4 hours.

FOR THE ALMOND DACQUOISE

Preheat the oven to 360°F (180°C). In an electric stand mixer fitted with a whisk attachment, whip the egg whites, then add the superfine sugar and beat until stiff. Sift together the ground almonds and confectioners' sugar, then fold them into the beaten egg whites using a silicone spatula. Spread onto a sheet of parchment paper to a thickness of ⅜ inch (1 cm) and bake for 12 minutes. Let cool, then use a cookie cutter to cut out 2½-inch (6-cm)-diameter disks.

FOR ASSEMBLY AND FINISHING

Use a wire whisk to whip the vanilla ganache, then use to fill 2⅜-inch (7-cm)-diameter silicone half-dome molds halfway. Place the mango centers in the middle, then cover with a thin layer of the ganache. Place the almond dacquoise on top. Freeze for 4 hours.

Melt the chocolate and mix it with the titanium dioxide. Temper as described on page 317, then spread onto a Rhodoïd acetate sheet. Let set a little, then use a knife to cut into irregular triangles. Turn the acetate sheet over onto a sheet of parchment paper, then place a heavy, flat baking sheet on top to prevent it from warping. Refrigerate for 10 minutes, then remove the triangles, breaking them apart. Freeze a few triangles for 1 minute, then sprinkle with the silver luster dust. Leave the others white. Make the titanium white spray mixture as described on page 317. Unmold the assemblies and spray them with an airbrush. Arrange the pieces of titanium white and silver chocolate on top. Freeze for 30 minutes.

FOR THE PASSION FRUIT SHERBET

1¼ cups (250 g) superfine sugar
½ cup (100 g) glucose powder
1 tablespoon (15 g) super neutrose
2 cups (500 g) milk
2 cups (500 g) passion fruit puree
seeds of 6 passion fruit

FOR THE RAVIOLI DOUGH

2⅓ cups (300 g) cake flour
14 large (235 g) egg yolks
1¼ cups (50 g) cilantro leaves

FOR THE CILANTRO PESTO

1¼ cups (50 g) fresh cilantro
¼ cup (30 g) fresh almonds, chopped
¼ cup (80 g) olive oil
2 tablespoons (2 g) crushed ice

FOR THE RAVIOLI FINISHING

16 mango balls
1 tablespoon (15 g) superfine sugar
2 tablespoons (5 g) chopped fresh cilantro

FOR THE ASSEMBLY AND FINISHING

1 mango (11¼ ounces/320 g)
2 cups (80 g) fresh cilantro leaves

FOR THE PASSION FRUIT SHERBET

The previous day, in a saucepan, bring 2 cups (500 g) water to a boil. Mix the superfine sugar with the glucose powder and super neutrose, then add to the saucepan. Transfer to another container and refrigerate for 30 minutes. Once the mixture is cold, add the milk, passion fruit puree, and passion fruit seeds. Blend with an immersion blender, then pour into a pan. Refrigerate for 24 hours.
The next day, blend again with the immersion blender, then churn to make the sherbet.

FOR THE RAVIOLI DOUGH

In an electric stand mixer fitted with a whisk attachment, process the flour, egg yolks, and cilantro until completely blended, then lay a sheet of plastic wrap onto the surface of the mixture. Refrigerate for at least 3 hours.

FOR THE CILANTRO PESTO

Using an immersion blender, blend the cilantro, fresh almonds, oil, and crushed ice. Set aside.

FOR THE RAVIOLI FINISHING

Roll the ravioli dough to a thickness of 1/32 inch (1 mm), then use a cookie cutter to cut out 4-inch (10-cm)-diameter disks. Place a mango ball in the middle of each disk and fold up into a three-sided pyramid, lifting the edges to the middle to enclose the mango ball inside the ravioli. Refrigerate.
In a saucepan, combine the superfine sugar and cilantro with 1⅔ cups (400 g) water and bring to a boil. Drop the ravioli into the simmering broth and cook for 3 minutes.

FOR ASSEMBLY AND FINISHING

Peel the mango and cut the flesh into dice. Arrange the mango on serving plates. Spread the cilantro pesto over the passion fruit sherbet, then scoop out curls to make elegant balls. Place these on top of the diced mango. Arrange two mango ravioli on each plate, then garnish with a few cilantro leaves.

PREPARATION TIME: 2 HOURS

SERVES 8

COOKING TIME: 20 MINUTES

RESTING TIME: 24 HOURS PLUS 3 HOURS 20 MINUTES

BER

RIES

CRANBERRY

In season
August and September

Selection
the fruit should be scented, swollen, and have a smooth skin

Average weight
a few grams

Storage
at room temperature for several days

Flavor pairings
red currant, thyme, cinnamon

BLACK CURRANT

In season

August and September

Selection

check that the fruit at the bottom of the basket are in a good state and that there is no mold

Average weight

a few grams

Storage

in the refrigerator vegetable drawer for 24 to 48 hours; take them out 30 minutes before eating

Flavor pairings

strawberry, raspberry, blueberry

CHERRY

In season

June

Selection

the fruit should be shiny and fleshy, with a very green stem that is still attached

Average weight

a few grams

Storage

at room temperature for 3 days, or in the refrigerator vegetable drawer if it is warm weather for up to 5 days; take them out 20 minutes before eating

Flavor pairings

kirsch, tarragon, pistachio

STRAWBERRY

In season

April to June

Selection

well-scented, shiny,
and with the stem still attached

Average weight

⅜ ounce (10 g)

Storage

in the refrigerator for up to 48 hours; take them out 20 minutes before eating

Flavor pairings

basil, chocolate, avocado

RASPBERRY

In season

July to September

Selection

the berries should be fleshy, velvety, and completely intact

Average weight

a few grams

Storage

in the refrigerator for up to 48 hours

Flavor pairings

thyme, cream cheese, pistachio

RED CURRANT

In season
June to September

Selection
the currants should be fleshy and intact

Average weight
a few grams

Storage
in the lower part of the refrigerator for 2 to 3 days

Flavor pairings
lemon, peach, apricot

PREPARATION TIME: 2 HOURS

SERVES 6

COOKING TIME: 30 MINUTES

RESTING TIME: 12 HOURS PLUS 1 HOUR 30 MINUTES

CRANBERRY

FOR THE VANILLA MOUSSE

6 ounces (172 g) white couverture chocolate, chopped
2 teaspoons (6 g) gelatin powder
3¼ cups (775 g) whipping cream
3 vanilla beans

FOR THE PUFF PASTRY

Kneaded butter (beurre manié)
1½ cups (11½ ounces/330 g) dry unsalted butter (84% fat content)
1 cup plus 2 tablespoons (135 g) pastry flour

Water dough (détrempe)
½ cup (130 g) water
2 teaspoons (12 g) salt
½ teaspoon (3 g) distilled white vinegar
½ cup (1 stick/102 g) unsalted butter, softened
2⅔ cups (315 g) pastry flour

FOR THE CRANBERRY JUICE

4 cups (400 g) frozen cranberries
¼ cup (40 g) superfine sugar

FOR THE CRANBERRY COMPOTE

2½ tablespoons (40 g) cranberry juice (see above)
¼ cup (40 g) superfine sugar
2 cups (200 g) frozen cranberries
1 tablespoon (15 g) glucose powder
¾ teaspoon (2 g) pectin NH
⅜ teaspoon (2 g) tartaric acid
2½ teaspoons (8 g) cornstarch

FOR THE VANILLA MOUSSE

The previous day, soak the gelatin in 3 tablespoons (42 g) cold water to soften. Heat one-third of the cream. Cut the vanilla beans in half lengthwise and scrape out the seeds, and add both seeds and pods and gelatin to the cream to infuse for 30 minutes. Pass through a conical sieve. Pour over the chopped chocolate. Use an immersion blender to blend. Refrigerate for at least 12 hours.

FOR THE PUFF PASTRY

The next day, make a dough using six simple turns: Start by rolling the puff pastry dough into a rectangle three times as long as it is wide. Make a simple turn by lifting the two ends and folding the dough into thirds, letter style. Refrigerate for 1 hour. Repeat this process five times, making sure to refrigerate the dough for a full hour between each turn. Preheat the oven to 360°F (180°C). Once the dough is prepared, roll to a thickness of 1/8 inch (3 mm). Place the rolled-out dough between two baking sheets and bake for 30 minutes. Once the baking is complete, cut into four 4½ by 8-inch (11 by 20-cm) rectangles. Return to the oven at 360°F (180°C) for 10 minutes.

FOR THE CRANBERRY JUICE

Preheat the oven to 210°F (100°C). Put the frozen cranberries and superfine sugar in a heatproof dish, then cover with several layers of oven-safe plastic wrap. Cook in the oven for 2 hours at 210°F (100°C). Strain the mixture using a cloth. Refrigerate for about 1 hour.

FOR THE CRANBERRY COMPOTE

In a saucepan, heat 2½ tablespoons (40 g) of the obtained cranberry juice with the superfine sugar. Bring to a boil and cook until syrupy. Then add the frozen cranberries. Combine the glucose, pectin, and tartaric acid in a separate bowl.

When the cranberries start to release their juices and the mixture is warm, add the glucose mixture. Heat to 215°F (102°C), then stir in the starch mixed with 1 tablespoon (15 g) water. Boil for 1 minute and cool rapidly by pouring the mixture into a shallow container and putting it in the freezer until cold.

FOR ASSEMBLY

In an electric stand mixer fitted with a whisk attachment, whip the vanilla mousse, then use to fill a pastry bag with a plain tip. On the first rectangle of pastry, pipe three lines of the vanilla mousse along its length, alternate with three lines of the compote. Repeat with the remaining rectangles and layer up to create the millefeuille.

FOR THE BLACK CURRANT JUICE

4½ cups (500 g) frozen black currants
½ cup (80 g) superfine sugar

FOR THE BLACK CURRANT SORBET

9 cups (1 kg) fresh wild black currants
1 cup (210 g) superfine sugar
1 cup (250 g) black currant juice
3½ tablespoons (50 g) trimoline (inverted sugar)

FOR THE BLACK CURRANT COMPOTE

⅔ cup (160 g) black currant juice
¾ cup (120 g) superfine sugar
5 cups (500 g) frozen black currants
⅓ cup (80 g) glucose powder
2¾ teaspoons (8 g) pectin NH
1⅜ teaspoons (8 g) tartaric acid
3½ tablespoons (30 g) starch

FOR ASSEMBLY AND FINISHING

1½ cups (150 g) black currants

FOR THE BLACK CURRANT JUICE

The previous day, put the frozen black currants and the superfine sugar in a pan or heatproof dish and cover with several layers of oven-safe plastic wrap. Cook in a bain-marie or steam oven at 210°F (100°C) for 4 hours. Strain through an apron or cloth. Do not press, so that the juice remains clear. Refrigerate.

FOR THE BLACK CURRANT SORBET

The same day, combine the black currants with 1 scant cup (200 g) of the superfine sugar, setting 1 tablespoon sugar aside, and let stand for 1 day at room temperature.

In a saucepan, heat the black currant juice with the trimoline. Sprinkle in the remaining 1 tablespoon (10 g) sugar, stir, and bring to a boil. Let this syrup stand for 1 day. Churn to make the sorbet.

FOR THE BLACK CURRANT COMPOTE

In a saucepan, heat the black currant juice (making sure to reserve some for finishing) and the superfine sugar to 240°F (115°C), then add the frozen black currants. When they start to release their juices and the mixture is warm, stir in the glucose mixed with the pectin and tartaric acid. Heat to 215°F (102°C), then stir in the starch mixed with ¼ cup (60 g) water. Boil for 1 minute, then pour into a shallow container. Refrigerate for 30 minutes.

FOR ASSEMBLY AND FINISHING

Spread the compote over the sorbet, then shape into a quenelle. Mix the fresh black currants with the reserved black currant juice and serve with the sorbet.

PREPARATION TIME: 2 HOURS

SERVES 10

COOKING TIME: 4 HOURS

RESTING TIME: 24 HOURS PLUS 30 MINUTES

PREPARATION TIME: 3 HOURS 30 MINUTES

SERVES 10

COOKING TIME: 40 MINUTES

RESTING TIME: 24 HOURS PLUS 3 HOURS

CHERRY

FOR THE TARTLET SHELLS

1 quantity (1¼ pounds/590 g) sweet dough (see page 312)

FOR THE TARRAGON GANACHE

1¼ teaspoons (4 g) gelatin powder
1½ cups (375 g) whipping cream
2 cups (100 g) fresh tarragon
3¼ ounces (90 g) white couverture chocolate, chopped
2 teaspoons (10 g) kirsch

FOR THE CHERRY PRESERVES

2½ cups (350 g) cherries
1 drizzle olive oil
3½ tablespoons (50 g) kirsch
1 cup (125 g) Morello cherries
2½ tablespoons (35 g) trimoline (inverted sugar)
2½ teaspoons (9 g) cornstarch
1½ tablespoons (20 g) superfine sugar
1⅜ teaspoons (4 g) pectin NH
Zest of 1 lime
½ cup (135 g) Morello cherry juice

FOR THE EGG WASH

6 large (100 g) egg yolks
1½ tablespoons (25 g) whipping cream

FOR THE ALMOND-TARRAGON CREAM

½ quantity (5¼ ounces/150 g) almond cream (see page 314)
1 tablespoon (18 g) rum
Zest of 1 lime
3 tablespoons (10 g) chopped fresh tarragon

FOR ASSEMBLY AND FINISHING

Red coating
1¼ cups (300 g) coating mixture (see page 317)
4 teaspoons (20 g) red food coloring
1 cup (100 g) finely chopped toasted almonds (see page 317)
10 (2½-inch/6-cm) chocolate stems (see page 317)
Green luster dust

FOR THE TARTLET SHELLS

The previous day, make the sweet dough for the tartlet shells as described on page 312 and let dry in the refrigerator for 1 day.

FOR THE TARRAGON GANACHE

Soak the gelatin in 2 tablespoons (25 g) cold water to soften. In a saucepan, heat ¾ cup (175 g) of the cream with the tarragon, without bringing to a boil. Melt the chocolate, then pour the hot cream over and blend together. Add the gelatin. Stir in the remaining cold cream and the kirsch, then use an immersion blender to blend. Refrigerate for 12 hours.

FOR THE CHERRY PRESERVES

Stem, halve, and pit the cherries. In a skillet, sear 1½ cups (200 g) of the halved cherries in a drizzle of oil, then flambé them with kirsch. Add the Morello cherries and trimoline. Combine the starch, superfine sugar, and pectin, add the mixture to the skillet, and stir. Boil for 2 minutes, then pour into a container and let cool. Meanwhile, cut the remaining 1 cup (150 g) halved cherries in half again.

Once the mixture has cooled, add the cherry quarters, lime zest, and Morello cherry juice. Use the preserves to fill 1¼-inch (3.5-cm)-diameter silicone half-dome molds and freeze for 1 hour. Set aside the remaining preserves for finishing the tartlets.

FOR THE EGG WASH

Preheat the oven to 320°F (160°C). Blind bake the tartlet shells for 20 minutes. Mix the egg yolks with the cream, brush the shells with the mixture, and return to the oven for 5 minutes.

FOR THE ALMOND-TARRAGON CREAM

Make the almond cream as described on page 314, and use to fill the tartlet shells. Bake in the oven for 5 minutes, then let cool.

FOR ASSEMBLY AND FINISHING

Transfer the tarragon ganache into 1¾-inch (4.5-cm)-diameter silicone half-dome molds, insert a cherry preserves center, and smooth with an offset spatula. Freeze for 3 hours, then sculpt into a cherry shape. Make the red coating as described on page 317. Dip the cherry shapes into the red coating, then let harden. Airbrush them with the same red coating. Fill the tartlet shells to the top with the remaining preserves and smooth. Place the cherry shapes on top and arrange the toasted almonds around the edge of each tartlet. Pierce the center of the cherries with a hot toothpick. Make the 2½-inch (6-cm) chocolate stems as described on page 317, dust with green luster dust, and place one at the center of each cherry.

CHERRY TART

FOR THE TART SHELL

1 quantity (1¼ pounds/590 g) sweet dough (see page 312)

FOR THE EGG WASH

6 large (100 g) egg yolks
1½ tablespoons (25 g) whipping cream

FOR THE ALMOND-TARRAGON CREAM

1 quantity (10½ ounces/300 g) almond cream (see page 314)
½ cup (25 g) fresh tarragon

FOR THE PASTRY CREAM

⅓ cup (90 g) milk
2 teaspoons (10 g) whipping cream
1 vanilla bean
1 extra-large (20 g) egg yolk
2½ teaspoons (10 g) superfine sugar
1 teaspoon (5 g) custard powder
2 teaspoons (5 g) all-purpose flour
1 teaspoon (6 g) cocoa butter
1 tablespoon (10 g) gelatin powder
2 teaspoons (10 g) unsalted butter
2 teaspoons (10 g) mascarpone cheese

FOR THE CHERRY PRESERVES

3⅔ cups (500 g) Burlat cherries
½ cup (100 g) superfine sugar
3½ tablespoons (50 g) lemon juice
¼ teaspoon (1 g) ascorbic acid
3½ teaspoons (10 g) pectin NH

FOR THE TARRAGON PESTO

4 cups (200 g) fresh tarragon
2 tablespoons (30 g) almond paste
2½ tablespoons (40 g) honey
2 tablespoons (25 g) yuzu juice
A little ice
⅔ cup (150 g) olive oil

FOR ASSEMBLY AND FINISHING

1 cup (150 g) fresh Burlat cherries
1 drizzle olive oil
1 pinch superfine sugar

FOR THE TART SHELL

The previous day, make the sweet dough for the tart shell as described on page 312 and let dry in the refrigerator for 1 day.

The next day, preheat the oven to 320°F (160°C) and blind bake the tart shell for 20 minutes.

FOR THE EGG WASH

Beat the egg yolks with the cream and brush the shell with the mixture. Return to the oven for 10 minutes.

FOR THE ALMOND-TARRAGON CREAM

Make the almond cream as described on page 314. Wash and chop the tarragon, then stir into the almond cream. Transfer to a pastry bag and pipe the cream into the tart shell. Bake for 10 minutes.

FOR THE PASTRY CREAM

Make the pastry cream as described on page 314, adjusting the amounts to fit this recipe. Refrigerate for 30 minutes. Transfer to a pastry bag and pipe into the tart shell on top of the layer of cooked almond-tarragon cream.

FOR THE CHERRY PRESERVES

Pit the cherries and cut them into eighths. Cook over low heat with 1/3 cup (80 g) of the superfine sugar, the lemon juice, and ascorbic acid and reduce for about 10 minutes to the desired consistency. Combine the remaining sugar with the pectin and add to the cherry mixture. Boil for 1 minute, then remove from the heat. Spread the preserves on the tart.

FOR THE TARRAGON PESTO

Using a blender, combine the tarragon, almond paste, honey, yuzu juice, and a little ice to preserve the chlorophyll, then whisk with the oil as if making a vinaigrette. Dot the tarragon pesto over the cherry preserves.

FOR ASSEMBLY AND FINISHING

Stem, halve, and pit the fresh cherries. Cook them with a little oil and a pinch of superfine sugar, then arrange them over the surface of the tart on top of the preserves layer.

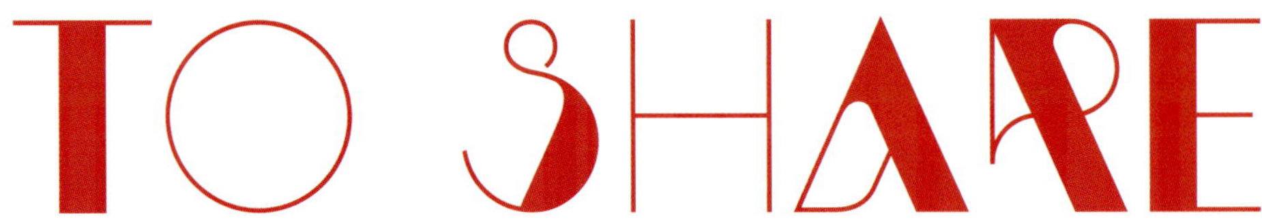

PREPARATION TIME: 2 HOURS

SERVES 10

COOKING TIME: 35 MINUTES

RESTING TIME: 24 HOURS PLUS 30 MINUTES

CHERRY

FOR THE RAW MILK-ESPELETTE PEPPER ICE CREAM

4½ cups (1 liter) raw milk
2 tablespoons (10 g) Espelette pepper
½ cup (100 g) packed light brown sugar
1½ tablespoons (20 g) superfine sugar
⅔ cup (160 g) crème fraîche

FOR THE MORELLO CHERRY JUICE AND MARINADE

6½ cups (2¼ pounds/1 kg) frozen Morello cherries
1 cup (200 g) superfine sugar

FOR THE BEET PAPER

6 red beets (1 pound 2 ounces/500 g)
3¾ large (125 g) egg whites (½ cup)

FOR THE BREAD CHIPS

7 ounces (200 g) frozen bread

FOR THE CANDIED ALMONDS

1¾ cups (250 g) almonds
¼ cup (40 g) superfine sugar

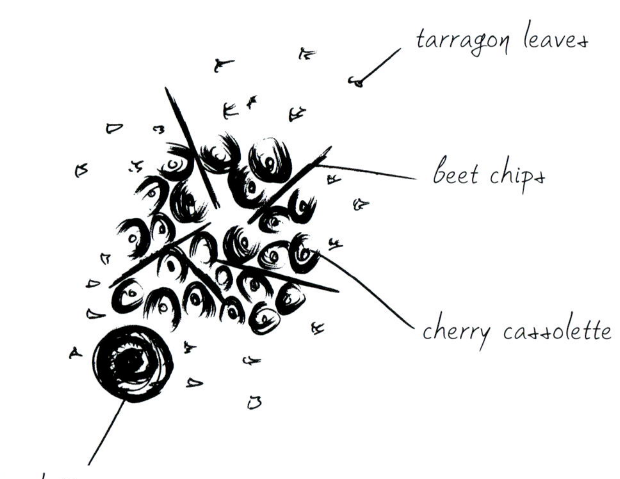

FOR THE KIRSCH PASTRY CREAM (SEE PAGE 314)

1½ teaspoons (5 g) gelatin powder
1¼ cups (300 g) milk
2½ tablespoons (40 g) whipping cream
2 vanilla beans
3½ large (60 g) egg yolks (¼ cup)
⅓ cup (60 g) superfine sugar
2½ teaspoons (15 g) custard powder
2 tablespoons (15 g) all-purpose flour
1½ tablespoons (20 g) cocoa butter
3 tablespoons (40 g) unsalted butter
1½ tablespoons (20 g) mascarpone cheese
2½ tablespoons (35 g) kirsch

FOR THE CHERRY PRESERVES

3⅔ cups (500 g) Burlat cherries
½ cup (100 g) superfine sugar
3½ tablespoons (50 g) lemon juice
¼ teaspoon (1 g) ascorbic acid
3½ teaspoons (10 g) pectin NH

FOR THE TARRAGON PESTO

4 cups (200 g) fresh tarragon
2 tablespoons (30 g) almond paste
2½ tablespoons (40 g) honey
2 tablespoons (25 g) yuzu juice
A little ice
⅔ cup (150 g) olive oil

FOR THE CHERRY CASSOLETTE

3⅓ cups (500 g) cherries
1 drizzle olive oil
⅓ cup (15 g) chopped fresh tarragon

Continued

BEETS

PREPARATION TIME: 3 HOURS

SERVES 10

COOKING TIME: 12 HOURS PLUS 5 TO 6 HOURS

RESTING TIME: 24 HOURS PLUS 30 MINUTES

FOR THE RAW MILK-ESPELETTE PEPPER ICE CREAM

The previous day, heat the milk with the Espelette pepper. Once it is hot, pour in the sugars and boil for about 1 minute. Pour into a shallow container and refrigerate. Combine the crème fraîche and the cold mixture, use an immersion blender to blend, and keep in the refrigerator for 1 day. Churn to make the ice cream.

FOR THE MORELLO CHERRY JUICE AND MARINADE

Defrost the Morello cherries and put them in a pan or on a baking sheet, mix with the superfine sugar, and cover with oven-safe plastic wrap. Cook for 12 hours at 200°F (95°C).

The next day, put the cherry-sugar mixture into a perforated pan, cover with a cloth, and collect only the clear juice.

FOR THE BEET PAPER

Preheat the oven to 175°F (80°C). Put the red beets through a juicer, keeping only the pulp that is left. In a powerful blender, process the beet pulp and egg whites until a smooth, fine mixture forms. Use a rolling pin to roll this mixture to a thickness of 1/16 inch (2 mm) between two acetate sheets. Dry in the oven at 175°F (80°C) for 3 to 4 hours.

FOR THE BREAD CHIPS

Remove the bread from the freezer a few minutes before use. Cut into thin slices using a deli slicer set at a thickness of lower than 2 or using an adjustable-blade slicer or mandoline. Place the bread chips on a lightly greased baguette baking mold, then dry in the oven at 175°F (80°C) for at least 2 hours.

FOR THE CANDIED ALMONDS

Preheat the oven to 300°F (150°C). Cut the almonds in half, then dry in the oven for 15 minutes.

Heat 1½ tablespoons (20 g) water and the superfine sugar to 250°F (120°C), then pour over the hot almonds. Candy without letting them caramelize. Coarsely chop some of the candied almonds for finishing.

FOR THE KIRSCH PASTRY CREAM

Make the pastry cream as described on page 314, adjusting the amounts to fit this recipe. Refrigerate for 30 minutes, then add the kirsch and whip.

FOR THE CHERRY PRESERVES

Pit the cherries and cut into eighths. Cook them over low heat with 1/3 cup (80 g) of the sugar, the lemon juice, and ascorbic acid. Reduce over low heat for about 10 minutes. Add the remaining 1½ tablespoons (20 g) sugar mixed with the pectin and boil for 1 minute before removing from the heat.

FOR THE TARRAGON PESTO

Put the tarragon, almond paste, honey, and yuzu juice in a powerful blender. Add a little ice to preserve the chlorophyll and blend until a smooth paste forms. Whisk with the oil as if making a vinaigrette.

FOR THE CHERRY CASSOLETTE

Stem, halve, and pit the cherries. Cook them in a drizzle of oil with the tarragon.

FOR ASSEMBLY AND FINISHING

Distribute the pastry cream and cherry preserves on serving plates. Arrange the candied almonds, a quenelle of Espelette pepper ice cream, and then the cherry cassolette on top. Insert the bread chips and slivers of beet paper into the cherries and dot the tarragon pesto over the cherry preserves. Serve the hot Morello cherry juice on the side.

STRAWBERRY

FOR THE STRAWBERRY JUICE (SEE PAGE 315)

3½ cups (500 g) frozen strawberries
1½ tablespoons (20 g) superfine sugar

FOR THE STRAWBERRY SORBET

2¼ pounds (1 kg) fresh strawberries
1 cup (200 g) superfine sugar

FOR THE MERINGUE TUILES

6 large (200 g) egg whites
1 cup (200 g) superfine sugar
1⅔ cups (200 g) confectioners' sugar
Strawberry powder

FOR THE STRAWBERRY PRESERVES

1½ cups (300 g) superfine sugar
3½ cups (500 g) frozen strawberries
3¼ cups (500 g) ripe Ciflorette strawberries
½ cup (100 g) glucose powder
2 teaspoons (6 g) pectin NH
1 teaspoon (6 g) tartaric acid

FOR THE STRAWBERRY CHANTILLY CREAM

2 cups (500 g) whipping cream
1½ tablespoons (10 g) strawberry powder

FOR ASSEMBLY AND FINISHING

1½ cups (250 g) fresh strawberries
8 teaspoons olive oil

TIP

Create an elegant assembly by bearing in mind the temperature of each product.

FOR THE STRAWBERRY JUICE

The previous day, make the strawberry juice as described on page 315.

FOR THE STRAWBERRY SORBET

Mix the whole strawberries with the sugar and let stand in a warm place overnight.

The next day, use an immersion blender to blend. Churn to make the sorbet.

FOR THE MERINGUE TUILES

Preheat the oven to 160°F (70°C). Make a French meringue as described on page 314. Using a spatula, make 1 by 8-inch (3 by 20-cm) strips with the meringue mixture on a sheet of parchment paper. If necessary, trim the ends of the strips with the point of a knife or a toothpick. Dust lightly with strawberry powder. Bake for 1 to 2 hours, until dry.

FOR THE STRAWBERRY PRESERVES

Strain the strawberry juice and cook ⅔ cup (150 g) in a saucepan with the superfine sugar to 240°F (115°C), then add the frozen and fresh strawberries. Combine the glucose, pectin, and tartaric acid. When the strawberries start to release their juices and the mixture is warm, mix in the glucose mixture and cook to 220°F (104°C). Cool rapidly by pouring the mixture into a wide shallow pan or dish.

FOR THE STRAWBERRY CHANTILLY CREAM

Cook ⅔ cup (150 g) of the strawberry juice until it is reduced by about half, then use a blender to combine with the cream and the strawberry powder for 30 seconds.

FOR ASSEMBLY AND FINISHING

Cut the strawberries into thin slices and arrange them in an overlapping circle. Just before serving, mix the remaining strawberry juice with about a teaspoon oil and drizzle over the plate. Arrange the sorbet by making a "swirl" with a soup spoon, add a little strawberry preserves, then use a pastry bag fitted with a no. 20 plain tip to pipe a dome of Chantilly cream and apply on the side. Arrange a few meringue tuiles in the dessert.

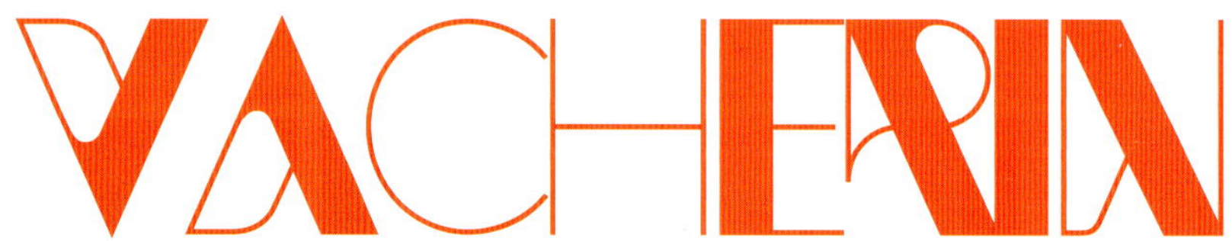

PREPARATION TIME: 1 HOUR

SERVES 8

COOKING TIME: 2 HOURS

RESTING TIME: 24 HOURS

PREPARATION TIME: 3 HOURS 30 MINUTES

SERVES 10

COOKING TIME: 35 MINUTES

RESTING TIME: 24 HOURS PLUS 4 HOURS

STRAWBERRY

FOR THE TARTLET SHELLS

1 quantity (1¼ pounds/590 g) sweet dough (see page 312)

FOR THE BASIL GANACHE

1½ teaspoons (5 g) gelatin powder
1½ cups (375 g) whipping cream
3⅓ cups (100 g) fresh basil
3¼ ounces (90 g) white couverture chocolate, chopped
½ teaspoon (0.5 g) Espelette pepper

FOR THE STRAWBERRY JELLY

1¼ cups (300 g) strawberry juice (see page 315)
1 tablespoon (12.5 g) superfine sugar
2 teaspoons (6 g) pectin NH

FOR THE EGG WASH

6 large (100 g) egg yolks
1½ tablespoons (25 g) whipping cream

FOR THE STRAWBERRY COMPOTE

2½ cups (400 g) strawberries
⅔ cup (20 g) fresh basil, chopped

FOR THE ALMOND-STRAWBERRY CREAM

½ quantity (5¼ ounces/150 g) almond cream (see page 314)
⅔ cup (100 g) thinly sliced strawberries

FOR ASSEMBLY AND FINISHING

Red coating

1¼ cups (300 g) coating mixture (see page 317)
2 teaspoons (12 g) red fat-soluble food coloring

Red glaze

1¼ cups (300 g) neutral glaze (see page 317)
4 teaspoons (20 g) strawberry-red water-soluble food coloring
⅜ ounce (10 g) titanium dioxide

Sesame seeds

Continued

STRAWBERRY

FOR THE TARTLET SHELLS

The previous day, make the dough for the tartlet shells as described on page 312 and refrigerate for 1 day.

FOR THE BASIL GANACHE

Soak the gelatin in 2 tablespoons (25 g) cold water to soften. Heat $\frac{1}{3}$ cup (85 g) of the cream with the basil without bringing to a boil, then add the gelatin. Pour over the chopped chocolate, blending them together, then add the remaining cold cream and the Espelette pepper. Use an immersion blender to blend. Refrigerate for 12 hours.

FOR THE STRAWBERRY JELLY

Heat the strawberry juice. Mix the superfine sugar with the pectin, then sprinkle the mixture over the strawberry juice while whisking. Bring to a boil, then simmer for 2 minutes. Pour the mixture into a shallow pan and refrigerate to cool more rapidly. Once completely cool, use an immersion blender to blend, being careful not to beat in any air.

FOR THE EGG WASH

The next day, preheat the oven to 320°F (160°C) and blind bake the tartlet shells for 20 minutes. Beat the egg yolks with the cream and brush the shells with the mixture. Return to the oven for 5 minutes, until golden.

FOR THE STRAWBERRY COMPOTE

Coarsely crush the strawberries with an electric mixer and let drain in a conical sieve. Use an immersion blender to blend them into the strawberry gelatin, then add the basil. Transfer the mixture to $1\frac{1}{4}$-inch (3.5-cm)-diameter silicone half-dome molds and freeze for 1 hour.

FOR THE ALMOND-STRAWBERRY CREAM

Make the almond cream as described on page 314. Fill the tartlet shells, then arrange the strawberry slices on top. Bake in the oven for 5 minutes, then let cool.

FOR ASSEMBLY AND FINISHING

In the chilled bowl of an electric stand mixer fitted with a whip attachment, whip the basil ganache, then transfer to 1¾-inch (4.5-cm)-diameter silicone half-dome molds. Insert a strawberry compote center, then smooth and freeze for 3 hours. Once frozen, add a little ganache on top and sculpt into a strawberry shape. Make the red coating as described on page 317 and the red glaze as described on page 317, then dip the strawberry shapes into first the red coating, then the red glaze. Arrange the sesame seeds to resemble strawberry seeds, and place the sculpted strawberries on top of the tartlets.

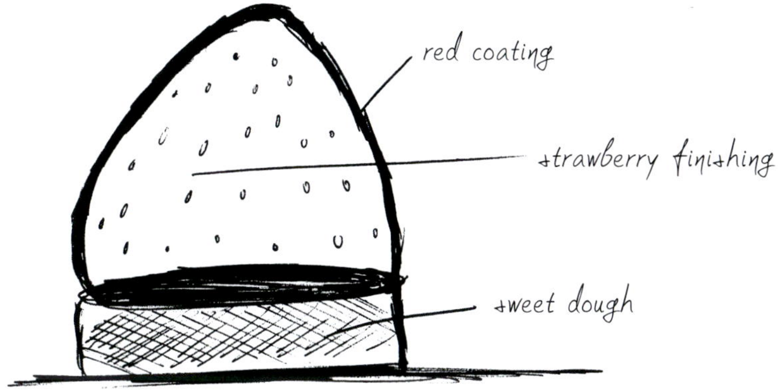

PREPARATION TIME: 2 HOURS

SERVES 8 TO 10

COOKING TIME: 45 MINUTES

RESTING TIME: 24 HOURS PLUS 30 MINUTES

STRAWBERRY–

FOR THE TART SHELL

1 quantity (1¼ pounds/590 g) sweet dough (see page 312)

FOR THE EGG WASH

6 large (100 g) egg yolks
1½ tablespoons (25 g) whipping cream

FOR THE ALMOND-STRAWBERRY CREAM

1 quantity (10½ ounces/300 g) almond cream (see page 314)
⅓ cup (50 g) finely sliced strawberries

FOR THE STRAWBERRY PRESERVES

1 tablespoon (15 g) strawberry juice (see page 315)
2½ tablespoons (30 g) superfine sugar
1 cup (150 g) ripe Ciflorette strawberries, hulled
2 teaspoons (10 g) glucose powder
2 teaspoons (6 g) pectin NH
1 teaspoon (6 g) tartaric acid

FOR THE PASTRY CREAM

1¼ cups (300 g) milk
2½ teaspoons (35 g) whipping cream
1 vanilla bean
3½ large (60 g) egg yolks (¼ cup)
3 tablespoons (35 g) superfine sugar
1 tablespoon (18 g) custard powder
2½ tablespoons (18 g) all-purpose flour
1½ tablespoons (20 g) cocoa butter
5 teaspoons (16 g) gelatin powder
⅓ cup (72 g) water
2¾ tablespoons (40 g) unsalted butter
1½ tablespoons (20 g) mascarpone cheese

FOR THE BASIL PESTO

4 cups (125 g) fresh basil
1 tablespoon (15 g) almond paste
⅓ cup (75 g) olive oil
1½ tablespoons (20 g) honey
1 tablespoon (14 g) yuzu juice
A little ice

FOR ASSEMBLY AND FINISHING

1¼ cups (180 g) fresh strawberries
2 teaspoons (10 g) olive oil

FOR THE TART SHELL

The previous day, make the sweet dough for the tart shell as described on page 312. Let dry in the refrigerator for 1 day.

The next day, bake blind for 25 minutes at 320°F (160°C).

FOR THE EGG WASH

Beat the egg yolks with the cream. Brush a thin layer of the mixture over the prebaked tart shell, then return to the oven for 10 minutes, until golden.

FOR THE ALMOND-STRAWBERRY CREAM

Make the almond cream as described on page 314. Fill the tart shell with the mixture, then arrange the strawberry slices on top. Bake in the oven for 10 minutes, then let cool.

FOR THE STRAWBERRY PRESERVES

In a saucepan, heat the strawberry juice and the superfine sugar to 240°F (115°C), then add the whole strawberries. When they start to release their juices and the mixture is warm, stir in the glucose mixed with the pectin and tartaric acid. Heat the mixture to 220°F (104°C), then pour into a shallow pan to cool rapidly and refrigerate.

FOR THE PASTRY CREAM

Make the pastry cream as described on page 314, adjusting the amounts to fit this recipe, and refrigerate for 30 minutes.

FOR THE BASIL PESTO

Using a powerful blender, combine the basil, almond paste, oil, honey, and yuzu juice, adding a little ice to preserve the chlorophyll.

FOR THE ASSEMBLY AND FINISHING

Once the tart shell is cooked and has cooled, fill with the pastry cream then the strawberry preserves. Marble with the pesto. Cut the fresh strawberries into thin slices and combine gently with the oil in a large bowl. Arrange the strawberry slices on top of the tart. Serve at room temperature.

FRAISIER

FOR THE VANILLA MOUSSE

2 teaspoons (6 g) gelatin powder
3¼ cups (775 g) whipping cream
3 vanilla beans
6 ounces (172 g) white couverture chocolate, chopped

FOR THE STRAWBERRY PRESERVES

⅓ cup (75 g) strawberry juice (see page 315)
¾ cup (150 g) superfine sugar
1⅔ cups (250 g) frozen strawberries
1½ cups (250 g) ripe Ciflorette strawberries, hulled
¼ cup (50 g) glucose powder
1 teaspoon (3 g) pectin NH
½ teaspoons (3 g) tartaric acid

FOR THE LADYFINGER

8 large (140 g) egg yolks
6⅓ large (210 g) egg whites (¾ cup plus 2 tablespoons)
1 cup (185 g) superfine sugar
1½ cups (185 g) flour, sifted
Confectioners' sugar

FOR THE RED SPRAY

1 cup (200 g) spray mixture (see page 317)
4 teaspoons (20 g) red fat-soluble food coloring

FOR ASSEMBLY AND FINISHING

2 cups (300 g) fresh Ciflorette strawberries, plus one for garnish
Zest of 1 lime
3½ tablespoons (50 g) neutral glaze (see page 317)
Gold leaf

TIP

Be careful not to freeze the fraisier cake for too long. Only the vanilla mousse can be frozen, not the strawberries.

FOR THE VANILLA MOUSSE

The previous day, soak the gelatin in 3 tablespoons (42 g) cold water. Heat one-third of the cream, halve the vanilla beans lengthwise and scrape out the seeds, then add both the seeds and pods to the cream to infuse for 30 minutes. Pass through a conical sieve, then add the drained gelatin. Pour over the chopped chocolate and blend together using an immersion blender. Refrigerate for at least 12 hours.

FOR THE STRAWBERRY PRESERVES

The next day, in a saucepan, heat the strawberry juice and sugar to 240°F (115°C), then add the frozen strawberries and whole Ciflorette strawberries. When they start to release their juices and the mixture is warm, stir in the glucose powder mixed with the pectin and tartaric acid. Heat the mixture to 220°F (104°C), then pour into a pan to cool rapidly and refrigerate.

FOR THE LADYFINGER

Preheat the oven to 360°F (180°C). In an electric stand mixer with a whisk attachment, beat the egg yolks and set aside. Next, whip the egg whites to form soft peaks, add the superfine sugar, and beat until stiff. Using a silicone spatula, fold the whipped yolks and whites together, then fold in the sifted flour. Use the mixture to fill a pastry bag fitted with a no. 18 plain tip. Pipe a 5½-inch (14-cm)-diameter ring on a pan covered with parchment paper, then fill the ring with the mixture. Dust with the confectioners' sugar, then bake for 10 to 12 minutes.

FOR ASSEMBLY AND FINISHING

Hull and halve the strawberries. In the chilled bowl of an electric stand mixer fitted with a whisk attachment, whip the vanilla mousse. Line the inside of a 6-inch (16-cm)-diameter by 1.5-inch (4.5-cm)-deep cake ring with a Rhodoïd acetate strip. Place the ladyfinger disk at the bottom of the ring, then pipe the whipped vanilla mousse around the edge. Spread the strawberry preserves over the ladyfinger disk, then arrange the halved strawberries in the middle, leaving ⅜ inch (1 cm) of mousse around the edge. Using a Microplane, zest the lime over the strawberries. Cover with vanilla mousse and use a spatula to spread. Freeze for 20 minutes. Gently remove the fraisier cake from the ring, then shape the edges by hand until well defined. Make the red spray (see page 317) and airbrush the cake. Airbrush a thin layer of warm neutral glaze and decorate with a fresh strawberry and the gold leaf.

PREPARATION TIME: 1 HOUR

SERVES 8

COOKING TIME: 20 MINUTES

RESTING TIME: 12 HOURS PLUS 50 MINUTES

RASPBERRY

FOR THE TART SHELL

1 quantity (1¼ pounds/590 g) sweet dough (see page 312)

FOR THE EGG WASH

6 large (100 g) egg yolks
1½ tablespoons (25 g) whipping cream

FOR THE ALMOND-RASPBERRY CREAM

1 quantity (10½ ounces/300 g) almond cream (see page 314)
2 teaspoons (9 g) rum
⅓ cup (40 g) raspberries
2 tablespoons (30 g) olive oil

FOR THE PASTRY CREAM

1¼ cups (300 g) milk
2½ tablespoons (35 g) whipping cream
1 vanilla bean
3½ large (60 g) egg yolks (¼ cup)
2½ tablespoons (35 g) superfine sugar
1 tablespoon (18 g) custard powder
2½ tablespoons (18 g) all-purpose flour
1½ tablespoons (20 g) cocoa butter
5 teaspoons (16 g) gelatin powder
⅓ cup (72 g) water
2¾ tablespoons (40 g) unsalted butter
1½ tablespoons (20 g) mascarpone cheese

FOR ASSEMBLY AND FINISHING

¼ quantity (3½ ounces/100 g) raspberry seed mixture (see page 315)
1½ cups (180 g) fresh raspberries
2 tablespoons (30 ml) olive oil

FOR THE TART SHELL

The previous day, make the sweet dough for the tart shell as described on page 312. Let dry in the refrigerator for 1 day.
The next day, preheat the oven to 320°F (160°C) and blind bake the tart shell for 25 minutes.

FOR THE EGG WASH

Mix the egg yolks with the cream, then brush the prebaked tart shell with the mixture. Return to the oven for 10 minutes, until golden.

FOR THE ALMOND-RASPBERRY CREAM

Make the almond cream as described on page 314. Fill the tart shell with the cream, then place the fresh raspberries on top. Bake for 10 minutes, then drizzle the oil over the tart and let cool.

FOR THE PASTRY CREAM

Make the pastry cream as described on page 314, adjusting the amounts to fit this recipe, and refrigerate for 30 minutes. Fill the tart shell with the chilled pastry cream on top of the almond-raspberry cream layer.

FOR ASSEMBLY AND FINISHING

Make the raspberry seed mixture as described on page 315, then spread it over the pastry cream layer. Cut the fresh raspberries in half and arrange on top of the tart. Finish with a drizzle of oil. Serve at room temperature.

PREPARATION TIME: 2 HOURS

SERVES 8 TO 10

COOKING TIME: 45 MINUTES

RESTING TIME: 24 HOURS

RASPBERRY-THYME

FOR THE PUFF PASTRY

Kneaded butter (beurre manié)
3 cups (1½ pounds/670 g) unsalted dry butter (84% fat content)
2¼ cups (270 g) pastry flour

Water dough (détrempe)
1½ tablespoons (25 g) salt
1 teaspoon (6 g) distilled white vinegar
¾ cup plus 2 tablespoons (1¾ sticks/200 g) unsalted butter, softened
5¼ cups (630 g) pastry flour

FOR THE ALMOND-THYME CREAM

⅘ quantity (8½ ounces/240 g) almond cream (see page 314)
2 teaspoons (8 g) rum
3 tablespoons (20 g) raspberries
¼ cup (10 g) fresh thyme, chopped

FOR THE RASPBERRY WHIPPED CREAM

2 cups (500 g) whipping cream
3½ tablespoons (50 g) mascarpone cheese
1½ tablespoons (17.5 g) superfine sugar
2 tablespoons (20 g) raspberry juice (see page 315)

FOR THE CREAM PUFFS

1 quantity (14 ounces/400 g) choux paste (see page 312)

FOR THE RED CRUMB DOUGH

½ cup (1 stick 100 g) unsalted butter
1 cup (125 g) all-purpose flour
½ cup (125 g) packed light brown sugar
1 teaspoon (5 g) red fat-soluble food coloring

FOR THE RASPBERRY PASTRY CREAM

2 teaspoons (6 g) gelatin powder
5⅓ large (90 g) egg yolks (⅓ cup)
½ cup (90 g) superfine sugar
1½ tablespoons (25 g) custard powder
3½ tablespoons (25 g) all-purpose flour
2 cups (500 g) raspberry juice (see page 315)
2 tablespoons (30 g) cocoa butter
⅓ cup plus 1 tablespoon (90 g) Casanova olive oil

FOR THE THYME PESTO

2 cups (100 g) fresh thyme
2 tablespoons (30 g) olive oil
⅜ teaspoon (2 g) fine salt
½ teaspoon (1 g) ground black pepper
4 teaspoons (20 g) lemon juice

FOR THE THYME SUGAR

2½ cups (500 g) isomalt
1 cup (50 g) fresh thyme

FOR ASSEMBLY AND FINISHING

1⅔ cups (200 g) raspberries, thinly sliced in halves

Continued

SAINT-HONORÉ CAKE

PREPARATION TIME: 3 HOURS

SERVES 8

COOKING TIME: 1 HOUR

RESTING TIME: 24 HOURS PLUS 2 HOURS 30 MINUTES

RASPBERRY-THYME

FOR THE PUFF PASTRY

The previous day, make the puff pastry dough for a Saint-Honoré cake as described on page 313, then let rest for 24 hours. The next day, carry out the cutting and cooking stages as described on page 313.

FOR THE ALMOND-THYME CREAM

Make the almond cream as described on page 314, adding the rum. Transfer to a pastry bag and refrigerate for 30 minutes. Preheat the oven to 340°F (170°C). Top the puff pastry with a thin layer of almond cream, then arrange pieces of raspberries and the thyme on the top and bake for 5 minutes.

FOR THE RASPBERRY WHIPPED CREAM

Combine the cream, mascarpone, superfine sugar, and raspberry juice, then use an immersion blender to blend. Refrigerate for 1 hour.

FOR THE CREAM PUFFS

Make the Saint-Honoré choux paste and pipe the cream puffs as described on page 312.

FOR THE RED CRUMB DOUGH

In an electric stand mixer fitted with a flat beater attachment, beat the butter with the flour, brown sugar, and food coloring until a dough forms. Be careful not to let it stiffen too much. Use a rolling pin to roll to a thickness of 1/16 inch (2 mm) between two sheets of parchment paper. Freeze for 15 minutes, then use a cookie cutter to cut out ¾-inch (2-cm)-diameter circles. Preheat the oven to 360°F (180°C). Place a crumb disk on each cream puff. Bake the cream puffs for 10 minutes, then reduce the oven temperature to 320°F (160°C) and bake for another 5 minutes.

SAINT-HONORÉ CAKE

FOR THE RASPBERRY PASTRY CREAM

Soak the gelatin in 3 tablespoons (42 g) cold water to soften. Whisk the egg yolks with the superfine sugar, custard powder, and flour until pale. Bring the raspberry juice to a boil and pour over the egg yolk mixture, then return to the saucepan and boil for 2 minutes. Remove from the heat and add the cocoa butter and gelatin. Use an immersion blender to mix, then an electric stand mixer fitted with a flat beater attachment to smooth the mixture. Add the oil. Refrigerate for 30 minutes.

FOR THE THYME PESTO

Put the thyme, oil, fine salt, pepper, and lemon juice in a deep bowl, then use an immersion blender to mix. Transfer to a vacuum-sealed pastry bag and set aside.

FOR THE THYME SUGAR

In a saucepan, heat the isomalt to 340°F (170°C), then add the thyme. Remove from the heat and dip the cream puffs in the mixture to glaze. Place in 1-inch (2.5-cm)-diameter silicone half-dome molds for a few minutes for the sugar to harden, then unmold.

FOR ASSEMBLY AND FINISHING

Top the pastry layer with the raspberry pastry cream and dot the thyme pesto over the top. Pipe a dot of the pesto on the cream puffs, then use a pastry bag fitted with a small plain tip to pipe the raspberry pastry cream into the cream puffs. Place the cream puffs around the edge of the cream and cover with the raspberries. In an electric stand mixer fitted with a whisk attachment, whip the raspberry whipped cream, then use it to fill a pastry bag with a no. 20 Saint-Honoré tip. Pipe the whipped cream over the raspberries, then finish by placing a last cream puff on top.

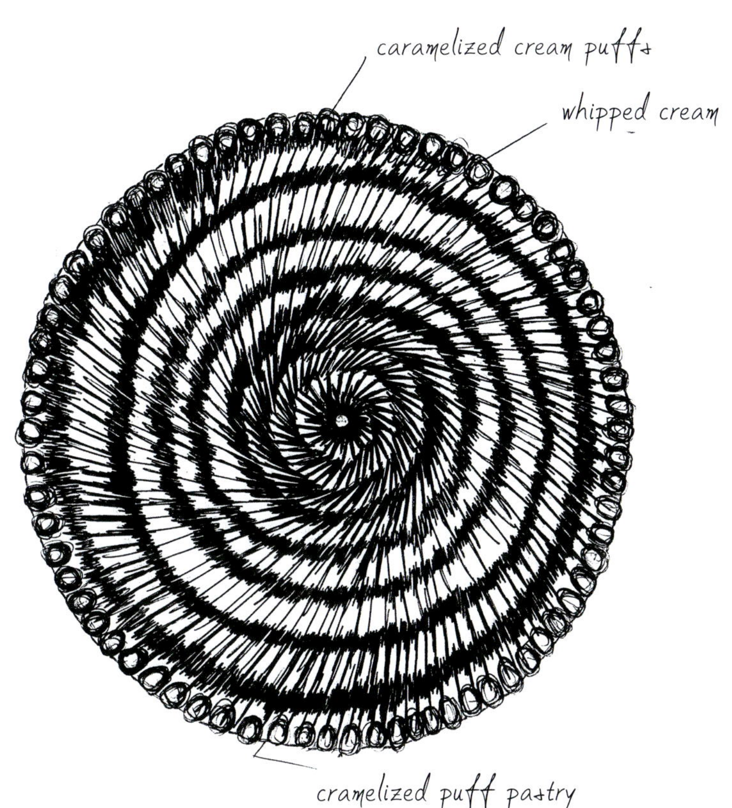

PREPARATION TIME: 1 HOUR 30 MINUTES

SERVES 10

COOKING TIME: 20 MINUTES

RESTING TIME: 12 HOURS PLUS 5 HOURS 30 MINUTES

FOR THE BRIOCHE DOUGH
4 cups (510 g) all-purpose flour
2 teaspoons (10 g) salt
3½ tablespoons (40 g) superfine sugar
⅓ (20 g) cake yeast, or 2¼ teaspoons active dry yeast (dissolved in milk or water)
⅔ cup (150 g) milk
3 large (150 g) eggs
3½ tablespoons (50 g) unsalted butter, softened
1⅓ cups (10½ ounces/300 g) unsalted dry butter (84% fat content)

FOR THE RASPBERRY SEED MIXTURE
1¾ cups (250 g) frozen raspberries
¾ cup (150 g) superfine sugar
1¾ teaspoons (5 g) pectin NH
2 teaspoons (10 g) lemon juice
¾ teaspoon (2 g) gelatin powder

FOR THE BRIOCHE DOUGH

The previous day, in an electric stand mixer fitted with a dough hook attachment, knead the flour, salt, sugar, yeast, milk, eggs, and softened butter, until the mixture forms a smooth dough. Refrigerate for 12 hours.

The next day, roll out the chilled dough into a large rectangle. Flatten the butter by battering it with a rolling pin until you have a rectangle half the size of the dough rectangle, then place in the center of the dough. Fold over the dough to encase the butter, then roll into a new rectangle. Fold in three and refrigerate for 2 hours. Repeat two times, using the same chilling time between each, until the dough has been turned three times, then refrigerate for 1 hour. Finally, roll to a thickness of ³/₄ inch (3.5 mm) and cut ten 2½ by 5-inch (6 by 12-cm) rectangles. Cut each rectangle into three ³/₄ inch by 3½-inch (2 by 9-cm) strips, then braid them and curl into balls by hand. Put each ball into a 3-inch (8-cm)-diameter cake ring on a baking sheet, then let rise for 30 minutes in a warm place.

Preheat the oven to 340°F (170°C). When the brioches have risen, bake for 20 minutes, until golden.

FOR THE RASPBERRY SEED MIXTURE

Make the raspberry seed mixture as described on page 315, adjusting the amounts to fit this recipe. Transfer to a pastry bag without a tip. Make a hole on the bottom side of each brioche and fill with the raspberry seed mixture.

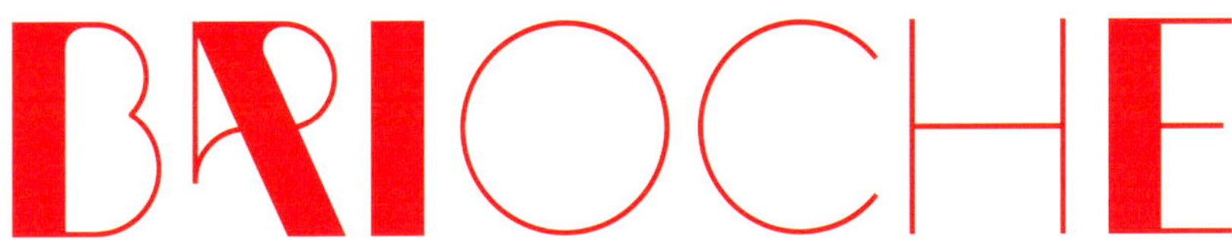

PREPARATION TIME: 2 HOURS

SERVES 8

COOKING TIME: 25 MINUTES

RESTING TIME: 12 HOURS PLUS 50 MINUTES

FRAMBOISIER

FOR THE HONEY MOUSSE

2 teaspoons (6 g) gelatin powder
3¼ cups (775 g) whipping cream
6 ounces (172 g) white couverture chocolate, chopped
⅓ cup (140 g) Béton honey

FOR THE RASPBERRY SPONGE CAKE

2½ tablespoons (50 g) Lubeca almond paste
1½ tablespoons (25 g) whipping cream
2 large (100 g) eggs
½ cup (100 g) superfine sugar
¾ cup (100 g) cake flour
1 cup (125 g) vanilla whipped cream (see page 314)
1⅔ cups (200 g) fresh raspberries

FOR THE ASSEMBLY AND FINISHING

2½ cups (300 g) fresh raspberries
½ quantity (5¼ ounces/150 g) raspberry seed mixture (see page 315)
Ground dried thyme

Red spray

1 cup (200 g) spray mixture (see page 317)
4 teaspoons (20 g) raspberry-red fat-soluble food coloring
3½ tablespoons (50 g) neutral glaze(see page 317)

FOR THE HONEY MOUSSE

The previous day, soak the gelatin in 3 tablespoons (42 g) cold water to soften. Heat one-third of the whipping cream, then add the gelatin and pour over the chocolate. Pass through a conical sieve, then add the honey. Add the remaining cold cream and use an immersion blender to blend together. Refrigerate for 12 hours.

FOR THE RASPBERRY SPONGE CAKES

The next day, preheat the oven to 360°F (180°C). Combine the almond paste and cream until smooth, then stir in the eggs and superfine sugar. Use a wire whisk to beat to ribbon consistency, then sprinkle in the flour and fold in the whipped cream using a silicone spatula. Place a 6½-inch (16-cm)-diameter by 2½-inch (6-cm)-deep greased cake ring on a baking sheet covered with a sheet of parchment paper. Pour the batter into the cake ring, place the raspberries on top, then bake for about 25 minutes.

FOR ASSEMBLY AND FINISHING

In the chilled bowl of an electric stand mixer fitted with a whisk attachment, whip the honey mousse, then transfer to a pastry bag. Cut the fresh raspberries in half. Line the inside of a 6½-inch (16-cm)-diameter by 1¾-inch (4.4-cm)-deep cake ring with a Rhodoïd acetate strip. Place the sponge cake in the bottom of the cake ring, then pipe the honey mousse around the edge and use a spatula to remove any air bubbles. Spread the raspberry seed mixture (see page 315) over the cake, then cover with as many raspberry halves as possible. Lightly dust with ground thyme, then cover the raspberries with the honey mousse. Use a spatula to smooth, then freeze for 20 minutes. Gently remove from the cake ring and shape the edge by hand until even. Using a pastry bag fitted with a no. 20 Saint-Honoré tip, cover the whole surface with honey mousse. Return to the freezer for 30 minutes. Make the red spray mixture as described on page 317, heat to 95°F (35°C), then airbrush the framboisier cake. Create a glossy effect on the framboisier cake by airbrushing with the neutral glaze, also at 95°F (35°C)..

RED CURRANT

FOR THE BRIOCHE

4 cups plus 2½ tablespoons (500 g) pastry flour
2 teaspoons (9 g) salt
⅓ cup (75 g) superfine sugar
½ (27.5 g) cake yeast, or 3¼ teaspoons active dry yeast (dissolved in milk or water)
1 teaspoon (6 g) vanilla extract
3 tablespoons (25 g) vanilla powder
6½ large (325 g) eggs (1⅓ cups)
1¾ cups (400 g) Bordier vanilla butter, chilled
1 egg, beaten

FOR THE CARAMEL SAUCE

1 cup (250 g) whipping cream
2 vanilla beans
1¼ cups (250 g) superfine sugar

FOR THE FRENCH TOAST MIXTURE

2¾ cups (650 g) raw vanilla milk
⅓ cup (100 g) whipping cream
4 large (200 g) eggs
¼ cup (50 g) superfine sugar
3½ tablespoons (50 g) unsalted butter
3½ tablespoons (50 g) grapeseed oil

FOR ASSEMBLY AND FINISHING

2 cups (250 g) fresh red currants

FOR THE BRIOCHE

The previous day, in an electric stand mixer fitted with a dough hook attachment, knead the flour, salt, superfine sugar, yeast, vanilla extract, vanilla powder, and eggs for 5 minutes on speed 1, then change to speed 2. When the dough begins to come away from the sides of the bowl, add the vanilla butter in three batches. Knead until the dough begins to come away from the sides again, then transfer to a greased mixing bowl. Let the dough rise for 1 hour 30 minutes at room temperature. Roll out, then refrigerate for 12 hours.

The next day, put 10½ ounces (300 g) of the brioche dough into a loaf pan and place in a turned-off oven with a saucepan of boiling water, or on top of a radiator, for 30 minutes. Remove from the oven and preheat the oven to 360°F (180°C). Brush with the beaten egg, then bake for 45 minutes.

FOR THE CARAMEL SAUCE

Heat the cream, split the vanilla beans, scrape out the seeds, and add both the seeds and pods to the cream to infuse for 15 minutes. In another saucepan, make a dry caramel with the superfine sugar, then pour over the infused cream. Boil for 2 minutes, then pass through a conical sieve.

FOR THE FRENCH TOAST MIXTURE

Mix the vanilla milk with the cream, eggs, and superfine sugar, then lightly mix with an immersion blender. Cut the brioche into slices, soak in the mixture, then let drip-dry. Fry on each side in a frying pan with the butter and grapeseed oil until golden brown.

FOR ASSEMBLY AND FINISHING

Serve the slices of French toast with the caramel sauce dotted with a few fresh red currants.

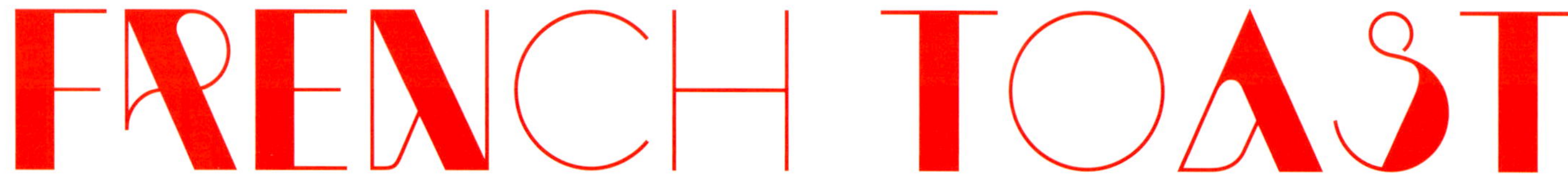

PREPARATION TIME: 1 HOUR 30 MINUTES

SERVES 10

COOKING TIME: 1 HOUR

RESTING TIME: 12 HOURS + 2 HOURS

WI
FRU

In season
July to October

Selection
the fruit should be scented, firm, and fleshy

Average weight
1¼ ounces (50 g)

Storage
at room temperature for 4 days; remove from the refrigerator 30 minutes before eating

Flavor pairings
Dolç Mataró sweet red wine, lavander, vanilla ice cream, rosemary

WILD STRAWBERRY

In season
June to September

Selection
the fruit should be well scented

Average weight
a few grams

Storage
in the refrigerator for up to 48 hours

Flavor pairings
lime, basil, cream cheese

BLACKBERRY

In season
July to October

Selection
the fruit should be scented, tender, almost soft

Average weight
a few grams

Storage
in the refrigerator vegetable drawer for 2 to 3 days

Flavor pairings
coconut, ginger, banana

BLUEBERRY

In season
June to September

Selection
check that there is no mold; the fruit should be scented and have a deep blue around the stem

Average weight
a few grams

Storage
in the refrigerator for up to 1 week

Flavor pairings
yogurt, raspberry, peach

GRAPE

In season
July to October

Selection
the fruit should be firm
with no blemishes; the stem should
be supple and brittle

Average weight
depending on the variety, a bunch
of grapes can weigh between 5 and
18 ounces (150 and 500 g)

Storage
in the refrigerator vegetable
drawer for up to 5 days

Flavor pairings
banana, rum, apple

RHUBARB

In season

April to July

Selection

the ends of the rhubarb stalks should be firm and without blemishes

Average weight

3 ounces (80 g)

Storage

in the refrigerator vegetable drawer for up to 3 days

Flavor pairings

strawberry, apple, ginger

FOR THE FIG LEAF SYRUP

1½ tablespoons (20 g) lavender honey
6 fig leaves, chopped

FOR THE POACHED FIGS

1¾ tablespoons (25 g) unsalted butter
8 Solliès figs
3 tablespoons (40 g) lavender honey
1 vanilla bean, split and scraped

FOR THE TARTLET SHELLS

1 quantity (1¼ pounds 590 g) sweet dough (see page 312)

FOR THE WHIPPED FIG LEAF GANACHE

1 teaspoon (3 g) gelatin powder
1⅓ cups (310 g) whipping cream
3 fig leaves, chopped
2½ ounces (70 g) white couverture chocolate, chopped

FOR THE FIG CENTERS

2 (100 g) fresh ripe figs

FOR THE EGG WASH

6 large (100 g) egg yolks
1½ tablespoons (25 g) whipping cream

FOR THE ALMOND-FIG CREAM

½ quantity (5¼ ounces/150 g) almond cream (see page 314)
2 teaspoons (9 g) rum
10 large slices fresh figs

FOR THE FIG PRESERVES

12 fresh figs (about 1 pound 6 ounces/625 g)
¼ cup (50 g) superfine sugar
¼ cup (50 g) glucose powder
1 teaspoon (3 g) pectin NH
½ teaspoon (3 g) tartaric acid

FOR ASSEMBLY AND FINISHING

Purple coating

2 cups (470 g) coating mixture (see page 317)
1 teaspoon (4 g) red fat-soluble food coloring
2 teaspoons (9 g) blue fat-soluble food coloring

Red glaze

1 drop (0.10 g) raspberry-red food coloring
3½ tablespoons (50 g) neutral glaze (see page 317)
1 cup (100 g) finely chopped toasted almonds (see page 317)
10 chocolate stems (see page 317

Continued

PREPARATION TIME: 3 HOURS 30 MINUTES

SERVES 10

COOKING TIME: 1 HOUR

RESTING TIME: 24 HOURS PLUS 3 HOURS 40 MINUTES

FIG

FOR THE FIG LEAF SYRUP

The previous day, in a saucepan, boil ¾ cup plus 2 tablespoons (200 g) water with the honey. Add the fig leaves and let infuse for 20 minutes. Pass through a conical sieve.

FOR THE POACHED FIGS

In a skillet, melt the butter, then add the whole figs. Stir to coat the figs with the butter, add the honey and vanilla bean seeds, cook for a few minutes, then add the fig leaf syrup. Heat for another few minutes, until the figs are slightly soft. Transfer to an airtight container with the cooking liquid and let macerate for 24 hours at room temperature.

FOR THE TARTLET SHELLS

Make the sweet dough for the tartlet shells as described on page 312 and let dry in the refrigerator for 1 day.

FOR THE WHIPPED FIG LEAF GANACHE

Soak the gelatin in 4 teaspoons (21 g) cold water to soften. Heat one-third of the cream with the chopped fig leaves, then let infuse for 20 minutes. Pass through a conical sieve and measure. Add cream to obtain a total of 1⅓ cups (310 g) and heat. Pour the hot cream over the chocolate, then add the gelatin. Use an immersion blender to blend. Refrigerate for 12 hours.

FOR THE FIG CENTERS

The next day, drain the poached figs and set aside the syrup for making the fig preserves. Coarsely chop the poached figs and fresh figs. Mix together and pour into 1¼-inch (3.5-cm)-diameter silicone half-dome molds. Freeze for 1 hour.

FOR THE EGG WASH

Preheat the oven to 320°F (160°C). Blind bake the tartlet shells for 20 minutes. Beat the egg yolks with the cream and brush the shells with the mixture. Return to the oven for 5 minutes.

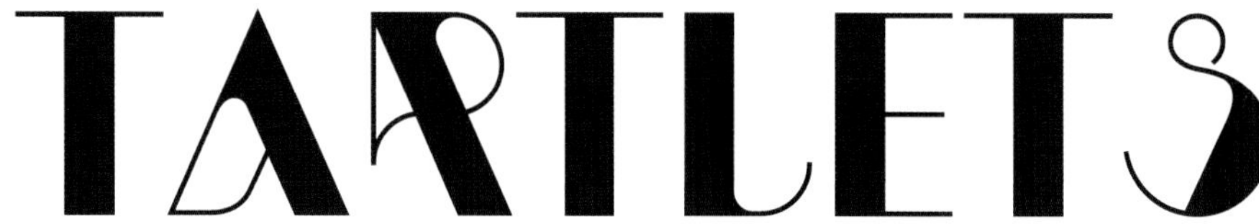

TARTLETS

FOR THE ALMOND-FIG CREAM

Make the almond cream as described on page 314 and use to fill the tartlet shells. Bake for 5 minutes, then let cool. Place a slice of fresh fig on top of each tartlet and bake for 10 minutes. Let cool.

FOR THE FIG PRESERVES

Cut 10 figs into quarters, then cut each quarter in two. Cut the remaining figs into small cubes. In a saucepan, heat ⅓ cup (75 g) of the reserved fig leaf — infused syrup and the sugar to 240°F (115°C). Add the fig eighths and cook over low heat. When the fruit starts to stew, let cool slightly, then add the glucose mixed with the pectin and tartaric acid. Heat to 200°F (95°C) and remove from the heat to let cool. Once the preserves have cooled, add the fig cubes and transfer to a pastry bag. Fill the tartlet shells to the top with the preserves and smooth.

FOR ASSEMBLY AND FINISHING

In the chilled bowl of an electric stand mixer fitted with a whisk attachment, whip the fig leaf ganache, then pipe into 1¾-inch (4.5-cm)-diameter silicone half-dome molds. Insert a frozen fig center, then cover to the top with ganache and smooth. Freeze for 3 hours. Unmold the fig domes, then pipe a little ganache at the top of each dome. Smooth to shape into fig shapes and return to the freezer for 20 minutes. Make the purple coating as described on page 317 and dip the fig shapes into the coating heated to 95°F (35°C). Airbrush with the same coating. Dilute a little red food coloring in ¼ teaspoon water, then mix with the neutral glaze. Heat the red glaze to 105°F (40°C) and airbrush to create little droplets. Place the fig shapes on the tartlet shells and arrange the toasted almonds around the edge. Make the chocolate stems as described on page 317 and secure them to the top of the figs.

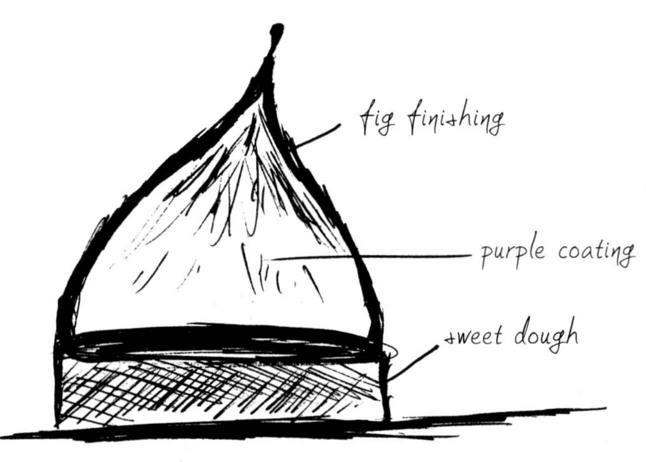

FOR THE POACHED FIGS

1 teaspoon (5 g) unsalted butter
8 ripe Solliès or Noire de Caromb figs
2 teaspoons (10 g) lavender honey
1 vanilla bean, split and scraped

FOR THE FIG COMPOTE

2 (100 g) fresh ripe figs

FOR THE CANDIED ALMONDS

⅔ cup (100 g) blanched almonds
3½ tablespoons (40 g) superfine sugar

FOR THE COOKIE DOUGH

½ cup (1 stick/120 g) unsalted butter
¼ teaspoon (1 g) red fat-soluble food coloring
¼ teaspoon (1 g) blue fat-soluble food coloring
⅓ cup (90 g) almond paste
½ cup (100 g) packed light brown sugar
1 cup plus 2 tablespoons (220 g) superfine sugar
1 teaspoon (4 g) fleur de sel
2 medium (90 g) eggs
3⅓ cups (420 g) all-purpose flour
2 teaspoons (8 g) baking soda
4 Ronde de Bordeaux figs

FOR ASSEMBLY AND FINISHING

20 fresh figs
1 drizzle olive oil

FOR THE POACHED FIGS

The previous day, in a skillet, melt the butter and add the whole figs. Stir to coat the figs with the butter, then add the honey and vanilla seeds. Heat for a few minutes until the figs are slightly soft. Transfer to an airtight container with the cooking liquid and let macerate for 24 hours at room temperature.

FOR THE FIG COMPOTE

The next day, drain the poached figs. Coarsely chop the poached figs and fresh figs. Mix together and transfer to a pastry bag without a tip.

FOR THE CANDIED ALMONDS

Preheat the oven to 320°F (160°C). Place the almonds on a baking sheet, then toast in the oven for 20 minutes. In a copper saucepan, heat 2 teaspoons (10 g) water and the sugar to 230°F (110°C). Add the almonds to coat and caramelize them. When they are well coated and the caramel has turned golden, transfer to a marble work surface or a lightly greased cutting board and let cool. Coarsely cut the almonds to slivers using a large knife.

FOR THE COOKIE DOUGH

Preheat the oven to 330°F (165°C). Beat the butter with the food colorings, almond paste, sugars, and fleur de sel, then beat in the eggs, one by one. Mix the flour and baking soda together, then mix into the butter mixture. Finally, mix in the fig pulp. Shape the dough by hand into approximately 1¼-ounce (35-g) balls, and roll in the candied almonds. Bake for 6 minutes.

FOR ASSEMBLY AND FINISHING

Cut the figs into eighths and cook on a baking sheet with the oil for 5 minutes. Once the cookies have baked for 6 minutes, place three cooked fig pieces on each, setting aside the remaining pieces. Shape the dough into 3-inch (8-cm)-diameter disks and return to the oven for 4 minutes. Spoon three dots of fig compote on top and bake for 1 minute more. Finally, after removing the cookies from the oven, place three pieces of the reserved cooked figs on each cookie and drizzle with a little oil.

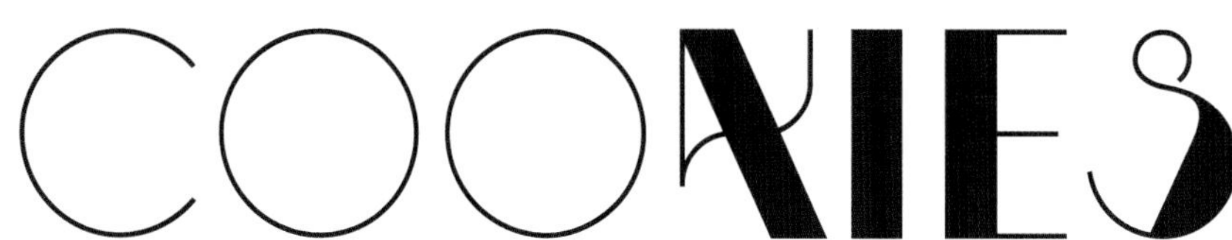

PREPARATION TIME: 1 HOUR

COOKING TIME: 35 MINUTES

SERVES 10

RESTING TIME: 24 HOURS

PREPARATION TIME: 2 HOURS

SERVES 8 TO 10

COOKING TIME: 45 MINUTES

RESTING TIME: 24 HOURS PLUS 20 MINUTES

FOR THE TART SHELL
1 quantity (1¼ pounds/590 g) sweet dough (see page 312)

FOR THE EGG WASH
6 large (100 g) egg yolks
1½ tablespoons (25 g) whipping cream

FOR THE ALMOND-FIG CREAM
1 quantity (10½ ounces/300 g) almond cream (see page 314)
¾ cup (45 g) fig pulp (3 figs)

FOR THE FIG LEAF SYRUP
2 teaspoons (7.5 g) superfine sugar
1 fig leaf, chopped

FOR THE FIG PRESERVES
1½ tablespoons (20 g) superfine sugar
5 (250 g) fresh figs
½ teaspoon (1.4 g) pectin NH
¼ teaspoon (1.4 g) tartaric acid

FOR THE DOLÇ MATARÓ GEL
½ cup (120 g) Dolç Mataró sweet red wine
½ teaspoon (1.5 g) agar powder
½ teaspoon (2.5 g) superfine sugar

FOR ASSEMBLY AND FINISHING
1½ cups (80 g) fig pulp
10 fresh figs

FOR THE TART SHELL

The previous day, make the sweet dough for the tart shell as described on page 312 and let dry in the refrigerator for 1 day.

The next day, blind bake the tart shell at 320°F (160°C) for 25 minutes.

FOR THE EGG WASH

Beat the egg yolks with the cream. Brush the mixture over the prebaked tart shell, then return to the oven for 10 minutes, until golden.

FOR THE ALMOND-FIG CREAM

Make the almond cream as described on page 314. Transfer to a pastry bag and pipe a layer of cream into the tart shell. Press pieces of fig pulp into the cream. Return to the oven for 10 minutes.

FOR THE FIG LEAF SYRUP

In a saucepan, boil 1/3 cup (75 g) water with the superfine sugar. Add the fig leaf and let infuse for 20 minutes. Pass through a conical sieve.

FOR THE FIG PRESERVES

In a saucepan, heat 2 tablespoons (30 g) of the fig leaf syrup and the superfine sugar to 240°F (115°C), then add the fresh figs and stew over low heat for 10 minutes. Let cool for a few minutes, then add the pectin and tartaric acid. Boil for 1 minute, then remove from the heat. Set aside.

FOR THE DOLÇ MATARÓ GEL

In a saucepan, heat the Dolç Mataró, add the agar mixed with the superfine sugar, and boil for 1 minute. Remove from the heat and refrigerate.

FOR ASSEMBLY AND FINISHING

Once the tart is cooked and has cooled, fill with the fig pulp, then decorate with the fig preserves and dot with the Dolç Mataró gelatin. Cut the fresh figs into slices and arrange on top of the tart.

FOR THE TARTLET SHELLS

1 quantity (1¼ pounds/590 g) sweet dough (see page 312)

FOR THE EGG WASH

6 large (100 g) egg yolks
1½ tablespoons (25 g) whipping cream

FOR THE ALMOND-WILD STRAWBERRY CREAM

1 quantity (10½ ounces/300 g) almond cream (see page 314)
⅔ cup (100 g) wild strawberries

FOR THE PASTRY CREAM

1¼ cups (300 g) milk
2½ tablespoons (35 g) whipping cream
1 vanilla bean
3½ large (60 g) egg yolks (¼ cup)
3 tablespoons (35 g) superfine sugar
1 tablespoon (18 g) custard powder
2½ tablespoons (18 g) all-purpose flour
1½ tablespoons (20 g) cocoa butter
5½ teaspoons (16 g) gelatin powder
⅓ cup (72 g) water
3 tablespoons (40 g) unsalted butter
1½ tablespoons (20 g) mascarpone cheese

FOR THE WILD STRAWBERRY PRESERVES

1 cup (150 g) wild strawberries
2½ tablespoons (30 g) superfine sugar
3½ tablespoons (45 g) olive oil
Zest and juice of 1 lime

FOR ASSEMBLY AND FINISHING

1¾ cups (250 g) wild strawberries

FOR THE TARTLET SHELLS

The previous day, make the sweet dough for the tart shell as described on page 312. Let dry in the refrigerator for 1 day.

The next day, preheat the oven to 320°F (160°C). Blind bake the tartlet shells for 20 minutes.

FOR THE EGG WASH

Beat the egg yolks with the cream, then brush the prebaked tartlet shells with the mixture. Return to the oven for 10 minutes, until golden.

FOR THE ALMOND-WILD STRAWBERRY CREAM

Make the almond cream as described on page 314. Transfer to a pastry bag and pipe into each tartlet shell. Press the wild strawberries into the cream. Return to the oven for 10 minutes.

FOR THE PASTRY CREAM

Make the cream as described on page 314, adjusting the amounts to fit this recipe, and refrigerate for 30 minutes. Fill the tartlet shells with the pastry cream, on top of the layer of almond – wild strawberry cream, shaping it into a dome on top.

FOR THE WILD STRAWBERRY PRESERVES

Using a fork, crush the wild strawberries with the superfine sugar, oil, and lime zest and juice. Transfer to a pastry bag without a tip, then garnish the pastry cream domes with the preserves.

FOR ASSEMBLY AND FINISHING

Arrange the wild strawberries over the cream domes, pointing outward.

PREPARATION TIME: 2 HOURS

SERVES 10

COOKING TIME: 45 MINUTES

RESTING TIME: 24 HOURS PLUS 30 MINUTES

PREPARATION TIME: 2 HOURS

SERVES 8 TO 10

COOKING TIME: 45 MINUTES

RESTING TIME: 24 HOURS

FOR THE TART SHELL
1 quantity (1¼ pounds/590 g) sweet dough (see page 312)

FOR THE EGG WASH
6 large (100 g) egg yolks
1½ tablespoons (25 g) whipping cream

FOR THE ALMOND-BLACKBERRY CREAM
1 quantity (10½ ounces/300 g) almond cream (see page 314)
⅓ cup (50 g) fresh blackberries
A few drops olive oil

FOR THE PASTRY CREAM
⅓ cup (90 g) milk
2 teaspoons (10 g) whipping cream
1 vanilla bean
1 extra-large (20 g) egg yolk
2 teaspoons (10 g) superfine sugar
1 teaspoon (5 g) custard powder
2 teaspoons (5 g) all-purpose flour
1½ teaspoons (6 g) cocoa butter
3½ teaspoons (10 g) gelatin powder
2 teaspoons (10 g) unsalted butter
2 teaspoons (10 g) mascarpone cheese

FOR THE BLACKBERRY PRESERVES
1⅓ cups (200 g) fresh blackberries
½ cup (100 g) superfine sugar
2 teaspoons (10 g) lemon juice
½ teaspoon (2 g) ascorbic acid
¾ teaspoon (2 g) pectin NH

FOR ASSEMBLY AND FINISHING
1¼ cups (180 g) wild blackberries
3 tablespoons (40 g) Casanova olive oil

FOR THE TART SHELL
The previous day, make the sweet dough for the tart shell as described on page 312. Let dry in the refrigerator for 1 day. The next day, blind bake the tart shell at 320°F (160°C) for 25 minutes.

FOR THE EGG WASH
Beat the egg yolks with the cream and brush the shell with the mixture. Return to the oven for 10 minutes.

FOR THE ALMOND-BLACKBERRY CREAM
Make the almond cream as described on page 314. Transfer to a pastry bag and pipe a layer of cream into the tart shell. Press the fresh blackberries into the cream. Return to the oven for 10 minutes. After removing from the oven, drizzle a few drops of oil over the hot tart.

FOR THE PASTRY CREAM
Make the pastry cream as described on page 314, adjusting the amounts to fit this recipe, and refrigerate for 30 minutes. Pipe into the tart shell on top of the layer of almond-blackberry cream.

FOR THE BLACKBERRY PRESERVES
In a saucepan, combine the blackberries with 1/3 cup (80 g) of the superfine sugar, the lemon juice, and ascorbic acid and cook over low heat for about 10 minutes, until reduced to the desired consistency. Add the remaining sugar mixed with the pectin, then boil for 1 minute. Remove from the heat and refrigerate for 30 minutes. Cover the tart with the preserves, spreading it over the pastry cream layer.

FOR THE ASSEMBLY AND FINISHING
Put the wild blackberries in a mixing bowl, add the oil, and mix gently to coat. Arrange them over the surface of the tart with the stem side down.

BLACKBERRY TART

BLUEBERRY

FOR THE WAFFLES

2 cups (500 g) milk
2 vanilla beans
1¾ cups (3½ sticks/400 g) unsalted butter
3⅔ cups (460 g) all-purpose flour
1 teaspoon (6 g) salt
6⅔ large (220 g) egg whites (¾ cup plus 2 tablespoons)
3½ tablespoons (40 g) superfine sugar
Brown sugar

FOR ASSEMBLY AND FINISHING

1¾ cups (250 g) fresh blueberries

FOR THE WAFFLES

Heat the milk, halve the vanilla beans lengthwise and scrape out the seeds, and add both seeds and pods to the milk to infuse for 20 minutes. Heat the butter until it browns. Mix the browned butter with the vanilla-infused milk and heat to 105°F (40°C). Put the flour and salt in a mixing bowl. Pour the butter mixture over the flour in three batches, using a wire whisk to mix each time to a smooth and elastic dough.

In an electric stand mixer fitted with a whisk attachment, whip the egg whites to soft peaks, then add the superfine sugar and beat until stiff. Gently mix the egg whites into the flour mixture.

Pour batter into a waffle iron, dust with a little brown sugar, and let cook for 4 minutes.

FOR ASSEMBLY AND FINISHING

Serve the waffles with the fresh blueberries.

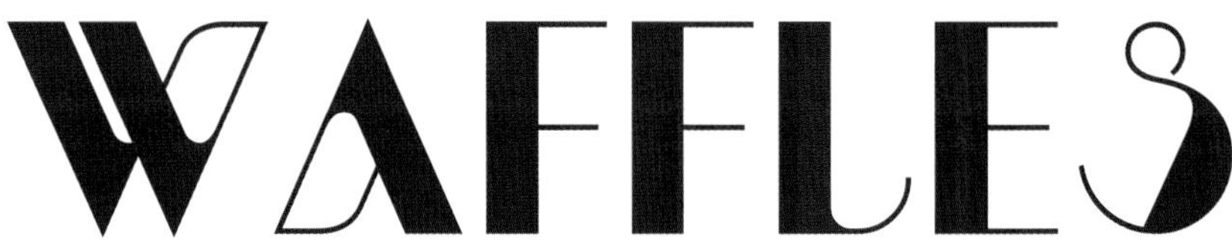

PREPARATION TIME: 30 MINUTES

SERVES 6

COOKING TIME: 4 MINUTES

RESTING TIME: 20 MINUTES

PREPARATION TIME: 2 HOURS

SERVES 8 TO 10

COOKING TIME: 45 MINUTES

RESTING TIME: 24 HOURS PLUS 30 MINUTES

FOR THE TART SHELL
1 quantity (1¼ pounds/590 g) sweet dough (see page 312)

FOR THE EGG WASH
6 large (100 g) egg yolks
1½ tablespoons (25 g) whipping cream

FOR THE ALMOND-BLUEBERRY CREAM
1 quantity (10½ ounces (300 g) almond cream (see page 314)
¼ cup (40 g) fresh blueberries
Olive oil

FOR THE PASTRY CREAM
⅓ cup (90 g) milk
2 teaspoons (10 g) whipping cream
1 vanilla bean
1 extra-large (20 g) egg yolk
2½ teaspoons (10 g) superfine sugar
1 teaspoon (5 g) custard powder
2 teaspoons (5 g) all-purpose flour
1½ teaspoons (6 g) cocoa butter
3½ teaspoons (10 g) gelatin powder
2 teaspoons (10 g) unsalted butter
2 teaspoons (10 g) mascarpone cheese

FOR THE BLUEBERRY PRESERVES
1⅓ cups (200 g) fresh blueberries
½ cup (100 g) superfine sugar
2 teaspoons (10 g) lemon juice
½ teaspoon (2 g) ascorbic acid
¾ teaspoon (2 g) pectin NH

FOR ASSEMBLY AND FINISHING
1¼ cups (180 g) wild blueberries
A few drops olive oil

FOR THE TART SHELL

The previous day, make the sweet dough as described on page 312. Let dry in the refrigerator for 1 day. The next day, blind bake the tart shell at 320°F (160°C) for 25 minutes.

FOR THE EGG WASH

Beat the egg yolks with the cream and brush the shell with the mixture. Return to the oven for 10 minutes.

FOR THE ALMOND-BLUEBERRY CREAM

Make the almond cream as described on page 314. Transfer to a pastry bag and pipe a layer of cream into the tart shell. Press the fresh blueberries into the cream. Return to the oven for 10 minutes. After removing from the oven, drizzle a few drops of oil over the hot tart.

FOR THE PASTRY CREAM

Make the pastry cream as described on page 314, adjusting the amounts to fit this recipe, and refrigerate for 30 minutes. Pipe into the tart shell on top of the layer of almond-blueberry cream.

FOR THE BLUEBERRY PRESERVES

In a saucepan, cook the blueberries with 1/3 cup (80 g) of the superfine sugar, the lemon juice, and ascorbic acid over low heat for about 10 minutes, until reduced to the desired consistency. Add the remaining sugar mixed with the pectin, then boil for 1 minute. Remove from the heat and refrigerate for 30 minutes. Cover the tart with the preserves, spreading it over the pastry cream layer.

FOR THE ASSEMBLY AND FINISHING

Put the wild blueberries in a mixing bowl, add the oil, and mix gently to coat. Arrange them over the surface of the tart.

PREPARATION TIME: 2 HOURS

SERVES 15

COOKING TIME: 15 MINUTES

RESTING TIME: 10 HOURS 35 MINUTES

RAISIN-

FOR THE DOUGH

8 cups (1 kg) all-purpose flour
3½ teaspoons (20 g) salt
⅔ cup (120 g) superfine sugar
⅓ cup (40 g) instant dry milk powder
⅔ (40 g) cake yeast, or 1½ tablespoons active dry yeast (dissolved in milk or water)
7 tablespoons (100 g) unsalted butter
2¼ cups (1 pound 2 ounces/500 g) unsalted dry butter (84% fat content)

FOR THE RAISINS

1⅓ cups (200 g) raisins
2 cups (500 g) warm water

FOR THE NOT-SO-SWEET PASTRY CREAM

1⅔ cups (400 g) milk
3½ tablespoons (50 g) whipping cream
2 vanilla beans
5¼ large (90 g) egg yolks (⅓ cup)
¼ cup (50 g) superfine sugar
1½ tablespoons (25 g) custard powder
3½ tablespoons (25 g) all-purpose flour
2½ tablespoons (30 g) cocoa butter
3½ teaspoons (10 g) gelatin powder
3½ tablespoons (50 g) unsalted butter
2¼ tablespoons (30 g) mascarpone cheese

FOR THE VANILLA PASTE

13 vanilla beans
⅓ cup (75 g) trimoline (inverted sugar)

FOR ASSEMBLY AND FINISHING

2½ tablespoons (20 g) vanilla powder

FOR THE DOUGH

In an electric stand mixer fitted with a dough hook attachment, knead the flour, salt, sugar, instant milk powder, yeast, 2 cups (460 g) water, and the 7 tablespoons (100 g) butter on speed 1 for 7 minutes. Let rise for 3 hours in the refrigerator. Roll out the chilled dough into a large rectangle. Using a rolling pin, flatten the dry butter until you have a rectangle half the size of the dough rectangle, then place in the center of the dough. Fold over the sides to encase the butter, then roll into a new rectangle. Fold in three and refrigerate for 2 hours. Repeat two times, using the same chilling time between each, until the dough has been turned three times, then refrigerate for 1 hour.

FOR THE RAISINS

Put the raisins in the warm water and let soften for 1 hour.

FOR THE NOT-SO-SWEET PASTRY CREAM

Make the pastry cream as described on page 314, adjusting the amounts to fit this recipe. Refrigerate for 30 minutes.

FOR THE VANILLA PASTE

Use a food processor to process the vanilla beans, then add the trimoline and 5 teaspoons (25 g) water. Remove the mixture and freeze for 15 minutes. Use a powerful blender to pulse at least 10 times. Make sure that the vanilla paste is still frozen when mixing it.

FOR ASSEMBLY AND FINISHING

Whisk the pastry cream to thin it and combine with the vanilla paste. Roll out the dough to a thickness of ⅛ inch (3.5 mm) and into a 12½ by 10-inch (32 by 25-cm) rectangle, then use an offset spatula to spread the pastry cream over the top. Add the swollen raisins and the vanilla powder, then roll the dough tightly into a cylinder. Roll the cylinder in the vanilla powder. Freeze for 20 minutes, then cut the cylinder into ¾-inch (2-cm) slices to obtain the raisin rolls. Cover with a cloth and let rise for 30 minutes in a warm place. Preheat the oven to 360°F (180°C). Put the raisin rolls into 4-inch (10-cm)-diameter cake rings on a baking sheet, then bake for 12 minutes.

KOUGLOF

FOR THE MARINATED GOLDEN RAISINS

1½ tablespoons (20 g) superfine sugar
1⅔ cups (335 g) golden raisins

FOR THE STARTER

2½ cups (325 g) cake flour
1½ teaspoons (5 g) active dry yeast

FOR THE DOUGH

1¼ cups (280 g) starter (see above)
2½ cups plus 1½ tablespoons (337.5 g) cake flour
⅓ cup plus 2 teaspoons (90 g) milk
2 teaspoons (9 g) liquid malt extract
½ cup (93 g) superfine sugar
¾ (46 g) cake yeast, or 5 teaspoons active dry yeast (dissolved in milk or water)
4 large (70 g) egg yolks
½ cup (1 stick/115 g) unsalted butter
1⅛ teaspoons (7 g) salt
½ teaspoon (2.5 g) lemon curd

FOR ASSEMBLY AND FINISHING

2 tablespoons (30 g) unsalted butter, for greasing
½ cup (50 g) sliced almonds
1½ tablespoons (20 g) superfine sugar
Melted butter

FOR THE MARINATED GOLDEN RAISINS

The previous day, in a saucepan, boil ½ cup (125 g) water with the superfine sugar. Transfer the syrup along with the raisins to an airtight container and refrigerate for 24 hours. Drain before using.

FOR THE STARTER

In an electric stand mixer fitted with a dough hook attachment, knead the flour, 1 cup (233 g) water, and the yeast on speed 1 for 5 minutes. Remove the mixture and let rise for 1 hour, then refrigerate for 24 hours.

FOR THE DOUGH

The next day, in an electric stand mixer fitted with a dough hook attachment, knead the starter with the flour, milk, malt extract, superfine sugar, yeast, and egg yolks for 5 minutes on speed 1, then add the butter and salt. When the dough is smooth, increase to speed 2 and knead until a veil forms (the dough is translucent) when the dough is stretched out into a thin sheet. Add the lemon curd and swollen marinated raisins. Let the dough rise for 2 hours at room temperature. Cut the dough into 1-pound (450-g) pieces and form into tight balls. Let rest for 10 minutes, then shape.

FOR ASSEMBLY AND FINISHING

Grease one 7-inch (18-cm)-diameter kouglof mold or six 3-inch (8-cm)-diameter molds or ramekins and line the bottom with sliced almonds and superfine sugar. Put the dough in the mold(s) and let rise for 45 minutes at room temperature. Preheat the oven to 360°F (180°C) and bake for 35 minutes. After removing from the oven, unmold and brush the surface of the kouglof(s) with the melted butter.

PREPARATION TIME: 2 HOURS

SERVES 6

COOKING TIME: 35 MINUTES

RESTING TIME: 1 HOUR PLUS 24 HOURS PLUS 2 HOURS 55 MINUTES

STRAWBERRY-

FOR THE ÉCLAIRS (SEE PAGE 318)

1 quantity (14 ounces/400 g) choux paste
1 drop (0.15 g) strawberry-red food coloring

Pink crumb dough
1 quantity (12¼ ounces/350 g) crumb dough
1 teaspoon (5 g) red fat-soluble food coloring

FOR THE SUGAR-COATED RHUBARB

5 rhubarb stalks
1½ cups (300 g) pearl sugar
2 large (30 g) egg whites
1 tablespoon (15 g) superfine sugar
1 teaspoon (5 g) vanilla sugar
1 teaspoon (5 g) honey

FOR THE STRAWBERRY-RHUBARB COMPOTE

⅓ cup (100 g) fresh strawberries
2 stalks (100 g) rhubarb

FOR THE STRAWBERRY PASTRY CREAM

1 cup (220 g) strawberry juice
1½ tablespoons (25 g) whipping cream
2 extra-large (40 g) egg yolks
¼ cup (45 g) superfine sugar
1½ tablespoons (12 g) all-purpose flour
2 teaspoons (12 g) custard powder
1¼ teaspoons (4 g) gelatin powder
5 teaspoons (24 g) water
1¾ tablespoons (25 g) unsalted butter
1½ tablespoons (22 g) cocoa butter
1 tablespoon (15 g) mascarpone cheese

FOR THE RED GLAZE

1 cup (250 g) white starch glaze (see page 319)
1 teaspoon (5 g) red water-soluble food coloring
2 tablespoons (10 g) edible copper luster dust

FOR ASSEMBLY AND FINISHING

Rhubarb chips (see page 316)

FOR THE SUGAR-COATED RHUBARB

The previous day, make the sugar-coated rhubarb as described on page 316 and let drain overnight over a bowl. (You could save the juice to use in a gelatin.)

FOR THE ÉCLAIRS

The next day, make the éclairs as described on page 318 with the pink crumb dough and bake for 20 minutes at 360°F (180°C). Dry at 320°F (160°C) for 15 minutes.

FOR THE STRAWBERRY-RHUBARB COMPOTE

Use a blender to puree the drained sugar-coated rhubarb. Cut the strawberries and raw rhubarb into small dice and combine with the blended rhubarb.

FOR THE STRAWBERRY PASTRY CREAM

Make the pastry cream as described on page 314, replacing the vanilla-infused milk with the strawberry juice and adjusting the amounts to fit this recipe, then refrigerate for 30 minutes. Use the mixture to fill a pastry bag fitted with a plain tip.

FOR THE RED STARCH GLAZE

Make the glaze as described on page 319, adding the edible copper luster dust at the same time as the coloring.

FOR THE ASSEMBLY AND FINISHING

Make four holes in the bottom of each éclair with the point of a knife. Pipe in a little pastry cream, then fill with the compote. Reheat the glaze to 80°F (27°C) in a microwave, then give the éclairs a first coat of glaze. Put in the freezer for 5 minutes, then give them another coat of glaze. Refrigerate for a few minutes. Just before serving, arrange the rhubarb chips on top.

PREPARATION TIME: 2 HOURS

SERVES 8

COOKING TIME: 35 MINUTES

RESTING TIME: 24 HOURS PLUS 2 HOURS

PREPARATION TIME: 2 HOURS

MAKES 10 SPHERES

COOKING TIME: 30 MINUTES

RESTING TIME: 24 HOURS PLUS 3 HOURS

RHUBARB

FOR THE SUGAR-COATED RHUBARB
5 rhubarb stalks
1½ cups (300 g) pearl sugar
1 large (30 g) egg white
1½ tablespoons (15 g) superfine sugar
1 teaspoon (5 g) vanilla sugar
1 teaspoon (5 g) honey

FOR THE WHIPPED GANACHE
2½ teaspoons (8 g) gelatin powder
8 stalks (400 g) rhubarb
2½ cups (600 g) whipping cream
7¾ ounces (220 g) white couverture chocolate, chopped

FOR THE RHUBARB GEL
2 tablespoons (25 g) superfine sugar
4 teaspoons (12 g) pectin NH

FOR ASSEMBLY AND FINISHING
White glaze (see page 317)
⅔ cup (140 g) milk
1¼ cups (290 g) whipping cream
2 cups (375 g) superfine sugar
⅓ cup (95 g) glucose powder
0.17 ounce (5 g) titanium dioxide
2½ tablespoons (25 g) cornstarch
3½ teaspoons (10 g) gelatin powder
¼ cup (55 g) water

White coating
1¼ cups (300 g) coating mixture (see page 317)
Rhubarb chips (see page 316)

FOR THE SUGAR-COATED RHUBARB
The previous day, make the sugar-coated rhubarb as described on page 316 and let drain overnight over a bowl.

FOR THE WHIPPED GANACHE
Soak the gelatin in 3 tablespoons (48 g) cold water to soften. Put the fresh rhubarb through a juicer to obtain 1⅔ cups (400 g) juice. Heat ¾ cup (200 g) of the cream with the rhubarb juice, stirring. Cover with plastic wrap and let infuse for 10 minutes. Pass through a conical sieve. Reheat, remove from the heat, and add the gelatin. Gradually pour over the chocolate, blending them together, then use an immersion blender to mix. Pour in the remaining cold cream and mix again. Refrigerate for at least 12 hours.

FOR THE RHUBARB GELATIN
The next day, retrieve the sugar-coated rhubarb and juice. In a saucepan, heat the juice, then add the sugar mixed with the pectin and use a wire whisk to combine. Bring to a boil and let simmer for 2 minutes. Transfer to a shallow pan and let cool completely in the refrigerator. Use an immersion blender to mix, being careful not to beat in any air. Add the cooked sugar-coated rhubarb. Transfer to 1¾-inch (4.5-cm)-diameter silicone half-dome molds, then freeze for 1 hour. Bring the two half-domes together to create spheres.

FOR ASSEMBLY AND FINISHING
In an electric stand mixer fitted with a whisk attachment, whip the chilled rhubarb ganache, then pipe into 2½-inch (5.5-cm)-diameter silicone half-dome molds. Pipe the rhubarb gel into the middle, then finish the assembly with the whipped rhubarb ganache, bringing the two parts of the mold together to create spheres. Freeze for 3 hours.

Make the white glaze as described on page 317, adjusting the amounts to fit this recipe. Also make the white coating as described on page 317. Unmold the set molds and smooth with warm hands. Dip into the white coating and then the white glaze. Refrigerate for 2 hours. Decorate with the rhubarb chips.

NU

NUTS

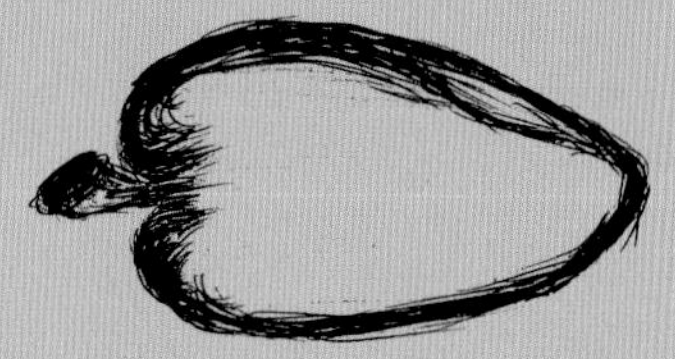

ALMOND

In season

September and October for the fresh nut, all year round for the dried nut

Selection

fresh almonds should be firm and scented, dried almonds should be hard and give off a faint scent

Average weight

a few grams

Storage

at room temperature for a few days for fresh almonds, away from light all year round for dried almonds

Flavor pairings

banana, nutmeg, apricot

CHESTNUT

In season

October

Selection

the nuts should be shiny and heavy, with no air bubbles under the skin

Average weight

¾ ounce (20 g)

Storage

in the refrigerator vegetable drawer for 5 to 6 days, and 4 to 5 days once peeled

Flavor pairings

hazelnut, lemon, chocolate

PEANUT

<u>In season</u>

All year round

<u>Selection</u>

the pod should be firm, with no marks

<u>Average weight</u>

a few grams

<u>Storage</u>

6 months in its pod; shelled and in a cool, dry space for 3 months

<u>Flavor pairings</u>

macadamia nut, chocolate, caramel

HAZELNUT

<u>In season</u>

September to November for the fresh nut, all year round for the dried nut

<u>Selection</u>

when fresh, it should be full, sticking to the shell; when dried, the shell should be smooth and shiny, with no cracks or holes

<u>Average weight</u>

a few grams

<u>Storage</u>

at room temperature for several weeks – even months – in the shell (fresh or dried); in a cool place, away from light, in an airtight container when shelled

<u>Flavor pairings</u>

caramel, honey, kiwi

WALNUT

<u>In season</u>

October and November for the fresh nut, all year round for the dried nut

<u>Selection</u>

the shell should be plump, and the kernels should not stick to the walls for the fresh nut; when dry, the nut should be heavy and full, with no holes

<u>Average weight</u>

⅜ ounce (10 g)

<u>Storage</u>

in the refrigerator vegetable drawer for 48 hours for the fresh nut;
at room temperature for the dry nut

<u>Flavor pairings</u>

honey, raisin, apple

COCONUT

<u>In season</u>

November to February

<u>Selection</u>

if you can hear liquid when shaking the nut, it means it is fresh and the flesh is tasty; the skin should not be moldy

<u>Average weight</u>

3¼ pounds (1.5 kg)

<u>Storage</u>

at room temperature; the flesh and coconut water keep for several days in the refrigerator

<u>Flavor pairings</u>

mango, Malibu rum, white chocolate

PECAN

<u>In season</u>

harvested from September to November, they can be eaten all year round

<u>Selection</u>

the shell should be plump, and the kernel should not stick to the walls of the shell

<u>Average weight</u>

⅜ ounce (10 g)

<u>Storage</u>

the pecan keeps best in its shell; once shelled, it must be kept in the refrigerator

<u>Flavor pairings</u>

caramel, orange, banana

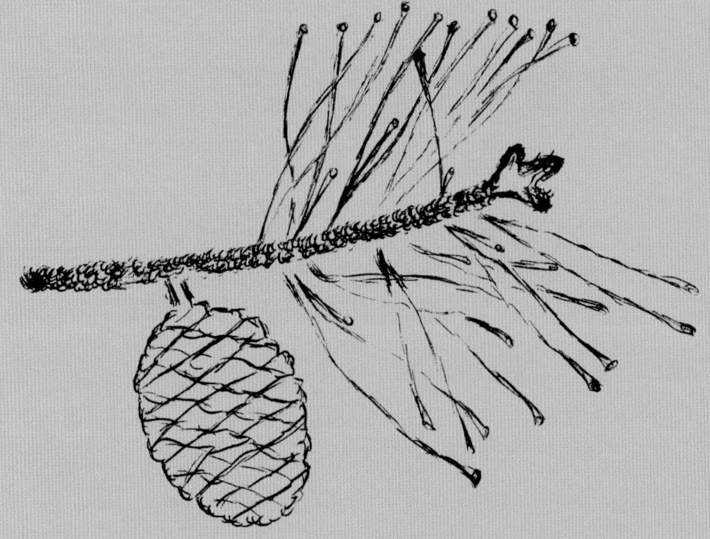

PINE NUT (PIGNOLI)

In season

All year round

Selection

the nut should be firm

Average weight

a few grams

Storage

for a few days in a cool,
dry place, in an airtight container

Flavor pairings

raisin, apple, nougat

PISTACHIO

In season

harvested from September
to October, they can be eaten
all year round

Selection

the nut must be dry to be ripe;
a good indication of ripeness
is a crack in the shell

Average weight

a few grams

Storage

they can be kept whole
for a few months in a cool place,
in an airtight container

Flavor pairings

cherry, apricot, strawberry

PREPARATION TIME: 1 HOUR 30 MINUTES

MAKES 10 SCONES

COOKING TIME: 15 MINUTES

RESTING TIME: 1 HOUR 15 MINUTES

FOR THE ALMOND SCONES

1¼ cups (150 g) all-purpose flour
1¼ cups (150 g) cake flour
1¼ tablespoons (15 g) baking powder
5 tablespoons (70 g) unsalted butter
⅓ cup (70 g) superfine sugar
4 teaspoons (15 g) trimoline (inverted sugar)
⅔ cup (160 g) milk
¼ cup (30 g) shelled fresh almonds

FOR THE ALMOND CRUMB DOUGH

½ cup (1 stick/110 g) unsalted butter
⅓ cup (75 g) superfine sugar
¾ cup (110 g) cake flour
¾ cup (75 g) sliced almonds
½ cup (75 g) whole almonds

FOR ASSEMBLY AND BAKING

1 large egg yolk

FOR THE ALMOND SCONES

Preheat the oven to 340°F (170°C). In an electric stand mixer fitted with a flat beater attachment, mix the flours, baking powder, butter, sugar, and trimoline. Gradually pour in the milk. Knead for 3 minutes on low speed, then 2 minutes on medium speed. Add the almonds, then mix on high speed. Stop the mixer and remove the dough. Use a rolling pin to roll to a thickness of 5/8 inch (15 mm), cover with plastic wrap, and freeze for 15 minutes to harden. Cut out 10 circles using a 2½-inch (6-cm)-diameter cookie cutter, then refrigerate for 1 hour.

FOR THE ALMOND CRUMB DOUGH

Rub the butter, sugar, and flour together by hand. Add the sliced and whole almonds. Set aside.

FOR THE ASSEMBLY AND BAKING

Preheat the oven to 340°F (170°C). Remove the scones from the refrigerator and brush with the beaten egg yolk. Place in 2⅝-inch (6.5-cm)-diameter greased cake rings on a baking sheet, then sprinkle about ¾ ounce (20 g) almond crumbs on each scone. Bake for 12 minutes, turning the baking sheet in the oven halfway through.

FOR THE CHOUX PASTE
1 quantity (14 ounces/400 g) choux paste (see page 312)

FOR THE MILK-SOAKED ALMONDS
12 whole almonds
½ cup (120 g) milk

FOR THE WHITE CRUMB DOUGH
½ cup plus 2 tablespoons (1¼ sticks/150 g) unsalted butter
1½ cups (187 g) all-purpose flour
¾ cup (187 g) packed light brown sugar
¼ ounce (9 g) titanium dioxide
½ cup (60 g) slivered almonds
3 tablespoons (20 g) chopped almonds
⅓ (10 g) large egg white (2 teaspoons)

FOR THE FRENCH BUTTERCREAM
3 tablespoons (45 g) milk
2 large (35 g) egg yolks
½ cup (105 g) superfine sugar
¾ cup plus 2 tablespoons (1¾ sticks/200 g) unsalted butter
1 large (30 g) egg white

FOR THE ALMOND PRALINE
2¾ cups (400 g) whole almonds
1 cup (200 g) superfine sugar
2 teaspoons (8 g) fleur de sel

FOR THE ALMOND PASTE
1¾ cups (250 g) whole almonds
2½ tablespoons (20 g) confectioners' sugar
½ teaspoon (2 g) fleur de sel

FOR THE ALMOND CREAM
1¼ cups (300 g) pastry cream (see page 314)

FOR THE TOASTED ALMONDS
⅔ cup (100 g) whole almonds

Continued

PARIS-BREST

PREPARATION TIME: 3 HOURS 30 MINUTES

SERVES 10

COOKING TIME: 2 HOURS

RESTING TIME: 4 HOURS

FOR THE CHOUX PASTE

Make and pipe the choux paste for Paris-Brest as described on page 312.

FOR THE MILK-SOAKED ALMONDS

Peel the almonds, reserving the skins. Dry the skins and set aside for the finishing. Soak the peeled almonds in the milk for 1 hour.

FOR THE WHITE CRUMB DOUGH

In an electric stand mixer fitted with a flat beater attachment, beat the butter with the flour, brown sugar, and titanium dioxide. Using a rolling pin or a pasta machine, roll the dough to a thickness of ¼ inch (5 mm). Freeze for 30 minutes. Meanwhile, mix the slivered and chopped almonds together and set aside.

Brush the frozen crumb dough with the egg white, then sprinkle the almonds over the top. Place a sheet of parchment paper over the top and use a rolling pin to press the almonds into the crumb dough. For individual Paris-Brests, cut out ten 2½-inch- (6-cm)-diameter disks and cut out the centers with a ¾-inch- (20-mm)-diameter plain piping tip. If you are making one large Paris-Brest, cut a 7¼-inch- (18-cm)-diameter disk with a 5-inch (12-cm)-diameter opening in the center.

FOR THE FRENCH BUTTERCREAM

In a saucepan, bring the milk to a boil. In a mixing bowl, whisk the egg yolks with ¼ cup (45 g) superfine sugar, then pour the boiling milk over them. Return the mixture to the saucepan and cook until thick enough to coat a spoon, about 180°F (83°C). In an electric stand mixer fitted with a whisk attachment, gradually pour this crème anglaise over the butter and whip. Set aside and clean the mixer bowl. Next, whip the egg white to soft peaks in the electric stand mixer fitted with a whisk attachment. Meanwhile, make a syrup by heating 4 teaspoons (20 g) water and the remaining sugar in a saucepan. When the syrup reaches a temperature of 250°F (121°C), pour it in a thin stream over the egg white while continuing to whip, until it cools, to make an Italian meringue. Using a silicone spatula, combine with the crème anglaise–butter mixture. Refrigerate for 30 minutes.

FOR THE ALMOND PRALINE

Preheat the oven to 300°F (150°C) and toast the almonds for 30 minutes. In a saucepan, cook the sugar and ¼ cup (64 g) water to form a caramel and, when it reaches 360°F (180°C), pour it over the almonds. Let cool. Use a food processor to pulse, then using an electric stand mixer fitted with a flat beater attachment, mix with the fleur de sel.

FOR THE ALMOND PASTE

Increase the oven temperature to 360°F (180°C) and toast the almonds for 15 to 20 minutes. In a powerful blender, mix them with the confectioners' sugar and fleur de sel until it forms a smooth almond paste.

FOR THE ALMOND CREAM

Make the pastry cream as described on page 314, refrigerate for 30 minutes, then whisk until smooth. Add 3 tablespoons (45 g) of the almond praline — setting aside the remainder for the assembly — and the almond paste. Use a whisk to whip the French buttercream until smooth, then gently combine with the first mixture. Refrigerate in a pan for 1 hour.

FOR THE TOASTED ALMONDS

Preheat the oven to 300°F (150°C) and toast the almonds for about 15 minutes, until they brown evenly.

FOR ASSEMBLY AND FINISHING

Increase the oven temperature to 360°F (180°C). Place the cut crumb pieces over the choux paste. Dust with confectioners' sugar and bake at 360°F (180°C) for 40 minutes, then reduce the temperature to 320°F (160°C) and dry for 10 minutes. Cool, then slice the Paris-Brest(s) in half. Flatten the bottom part and pipe the almond cream, using a fluted tip to make little swirls. Dot the almond praline six times on top, then garnish with the toasted almonds. Cut out the top part(s) using a cake ring or a cookie cutter to make them round, then place on top. Sprinkle with toasted almonds, the almond skins, and the milk-soaked almonds.

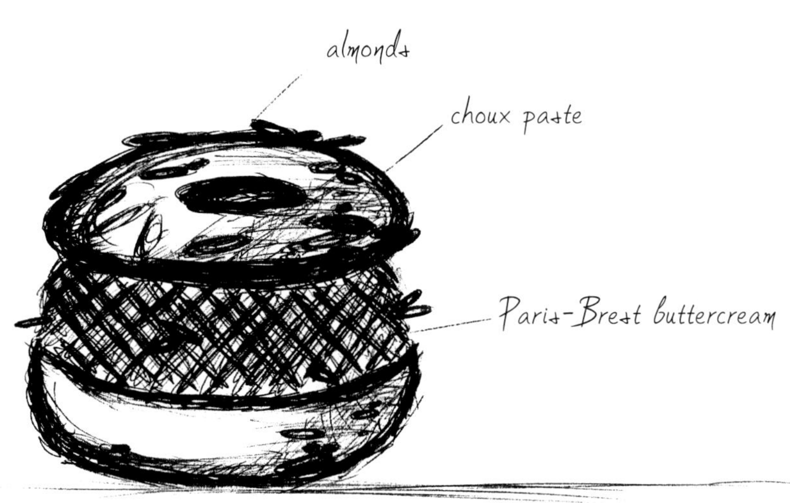

FOR THE ÉCLAIRS (SEE PAGE 318)

1 quantity (14 ounces/400 g) choux paste

White crumb dough

1 quantity (12¼ ounces/350 g) crumb dough
¼ ounce (9 g) titanium dioxide

White glaze

1¼ cups (300 g) white starch glaze (see page 317)

FOR THE ALMOND CHANTILLY CREAM

¼ cup (65 g) Lubeca almond paste
2 tablespoons (30 g) almond milk
1⅔ cups (400 g) whipping cream

FOR THE ALMOND PRALINE

½ cup (104 g) superfine sugar
1⅓ cups (200 g) whole almonds
Grapeseed oil

FOR THE ALMOND PASTE

1¾ cups (250 g) almonds
3½ cups (25 g) confectioners' sugar
½ teaspoon (2 g) fleur de sel

FOR ASSEMBLY AND FINISHING

Silver leaf pieces
40 peeled almond halves

FOR THE ÉCLAIRS

Make the éclairs as described on page 318 with the white crumb dough and bake for 20 minutes at 360°F (180°C). Let dry at 320°F (160°C) for 15 minutes. Make the white glaze as described on page 319.

FOR THE ALMOND CHANTILLY CREAM

In an electric stand mixer fitted with a whisk attachment, whisk the almond paste with the almond milk. Gradually add ¾ cup (200 g) of the cream, while whisking. Using a silicone spatula or a dough scraper, gather the mixture to the sides of the bowl, then use an immersion blender to mix. Add the remaining cream, mix again, and refrigerate for 1 hour in a pastry bag fitted with a 3/8-inch (8-mm) plain tip.

FOR THE ALMOND PRALINE

Preheat the oven to 340°F (170°C). In a saucepan, heat 2½ tablespoons (38 g) water and the superfine sugar to 230°F (110°C). Bake the almonds for 20 minutes, then add to the syrup. Coat and cook until a light caramel forms. Remove from the saucepan and let cool on a Silpat or parchment paper. Pulse in a small food processor to conserve the small pieces. Finally, adjust the consistency of the praline by adding the grapeseed oil. Use the mixture to fill a pastry bag fitted with a 3/8-inch (8-mm) plain tip.

FOR THE ALMOND PASTE

Preheat the oven to 360°F (180°C). Toast the almonds for 15 to 20 minutes. Mix with the confectioners' sugar and fleur de sel, then use a powerful blender to mix until a smooth almond paste forms.

FOR THE ASSEMBLY AND FINISHING

Make four holes in the bottom of each éclair with the point of a knife, then pipe in the almond Chantilly cream (not too whipped), then the praline to fill. Coat the top of the éclairs by dipping them in the white glaze at 80°F (27°C), then smooth them. To serve, decorate each éclair with the pieces of silver leaf and five almond halves.

PREPARATION TIME: 2 HOURS

SERVES 8

COOKING TIME: 1 HOUR 15 MINUTES

RESTING TIME: 2 HOURS 30 MINUTES

PREPARATION TIME: 3 HOURS

SERVES 6

COOKING TIME: 40 MINUTES

RESTING TIME: 4 DAYS

ALMOND GALETTE

FOR THE INVERSE PUFF PASTRY

Kneaded butter (beurre manié)

1¾ cups (225 g) cake flour
1¾ cups (225 g) all-purpose flour
2 pounds (900 g) unsalted dry butter (84% fat content)

Water dough (détrempe)

½ teaspoon (3 g) distilled white vinegar
1¾ tablespoons (20 g) fleur de sel
3⅓ cups (420 g) all-purpose flour
1 cup plus 2 tablespoons (5 ounces/140 g) unsalted dry butter (84% fat), at room temperature

FOR THE TOASTED ALMOND CREAM

¾ cup (80 g) ground almonds
4½ tablespoons (64 g) unsalted butter
⅓ cup (50 g) confectioners' sugar
2 teaspoons (11 g) custard powder
1 large (47 g) egg
2 tablespoons (35 g) almond milk
½ cup (113 g) whipping cream

FOR ASSEMBLY AND FINISHING

3½ tablespoons (50 g) Lubeca almond paste
⅓ cup (40 g) slivered almonds, toasted
1 large egg yolk, beaten

TIP

The cream should stay smooth. If necessary, you can give it a quick blast with a chef's kitchen torch to make sure that all the different elements are at the same temperature.

FOR THE INVERSE PUFF PASTRY

Make the kneaded butter (beurre manié)

Four days in advance, put the flours in the bowl of an electric stand mixer fitted with a flat beater attachment, then add the butter. Beat until a completely smooth mixture forms, but without making it too thick.

Make the water dough (détrempe)

Mix ¾ cup (180 g) water, the vinegar, and fleur de sel until the fleur de sel dissolves, then pour into the mixer bowl. Add the flour, then the butter. Mix in the electric stand mixer fitted with a dough hook attachment until a smooth dough forms, but without kneading.

After making the beurre manié and détrempe, refrigerate for 2 hours. Remove the beurre manié 10 minutes before the détrempe so that the two parts have the same consistency. Roll the beurre manié out to a thickness of 1¼ inches (3 cm), then cover with the détrempe. Turn twice, then refrigerate for 1 day. Repeat the process another three times, resting for 1 day every two turns.

FOR THE TOASTED ALMOND CREAM

On the day you're baking, preheat the oven to 360°F (180°C). Spread the ground almonds on a flat baking sheet and toast for 30 minutes in the oven. Let cool at room temperature. In a saucepan, brown half of the butter, then let cool. Transfer to the bowl of an electric stand mixer fitted with a flat beater attachment and add the other half of the butter. Mix together, then combine with the confectioners' sugar, custard powder, and toasted ground almonds while the mixer is running. Gradually add the egg and almond milk until a smooth mixture forms. Whisk the whipping cream and combine with the almond cream.

FOR ASSEMBLY AND FINISHING

Roll out the dough to ¼ inch thick and cut out two disks: one of 7½ inches (18 cm) in diameter and another of 8 inches (20 cm). On the first, layer the mixtures in the following order: 3½ tablespoons (50 g) almond paste, ⅔ cup (150 g) almond cream, ⅓ cup (40 g) toasted slivered almonds, and, finally, ½ cup (130 g) almond cream. Brush the edges with the egg yolk and place the second pastry disk on top. Gently press the edges together with your fingers. Using a 6½-inch (16-cm) cake ring, trim the galette, then turn it over. Brush the top with egg yolk a first time, let dry, then brush for a second time and score lines into the galette. Bake for 10 minutes at 360°F (180°C), then for 30 minutes at 320°F (160°C).

CHESTNUT

FOR THE TARTLET SHELLS
1 quantity (1¼ pounds/590 g) sweet dough (see page 312)

FOR THE EGG WASH
6 large (100 g) egg yolks
1½ tablespoons (25 g) whipping cream

FOR THE ALMOND-CHESTNUT CREAM
1 quantity (10½ ounces/300 g) almond cream (see page 314)
½ cup (150 g) chestnut paste (Agrimontana)
8 (75 g) candied chestnuts

FOR THE SMOKED CHESTNUT CREAM
½ cup (150 g) chestnut paste (Agrimontana)
⅔ cup (150 g) chestnut cream
Hay

FOR THE LEMON GEL
1½ cups (380 g) unstrained lemon juice
2 tablespoons (25 g) superfine sugar
1¼ tablespoons (10 g) agar powder

FOR THE CHESTNUT FOAM
1¼ cups (300 g) whipping cream

FOR ASSEMBLY AND FINISHING
1 cup (250 g) hazelnut praline (see page 316)
Chestnut chips (see page 316)

FOR THE TARTLET SHELLS

The previous day, make the dough for the tartlet shells as described on page 312. Let dry in the refrigerator for 1 day. The next day, preheat the oven to 320°F (160°C). Blind bake the tartlet shells for 20 minutes.

FOR THE EGG WASH

Beat the egg yolks with the cream, brush the shells with the mixture, and return to the oven for 5 minutes.

FOR THE ALMOND-CHESTNUT CREAM

Make the almond cream as described on page 314, adding the chestnut paste. Pipe into the prebaked tartlet shells and add the candied chestnuts. Return to the oven for 5 minutes.

FOR THE SMOKED CHESTNUT CREAM

Mix the chestnut paste and cream in a heatproof bowl. Put the hay in a Dutch oven and burn with a chef's kitchen torch. Place the bowl with the chestnut mixture in the Dutch oven, cover, and let smoke for 15 minutes. Transfer to a pastry bag and set aside.

FOR THE LEMON GEL

Heat the lemon juice with ½ cup (127 g) water, then add the superfine sugar mixed with the agar. Boil for 2 minutes, then let cool and use an immersion blender to mix.

FOR THE CHESTNUT FOAM

Using an immersion blender, blend the whipping cream with ¾ cup (200 g) of the smoked chestnut cream until mixed well. Transfer to a siphon and add two gas canisters, shaking well.

FOR ASSEMBLY AND FINISHING

Make the hazelnut praline as described on page 316 and spoon into the prebaked tartlets with the lemon gelatin. Add the chestnut foam on top of each tartlet, then arrange the chestnut chips on top.

PREPARATION TIME: 2 HOURS

SERVES 10

COOKING TIME: 30 MINUTES

RESTING TIME: 24 HOURS PLUS 15 MINUTES

PREPARATION TIME: 3 HOURS 30 MINUTES

SERVES 10

COOKING TIME: 40 MINUTES

RESTING TIME: 24 HOURS PLUS 3 HOURS 45 MINUTES

FOR THE TARTLET SHELLS

1 quantity (1¼ pounds/590 g) sweet dough (see page 312)

FOR THE CHESTNUT CENTERS

2¼ cups (550 g) milk
3 tablespoons (35 g) superfine sugar
5¼ large (90 g) egg yolks (⅓ cup)
24 (225 g) candied chestnuts, cut into pieces
1 cup (360 g) chestnut paste (Agrimontana)

FOR THE CHESTNUT PASTRY CREAM

1 cup (250 g) pastry cream (see page 314)
2 teaspoons (10 g) chestnut cream (store-bought)
2 teaspoons (10 g) chestnut paste (Agrimontana)

FOR THE MASCARPONE-CHESTNUT CREAM

1¼ teaspoons (4 g) gelatin powder
1 cup (240 g) UHT cream
6 large (100 g) egg yolks
¼ cup (50 g) superfine sugar
2 cups (500 g) mascarpone cheese
1¼ cups (400 g) chestnut paste (Agrimontana)

FOR THE EGG WASH

6 large (100 g) egg yolks
2 tablespoons (25 g) whipping cream

FOR THE ALMOND-CHESTNUT CREAM

½ quantity (150 g) almond cream (see page 314)
¼ cup (75 g) chestnut paste (Agrimontana)
6 (60 g) candied chestnuts

FOR THE LEMON GELATIN

1½ cups (380 g) fresh unfiltered lemon juice
3 tablespoons (35 g) superfine sugar
1¼ tablespoons (10 g) agar powder

FOR ASSEMBLY AND FINISHING

1¼ cups (300 g) chocolate-colored coating mixture (see page 317)
¾ cup (200g) hazelnut praline (see page 316)

<u>Chestnut mixture</u>

½ cup (150 g) chestnut paste (Agrimontana)
⅔ cup (150 g) (store-bought) chestnut cream

Confectioners' sugar
10 pieces candied chestnuts

FOR THE TARTLET SHELLS

The previous day, make the dough for the tartlet shells as described on page 312. Let dry in the refrigerator for 1 day.

FOR THE CHESTNUT CENTERS

The next day, heat the milk and add two-thirds of the superfine sugar. Whisk the egg yolks with the remaining sugar until the mixture turns pale. Pour the hot sweetened milk over the top, transfer to the saucepan, and cook until thick enough to coat a spoon, about 180°F (83°C), like for a crème anglaise. Rinse the candied chestnuts to remove the excess sugar, then add them to the hot crème anglaise along with the chestnut paste. Use an immersion blender to mix, then transfer the mixture to 1¼-inch (3.5-cm)-diameter silicone half-dome molds. Freeze for 1 hour.

FOR THE CHESTNUT PASTRY CREAM

Make the pastry cream as described on page 314, adding the chestnut cream and paste at the end to replace the mascarpone. Refrigerate for 30 minutes.

FOR THE MASCARPONE-CHESTNUT CREAM

Put the gelatin in 4½ teaspoons (24 g) cold water to hydrate. Heat the cream. Whisk the egg yolks with the superfine sugar until pale, then pour the hot cream over them. Return to the saucepan and heat to 180°F (83°C), like a crème anglaise. Add the gelatin to the mixture, then pour it over the mascarpone mixed with the chestnut pastry cream and chestnut paste. Use an immersion blender to mix well and refrigerate for 1 hour.

In an electric stand mixer fitted with a whisk attachment, whip the cold chestnut cream. Pour into 1¾-inch (4.5-cm)-diameter silicone half-dome molds. Insert a chestnut center, then cover with cream, setting aside the remaining cream for the tartlet assembly. Freeze for 3 hours.

FOR THE EGG WASH

Preheat the oven to 320°F (160°C). Blind bake the tartlet shells for 20 minutes. Beat the egg yolks with the cream, then brush the tartlet shells with the mixture. Return to the oven for 5 minutes.

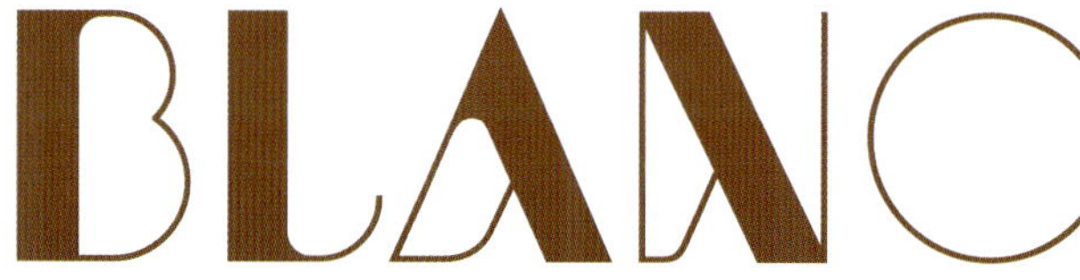

FOR THE ALMOND-CHESTNUT CREAM

Meanwhile, make the almond cream as described on page 314, adding the chestnut paste. Pipe into the prebaked tartlet shells and add the candied chestnuts. Return to the oven for 15 minutes, then let cool.

FOR THE LEMON GEL

Heat the lemon juice with ½ cup (127 g) water, then add the superfine sugar mixed with agar. Boil for 2 minutes, then let cool and use an immersion blender to mix.

FOR ASSEMBLY AND FINISHING

Once the domes are frozen, pipe a little more mascarpone-chestnut cream on top and smooth to give each Mont Blanc more height. Make the coating as described on page 317, then use to coat the surface of the Mont Blancs. Refrigerate.

Once the tartlet shells have cooled, fill with the almond-chestnut cream, then the hazelnut praline and lemon gel. Marble together by smoothing, then place a dome on each tartlet shell. Make the chestnut mixture by mixing the chestnut paste and cream, then transfer to a pastry bag fitted with a bird's nest tip. Pipe it neatly over the domes, using a cake decorating turntable, if possible. Dust with confectioners' sugar and, finally, place a piece of candied chestnut on top.

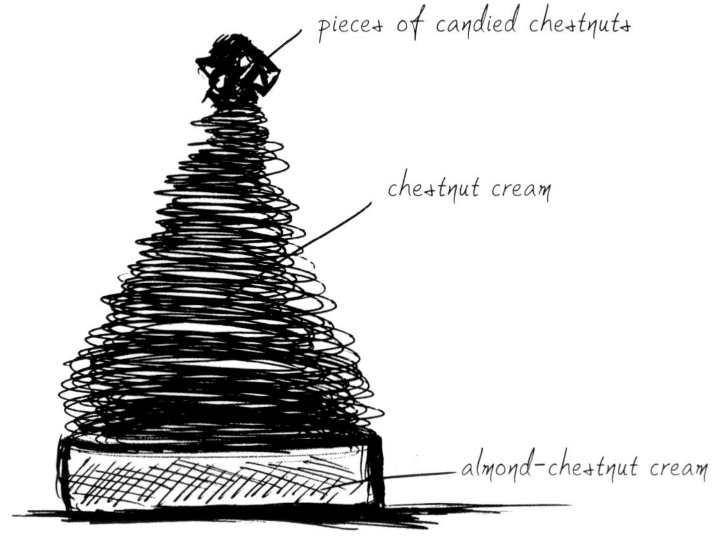

PREPARATION TIME: 3 HOURS

SERVES 8

COOKING TIME: 1 HOUR

RESTING TIME: 24 HOURS PLUS 4 HOURS 30 MINUTES

CHESTNUT,

FOR THE CHESTNUT ICE CREAM

2¼ cups (550 g) milk
3 tablespoons (35 g) superfine sugar
5¼ large (90 g) egg yolks (⅓ cup)
24 (225 g) candied chestnuts, cut into pieces
½ cup (180 g) chestnut paste (Agrimontana)

FOR THE CHESTNUT PASTRY CREAM

1 cup (250 g) pastry cream (see page 314)
2 teaspoons (10 g) chestnut cream (store-bought)
2 teaspoons (10 g) chestnut paste (Agrimontana)

FOR THE MASCARPONE-CHESTNUT CREAM

1¼ teaspoons (4 g) gelatin powder
1 cup (240 g) UHT cream
6 large (100 g) egg yolks
¼ cup (50 g) superfine sugar
2 cups (500 g) mascarpone cheese
⅔ cup (200 g) chestnut paste (Agrimontana)

FOR THE HAZELNUT PRALINE

1¾ cups (250 g) hazelnuts
1 cup (200 g) superfine sugar

FOR THE CHESTNUT TUILES

¾ cup (250 g) chestnut paste (Agrimontana)
1 cup (250 g) chestnut cream (store-bought)

FOR THE MERINGUE SOUFFLÉ

3¾ large (125 g) egg whites (½ cup)
⅔ cup (125 g) superfine sugar
1 cup (125g) confectioners' sugar
⅓ cup (30 g) cocoa powder

FOR THE SMOKED CHESTNUT CREAM

½ cup (150 g) chestnut paste (Agrimontana)
⅔ cup (150 g) chestnut cream (store-bought)
Hay

FOR THE LEMON GEL

1½ cups (380 g) unstrained lemon juice
3 tablespoons (25 g) superfine sugar
1¼ tablespoons (10 g) agar powder

FOR ASSEMBLY AND FINISHING

1¾ cups (300 g) milk chocolate-colored coating mixture (see page 317)
A few hazelnuts
A few lemon slices
Chestnut chips (see page 316)

Continued

HAZELNUT, AND LEMON

CHESTNUT,

FOR THE CHESTNUT ICE CREAM

The previous day, heat the milk, then add half the superfine sugar. Whisk the egg yolks with the remaining sugar until the mixture turns pale. Pour the hot sweetened milk over the top, transfer to the saucepan, and cook until thick enough to coat a spoon, about 180°F (83°C), like for a crème anglaise. Rinse the candied chestnuts to remove the excess sugar, then add them to the hot mixture along with the chestnut paste. Use an immersion blender to mix well and refrigerate for 1 day.

The next day, churn to make the ice cream.

FOR THE CHESTNUT PASTRY CREAM

Make the pastry cream as described on page 314, adding the chestnut cream and paste at the end to replace the mascarpone. Refrigerate for 30 minutes.

FOR THE MASCARPONE-CHESTNUT CREAM

Put the gelatin in 4½ teaspoons (24 g) cold water to hydrate. Heat the cream. Whisk the egg yolks with the superfine sugar until pale, then pour the hot cream over them. Return to the saucepan and heat to 180°F (83°C), like a crème anglaise. Add the gelatin to the hot mixture, then pour over the mascarpone mixed with the chestnut pastry cream and chestnut paste. Mix, then refrigerate for 1 hour.

FOR THE HAZELNUT PRALINE

Preheat the oven to 300°F (150°C). Toast the hazelnuts for 30 minutes. Heat the sugar and ⅓ cup (75 g) water to 250°F (120°C) to caramelize, then add the hazelnuts. Caramelize well, then pour onto a Silpat baking mat and let cool. In a food processor, pulse until it forms the texture of praline.

FOR THE CHESTNUT DOME ASSEMBLY

In an electric stand mixer fitted with a whisk attachment, whip the cold mascarpone-chestnut cream. Transfer into 1¼-inch (3.5-cm)-diameter silicone half-dome molds, then add a little hazelnut praline to make the melting center. Freeze for 3 hours.

HAZELNUT, AND LEMON

FOR THE CHESTNUT TUILES

Preheat the oven to 360°F (180°C). In an electric stand mixer fitted with a flat beater attachment, beat the chestnut paste and cream. Spread some of the mixture thinly in small dots on a baking sheet or Silplat to make the chestnut shavings. Spread the remaining mixture on a 16 by 24-inch (40 by 60-cm) baking sheet, then bake both for 15 minutes. In a food processor, pulse the larger baked piece to obtain the toasted chestnut powder.

FOR THE MERINGUE SOUFFLÉ

In the bowl of an electric stand mixer fitted with a flat beater attachment, whip the egg whites until they form soft peaks, then add the superfine sugar and beat until stiff. Use a silicone spatula to stir in the confectioners' sugar. Pipe out meringue balls onto a Silpat using a pastry bag fitted with a no. 12 plain tip. Cut the tops off using a pair of scissors dampened with warm water, dust with ¼ cup (25 g) of the toasted chestnut powder and the cocoa powder, then bake for 25 minutes at 250°F (120°C).

FOR THE SMOKED CHESTNUT CREAM

Mix the chestnut paste and cream in a heatproof bowl. Put hay in a Dutch oven and burn with a chef's kitchen torch. Place the bowl with the chestnut mixture in the Dutch oven, then cover and let smoke for 15 minutes. Transfer to a pastry bag and set aside to use in the assembly.

FOR THE LEMON GEL

Heat the lemon juice with ½ cup (127 g) water, then add the superfine sugar mixed with the agar. Boil for 2 minutes, then let cool and use an immersion blender to blend without mixing in any air.

FOR ASSEMBLY AND FINISHING

Make the milk chocolate–colored coating mixture as described on page 317, then coat the domes once frozen. Grate the hazelnuts over to create a woody effect. Line serving plates with the smoked chestnut cream and lemon gel, then add the lemon slices. Add some chestnut ice cream to the meringues and cover with the chestnut domes. Make an ice cream quenelle, then add the chestnut chips, halved hazelnuts, and crushed chestnut shavings.

PREPARATION TIME: 2 HOURS

SERVES 10

COOKING TIME: 30 MINUTES

RESTING TIME: 12 HOURS PLUS 6 HOURS 15 MINUTES

PEANUT

FOR THE PUFF PASTRY

2½ cups (315 g) cake flour
2½ cups (315 g) all-purpose flour
1 large (15 g) egg yolk
½ cup (40 g) instant dry milk powder
1 tablespoon (15 g) superfine sugar
⅓ (25 g) cake yeast, or 1 tablespoon active dry yeast (dissolved in milk or water)
¾ teaspoon (15 g) salt
3 tablespoons (40 g) unsalted butter, for the water dough (détrempe)
1 cup plus 2 tablespoons (8¾ ounces/250 g) unsalted dry butter (84% fat content)

FOR THE PEANUT FILLING

1⅔ cups (250 g) toasted peanuts, ground
⅓ cup (75 g) peanut paste
2 teaspoons (5 g) cornstarch
⅓ cup (75 g) packed dark brown sugar
⅓ cup (75 g) superfine sugar

FOR THE ASSEMBLY AND FINISHING

1 large egg yolk, beaten

FOR THE PUFF PASTRY DOUGH

The previous day, in an electric stand mixer fitted with a dough hook attachment, knead the flours, 1⅓ cups (340 g) water, the egg yolk, dry milk powder, sugar, yeast, salt, and butter for the détrempe on low speed for about 6 minutes. Roll the détrempe out into a large rectangle and transfer to a baking sheet lined with parchment paper. Refrigerate for 12 hours.

The next day, flatten the butter with a rolling pin, then shape it into a rectangle that is the same width as the détrempe, but two times shorter, and place in the middle of the détrempe. Fold over the edges of the chilled détrempe to completely encase the butter. Roll out the dough to a ¾-inch (2-cm)-thick rectangle, then fold in three and refrigerate for 2 hours. Repeat the process two times so that the dough receives three turns, letting it rest for 2 hours between each turn.

FOR THE PEANUT FILLING

In an electric stand mixer fitted with a flat beater attachment, beat the peanuts, peanut paste, starch, ¾ cup (175 g) water, the brown sugar, and superfine sugar until a smooth paste forms.

FOR ASSEMBLY AND FINISHING

Preheat the oven to 340°F (170°C). Using a rolling pin, roll out the dough to a thickness of about ⅛ inch (3 mm). Spread 13½ ounces (375 g) of the peanut filling over the rolled-out dough, leaving a ¾-inch (2-cm) border, and roll tightly. Freeze for 15 minutes to harden the cylinder, then cut into 1½-inch (4-cm) sections. Place in 4-inch (10-cm) cake rings lined with parchment paper. Brush with egg yolk, then bake for 30 minutes at 340°F (170°C), turning the baking sheet halfway through.

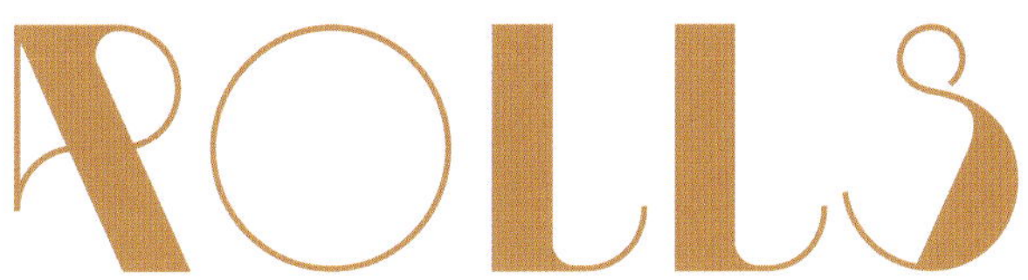

PEANUT

FOR THE CREAMY CARAMEL

¾ cup (200 g) cream
3½ tablespoons (50 g) milk
⅔ cup (155 g) glucose powder
1 vanilla bean, split and scraped
½ teaspoon (2 g) fleur de sel
½ cup (90 g) superfine sugar
5 tablespoons (70 g) unsalted butter

FOR THE COOKIE DOUGH

½ cup (1 stick/120 g) unsalted butter
¼ cup (70 g) peanut paste
¾ cup (190 g) packed dark brown sugar
¾ cup (140 g) superfine sugar
¾ teaspoon (4 g) salt
2 large (94 g) eggs
3 cups (370 g) all-purpose flour
2 teaspoons (8 g) baking powder

FOR THE CARAMELIZED PEANUTS

½ cup (85 g) superfine sugar
1⅔ cups (250 g) toasted salted peanuts
½ tablespoon (8 g) grapeseed oil

FOR THE SMOOTH PEANUT PRALINE

⅔ cup (130 g) superfine sugar
1⅔ cups (250 g) peanuts

FOR THE CREAMY CARAMEL

Heat the cream with the milk, ½ cup (100 g) of the glucose, the vanilla seeds and pod, and fleur de sel. Heat the superfine sugar and the remaining glucose to 365°F (185°C), then deglaze with the hot cream. Heat to 220°F (105°C), then pass through a conical sieve. When the temperature of the caramel has dropped to 160°F (70°C), add the butter. Use an immersion blender to mix, then refrigerate for about 3 hours.

FOR THE COOKIE DOUGH

Mix the butter with the peanut paste, brown sugar, superfine sugar, and salt, then combine with the eggs. Mix the flour and baking powder together, then add to the first mixture. Make balls of about 1¼ ounces (35 g) and refrigerate for 1 hour.

FOR THE CARAMELIZED PEANUTS

Preheat the oven to 340°F (170°C). In a copper saucepan, heat 1¾ tablespoons (25 g) water and the sugar to 230°F (110°C). Place the peanuts on a baking sheet, bake in the oven for 10 minutes, then add to the syrup. The peanuts will become coated and caramelize. When they are well coated with the caramel, transfer to a marble work surface or a lightly greased cutting board and let cool. Coarsely chop the peanuts into slivers.

FOR THE SMOOTH PEANUT PRALINE

Make a syrup by heating the superfine sugar and 3 tablespoons (45 g) water to 210°F (100°C). Toast the peanuts for 8 to 10 minutes at 340°F (170°C), then add to the syrup. Coat the nuts and cook until the whole mixture caramelizes. Remove from the saucepan and cool on a Silpat or parchment paper. Transfer to a food processor and pulse until it forms a fine smooth texture.

FOR BAKING

Lightly flatten the cookie dough balls on a baking sheet lined with parchment paper. Sprinkle the slivers of caramelized peanuts over them, then bake for 5 minutes at 330°F (165°C).

Once removed from the oven, pipe three dots of praline on each, then return to the oven for 2 minutes. Once baked, use a pastry bag to add three dots of creamy caramel and let it run slightly. Once cool, add three dots of praline and sprinkle some caramelized peanuts attractively over the top.

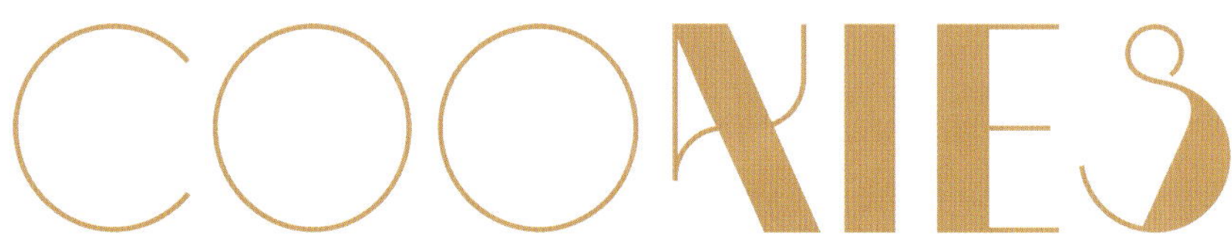

PREPARATION TIME: 2 HOURS

SERVES 10

COOKING TIME: 30 MINUTES

RESTING TIME: 4 HOURS

PREPARATION TIME: 3 HOURS 30 MINUTES

SERVES 10

COOKING TIME: 50 MINUTES

RESTING TIME: 2 HOURS

HAZELNUT

FOR THE CHOUX PASTE

1 quantity (14 ounces/400 g) choux paste (see page 312)

FOR THE BROWN CRUMB DOUGH

7 tablespoons (100 g) unsalted butter
¾ cup plus 2 tablespoons (110 g) all-purpose flour
½ cup (125g) packed light brown sugar
2½ tablespoons (15 g) cocoa powder
1 large (30 g) egg white
½ cup (50 g) chopped hazelnuts

FOR THE HAZELNUT PASTE

1¾ cups (250 g) toasted hazelnuts (see page 317)
1½ tablespoons (13.5 g) confectioners' sugar
⅛ teaspoon (0.5 g) fleur de sel

FOR THE HAZELNUT PRALINE CREAM

2 cups (500 g) pastry cream (see page 314)
⅓ cup (100 g) hazelnut praline (see page 316)
3 tablespoons (50 g) hazelnut paste (see above)
2 cups (500 g) buttercream (see page 314)

FOR ASSEMBLY AND FINISHING

Confectioners' sugar
¾ cup (100 g) toasted hazelnuts (see page 317)

FOR THE CHOUX PASTE

Make and pipe the choux paste for Paris-Brest as described on page 312.

FOR THE BROWN CRUMB DOUGH

In an electric stand mixer fitted with a flat beater attachment, beat the butter with the flour, brown sugar, and cocoa powder. Roll to a thickness of ¼ inch (5 mm) using a rolling pin. Freeze for 30 minutes. Brush the frozen crumb dough with the egg white, then sprinkle with the hazelnuts. Place a sheet of parchment paper over the top and use a rolling pin to press the hazelnuts into the dough. Cut out ten 2½-inch (6-cm)-diameter disks and cut out the centers with a ¾-inch (20-mm)-diameter plain tip for individual Paris-Brests. If you are making one large Paris-Brest, cut a 7¼-inch (18-cm)-diameter disk with a 5-inch (12-cm) opening in the center.

FOR THE HAZELNUT PASTE

In a blender, pulse the toasted hazelnuts with the confectioners' sugar and fleur de sel until a smooth paste forms.

FOR THE HAZELNUT PRALINE CREAM

Make the pastry cream as described on page 314, smooth, then add the hazelnut praline and hazelnut paste. Make the buttercream as described on page 314 and, in an electric stand mixer fitted with a whip attachment, whip until smooth. Gently combine with the first mixture. Set aside.

FOR ASSEMBLY AND FINISHING

Preheat the oven to 360°F (180°C). Place the cut crumb pieces over the choux paste. Dust with confectioners' sugar and bake for 40 minutes, then dry in the oven at 320°F (160°C) for 10 minutes. Let cool, then slice the Paris-Brest(s) in half. Flatten the bottom part of the choux pastry and use a pastry bag with a fluted tip to pipe the hazelnut praline cream onto it, making little swirls. Pipe six dots of the hazelnut praline on top. Cut the tops using a cake ring or cookie cutter so that they are well rounded, then place on top. Decorate the Paris-Brest(s) with the toasted hazelnuts.

HAZELNUT

FOR THE CROISSANTS

⅓ (17 g) cake yeast, or 2 teaspoons active dry yeast
½ cup (120 g) milk
2 cups (250 g) pastry flour
2½ tablespoons (30 g) superfine sugar
2½ tablespoons (10 g) instant dry milk powder
¾ teaspoon (4 g) salt
⅓ cup (3½ ounces/100 g) starter
4¾ tablespoons (67 g) unsalted butter
1 cup (7¼ ounces/210 g) unsalted dry butter (84% fat content), flattened

For the egg wash

1 large (20 g) egg yolk
1 teaspoon (5 g) egg white
1 teaspoon (5 g) lavender honey

FOR THE HAZELNUT PRALINE

1½ cups (200 g) whole hazelnuts
½ cup (100 g) superfine sugar
1 teaspoon (4 g) fleur de sel

FOR THE CROISSANTS

The previous day, in an electric stand mixer fitted with a dough hook, dissolve the yeast in the milk. Add the flour, superfine sugar, dry milk powder, salt, starter, and butter. Knead for 4 minutes on speed 1, then for 6 minutes on speed 2. Refrigerate for 24 hours.

The next day, use a rolling pin to roll out the dough into a large square, then place the unsalted dry butter in the middle and fold in the edges to encase it. Give it a half turn. Roll the dough into a rectangle, then fold in three to give a simple turn. Roll out thinly to better chill the dough, then freeze for 15 minutes. Give it a double turn. Roll out thinly again and refrigerate for 1 hour.

Roll the dough out to a thickness of ⅛ inch (3 mm), then cut ten triangles with a base of 2½ inches (6 cm) and a length of 8½ inches (22 cm). Roll the triangles on themselves from the base end to the point, to make croissants with five "layers." Preheat the oven to 210°F (100°C), then put a glass of water inside and turn off the oven. Put the croissants in the turned-off oven and let rise for 30 minutes.

Remove the croissants and preheat the oven to 375°F (190°C). Beat the egg yolk with the egg white and honey. Brush the pastries with this mixture. Bake for 6 minutes at 375°F (190°C), then for 6 minutes at 360°F (180°C).

FOR THE HAZELNUT PRALINE

Toast the hazelnuts at 300°F (150°C) for 30 minutes. Heat the superfine sugar and 2 tablespoons (32 g) water until it caramelizes at 360°F (180°C) and pour over the toasted hazelnuts. In a food processor, pulse the nuts to obtain the texture of praline, then mix with the fleur de sel in an electric stand mixer fitted with a flat beater attachment. Pipe the croissants with the praline from underneath once cooked.

PREPARATION TIME: 1 HOUR 30 MINUTES

SERVES 6

COOKING TIME: 45 MINUTES

RESTING TIME: 24 HOURS PLUS 1 HOUR 45 MINUTES

PREPARATION TIME: 3 HOURS 30 MINUTES

SERVES 10

COOKING TIME: 30 MINUTES

RESTING TIME: 24 HOURS PLUS 5 HOURS

HAZELNUT

FOR THE TARTLET SHELLS
1 quantity (1¼ pounds/590 g) sweet dough (see page 312)

FOR THE WHIPPED HAZELNUT GANACHE
1½ teaspoons (5 g) gelatin powder
1 cup (250 g) milk
½ cup (80 g) toasted hazelnuts (see page 317)
3½ ounces (100 g) white couverture chocolate, chopped
⅔ cup (160 g) hazelnut paste
2 cups (450 g) whipping cream

FOR THE CREAMY CARAMEL
1⅔ cups (400 g) whipping cream
⅓ cup (100 g) milk
1⅓ cups (310 g) glucose powder
2 vanilla beans, split and scraped
1 teaspoon (4 g) fleur de sel
1 cup (190 g) superfine sugar
½ cup plus 2 tablespoons (1¼ sticks/140 g) unsalted butter

FOR THE CARAMEL CENTERS
2 tablespoons (25 g) milk

FOR THE HAZELNUT PRALINE
1 cup (150 g) hazelnuts
½ cup (100 g) superfine sugar
⅛ teaspoon (1 g) fine salt

FOR THE EGG WASH
6 large (100 g) egg yolks
1½ tablespoons (25 g) whipping cream

FOR THE ALMOND-HAZELNUT CREAM
½ quantity (5¼ ounces/150 g) almond cream (see page 314)
½ cup (37.5 g) blended hazelnuts, finely crushed
⅓ cup (50 g) toasted hazelnuts (see page 317)

FOR ASSEMBLY AND FINISHING
1¼ cups (300 g) milk chocolate-colored coating mixture (see page 317)
Gold luster dust
1 cup (100 g) finely chopped toasted almonds (see page 317)

Continued

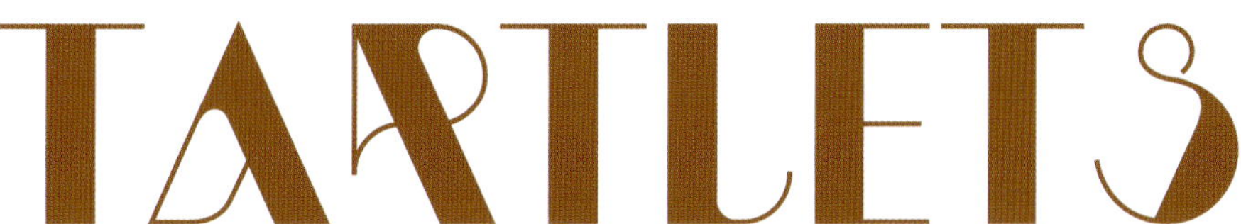

FOR THE TARTLET SHELLS

The previous day, make the dough for the tartlet shells as described on page 312 and refrigerate for 1 day.

FOR THE WHIPPED HAZELNUT GANACHE

Soak the gelatin in 2½ tablespoons (35 g) cold water to hydrate. Heat the milk, add the toasted hazelnuts, then use an immersion blender to break them into pieces and let infuse for 20 minutes. Pass the milk through a conical sieve and heat again. Pour the hot milk over the chocolate, blending them together, then add the gelatin. Mix with an immersion blender, then add the hazelnut paste and cream and mix again. Pour into a pan and seal by covering the surface of the ganache with plastic wrap. Refrigerate overnight.

FOR THE CREAMY CARAMEL

The next day, heat the cream, milk, ½ cup (100 g) of the glucose, the vanilla seeds and pods, and fleur de sel together. Heat the superfine sugar and remaining glucose to 365°F (185°C), then deglaze with the cream mixture. Heat to 220°F (105°C), then pass through a conical sieve. When the caramel cools to 160°F (70°C), add the butter in pieces. Use an immersion blender to mix.

FOR THE CARAMEL CENTERS

Thin ¾ cup (200 g) of the creamy caramel with the milk, then transfer into 1¼-inch (3.5-cm)-diameter silicone half-dome molds, filling two-thirds full. Freeze for 30 minutes.

FOR THE HAZELNUT PRALINE

Make the hazelnut praline as described on page 316 with the ingredient quantities listed, then use to fill the half-dome molds to the top, on top of the layer of half-frozen caramel. Return to the freezer for 1 hour.

FOR THE EGG WASH

Preheat the oven to 320°F (160°C). Blind bake the tartlet shells for 20 minutes. Beat the egg yolks with the cream and brush the shells with the mixture. Return to the oven for 5 minutes.

FOR THE ALMOND-HAZELNUT CREAM

Meanwhile, make the almond cream as described on page 314, replacing the almond powder with the blended hazelnuts. Fill the prebaked tartlet shells and sprinkle with the toasted hazelnuts. Return to the oven for 5 minutes.

FOR ASSEMBLY AND FINISHING

Gently whip the hazelnut ganache, then transfer to 1¾-inch (4.5-cm)-diameter silicone half-dome molds. Add the frozen caramel–hazelnut praline centers, smooth over the top, then freeze for 3 hours. Make the tip of the hazelnut by adding a little whipped ganache on top of the hardened domes, then return to the freezer for 30 minutes. Make the milk chocolate–colored coating as described on page 317, then dip half the hazelnuts in it to coat. Use a metal brush to lightly scratch into the surface. Apply the golden powder with a fine brush. Finally, sprinkle the toasted almonds around the tartlet.

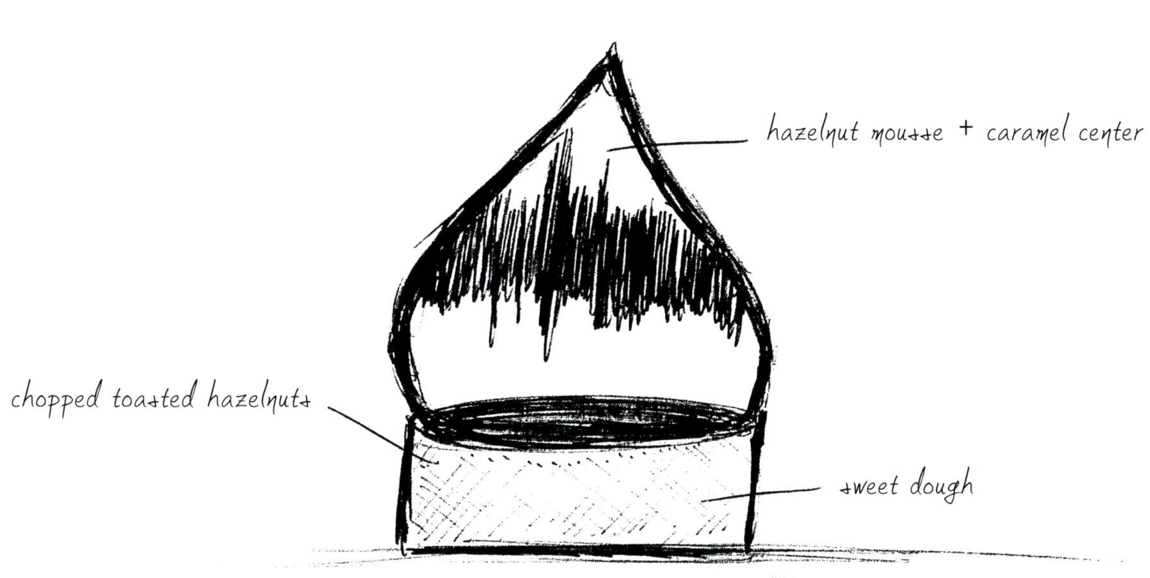

HAZELNUTS

FOR THE WHIPPED HAZELNUT GANACHE

1½ teaspoons (5 g) gelatin powder
¾ cup plus 2 tablespoons (220 g) milk
½ cup (80 g) toasted hazelnuts (see page 317)
3½ ounces (100 g) white couverture chocolate, chopped
⅓ cup (80 g) hazelnut paste
2 cups (450 g) whipping cream

FOR THE CREAMY CARAMEL

1⅓ cups (330 g) whipping cream
⅓ cup (85 g) milk
1 cup (255 g) glucose powder
3 vanilla beans, split and scraped
1 teaspoon (4 g) fleur de sel
¾ cup (150 g) superfine sugar
½ cup (1 stick/115 g) unsalted butter

FOR THE CARAMEL CENTERS

⅓ cup (80 g) milk

FOR THE HAZELNUT SPONGE CAKE

¼ cup (½ stick/50 g) unsalted butter
3½ tablespoons (50 g) hazelnut paste
4 large (70 g) egg yolks
⅓ cup (75 g) superfine sugar
2½ teaspoons (6 g) all-purpose flour
2½ teaspoons (6 g) cornstarch
3 large (100 g) egg whites
¼ cup (25 g) chopped hazelnuts

FOR THE ASSEMBLY AND FINISHING

⅔ cup (160 g) hazelnut praline (see page 316)
3⅓ cups (800 g) milk chocolate-colored coating mixture (see page 317)
Gold luster dust
10½ ounces (300 g) dark couverture chocolate, tempered (see page 317)

FOR THE WHIPPED HAZELNUT GANACHE

The previous day, soak the gelatin in 2 tablespoons (30 g) cold water to hydrate. Heat the milk, add the toasted hazelnuts, then use an immersion blender to break them into pieces and let infuse for 20 minutes. Pass the milk through a conical sieve and heat again. Pour the hot milk over the couverture chocolate, blending them together, then add the gelatin. Mix with an immersion blender, then add the hazelnut paste and cream, and mix again. Pour into a pan and seal by covering the surface of the ganache with plastic wrap. Refrigerate overnight.

FOR THE CREAMY CARAMEL

The next day, heat the cream, milk, 3½ tablespoons (50 g) of the glucose, the vanilla seeds and pods, and fleur de sel together. Heat the superfine sugar and the remaining glucose to 365°F (185°C), then deglaze with the hot cream mixture. Heat to 220°F (105°C), then pass through a conical sieve. When the caramel cools to 160°F (70°C), add the butter in pieces. Mix with an immersion blender.

FOR THE CARAMEL CENTERS

Thin 1¼ cups (300 g) of the creamy caramel with the milk, then transfer to 1¾-inch (4.5-cm)-diameter half-dome molds. Fill half of the half-dome molds with 2½ teaspoons (12 g) and the other half with 1 tablespoon (15 g). Freeze the second half for 1 hour 30 minutes and keep the first half at room temperature.

FOR THE HAZELNUT SPONGE CAKE

Preheat the oven to 175°F (80°C). In the bowl of an electric stand mixer fitted with a whisk attachment, beat the butter and hazelnut paste. Whip the egg yolks with 2 tablespoons (25 g) sugar until the mixture turns pale. Sift together the flour and starch. Use the electric stand mixer fitted with the clean whip attachment and a clean bowl to whip the egg whites, then add the remaining sugar and beat until stiff. Mix the egg yolk mixture with the butter-hazelnut paste mixture. Gently fold in the whipped egg whites, then add the sifted flour and starch. Once the mixture is combined, stop mixing. Using a rolling pin, roll out the mixture thinly on a baking sheet, then sprinkle with the hazelnuts. Bake for 13 minutes. Cut out 1½-inch (4-cm) sponge cake disks.

FOR ASSEMBLY AND FINISHING

Make the hazelnut praline as described on page 316. Spread it over the frozen caramel.

Add a sponge cake disk to the half-dome molds with the room-temperature caramel. Add the frozen caramel centers on top to make complete spheres, then return to the freezer for 3 hours.

Gently whip the hazelnut ganache, then transfer to 2¼-inch (5.5-cm)-diameter half-dome molds. Add the frozen caramel–hazelnut praline centers, use the ganache to complete the spheres, then freeze for 3 hours. Make the tip of the hazelnut by adding a little whipped ganache on top of the hardened spheres, then freeze for 30 minutes. Make the milk chocolate–colored coating as described on page 317, then dip the hazelnuts in it to coat. Use a metal brush to lightly score the surface. Apply the golden powder using a fine brush. Brush the tempered chocolate over 20 by 3¼-inch (25 by 8.5-cm) acetate sheets. Heat the bottom of the hazelnuts, then place them on the chocolate in the center of the acetate sheets. Fold up on both sides so that the chocolate sticks to the hazelnuts.

PREPARATION TIME: 2 HOURS

SERVES 8

COOKING TIME: 15 MINUTES

RESTING TIME: 12 HOURS PLUS 8 HOURS

PREPARATION TIME: 2 HOURS

SERVES 10

COOKING TIME: 40 MINUTES

RESTING TIME: 4 HOURS

PECAN-

FOR THE CREAMY CARAMEL

2½ tablespoons (40 g) whipping cream
2 teaspoons (10 g) milk
2 tablespoons (30 g) glucose powder
½ vanilla bean, scraped
1 pinch fleur de sel
1½ tablespoons (20 g) superfine sugar
1 tablespoon (15 g) unsalted butter

FOR THE COOKIE DOUGH

⅔ cup (1⅜ sticks/160 g) unsalted butter, softened
1 cup (200 g) packed light brown sugar
3 tablespoons (40 g) packed dark brown sugar
3½ tablespoons (40 g) superfine sugar
1 teaspoon (13 g) hazelnut paste
1½ large (75 g) eggs (⅓ cup), beaten, at room temperature
2½ cups (320 g) all-purpose flour
2 teaspoons (8 g) fleur de sel
¾ teaspoon (3.2 g) baking soda
1 cup (100 g) chopped hazelnuts

FOR THE CARAMELIZED PECANS

2 cups (200 g) pecans
¼ cup (50 g) superfine sugar

FOR THE PECAN PRALINE

1 cup (100 g) whole pecans
¼ cup (50 g) superfine sugar
½ teaspoon (2 g) fleur de sel

Continued

FOR THE CREAMY CARAMEL

Heat the cream, milk, 1½ tablespoons (20 g) of the glucose, the vanilla seeds and pod, and fleur de sel together. Meanwhile, heat the superfine sugar and the remaining glucose to 365°F (185°C), then deglaze with the hot cream mixture. Heat to 220°F (105°C), then pass through a conical sieve. When the temperature of the caramel drops to 160°F (70°C), add the butter. Use an immersion blender to smooth, then let cool. Transfer to a pastry bag fitted with a small tip and refrigerate for 3 hours.

FOR THE COOKIE DOUGH

Mix together the butter, sugars, and hazelnut paste. Add the eggs, then add the flour, fleur de sel, and baking powder. Add the hazelnuts. Measure out and shape 1¼-ounce (35-g) balls, place on a nonstick baking sheet, and refrigerate for 1 hour.

FOR THE CARAMELIZED PECANS

Preheat the oven to 300°F (150°C). Toast the pecans for 30 minutes. In a copper saucepan, heat the sugar and 1 tablespoon (15 g) water to 230°F (110°C), then immediately add the toasted pecans. Use a silicone spatula to stir and coat the nuts, cooking them until they caramelize. Pour out onto a baking sheet to cool.

FOR THE PECAN PRALINE

Toast the pecans in the oven at 300°F (150°C) for 30 minutes. Heat the superfine sugar with 1 tablespoon (15 g) water at 360°F (180°C) until it caramelizes, then immediately pour over the toasted pecans. Let cool and pulse with a food processor until it forms a paste, then mix with the fleur de sel in an electric stand mixer fitted with a flat beater attachment. Transfer to a pastry bag fitted with a small plain tip.

FOR BAKING

Preheat the oven to 330°F (165°C). Lightly flatten the balls of dough. Chop the caramelized pecans and place on top of the cookies. Bake for 5 minutes, then remove the baking sheet from the oven. Pipe three dots of pecan praline on each cookie, then bake again for 2 minutes. Pipe three dots of creamy caramel over the praline, so that it runs over the sides. Let cool, then pipe a little more caramel on the cookies. Cover with the chopped pecans, then add a few more dots of praline.

PREPARATION TIME: 2 HOURS

SERVES 8

COOKING TIME: 35 MINUTES

RESTING TIME: 1 HOUR

PECAN

FOR THE ÉCLAIRS (SEE PAGE 318)

1 quantity (14 ounces/400 g) choux paste

Caramel crumb dough

1 quantity (12¼ ounces/350 g) crumb dough
1/32 teaspoon (0.15 g) red fat-soluble food coloring
1/64 teaspoon (0.07 g) blue fat-soluble food coloring
1/64 teaspoon (0.6 g) yellow fat-soluble food coloring

FOR THE CARAMEL CHANTILLY CREAM

2 cups (500 g) whipping cream
½ cup (100 g) superfine sugar

FOR THE PECAN PRALINE

5 cups (500 g) pecans
2 cups (400 g) superfine sugar

FOR THE CARAMEL GLAZE

3½ teaspoons (10 g) gelatin powder
⅔ cup (140 g) milk
1¼ cups (290 g) whipping cream
⅓ cup (95 g) glucose powder
1 vanilla bean, split and scraped
1¾ cups plus 2 tablespoons (370 g) superfine sugar
3½ tablespoons (25 g) cornstarch

FOR ASSEMBLY AND FINISHING

⅔ quantity (14 ounces/400 g) crispy wafer cookie mixture (see page 319)
A few pecans

FOR THE ÉCLAIRS

Preheat the oven to 360°F (180°C). Make the éclairs as described on page 318 with the caramel crumb dough and bake for 20 minutes. Increase the oven temperature to 320°F (160°C), then return to the oven for about 15 minutes to dry the éclairs.

FOR THE CARAMEL CHANTILLY CREAM

Heat 1/3 cup (100 g) of the cream. Meanwhile, heat the sugar to 365°F (185°C), then deglaze with the heated cream. Use a blender to smooth, then gradually add the cold cream. Mix again to whip the cream. Transfer to a pastry bag fitted with a 3/8-inch (8-mm) plain tip and refrigerate.

FOR THE PECAN PRALINE

Lightly toast the pecans in the oven at 320°F (160°C). Heat the superfine sugar and 2/3 cup (150 g) water to 250°F (120°C), then add the toasted pecans. Caramelize until the mixture gives off a lot of steam. Let cool, then pulse in a food processor until it's a paste to make the pecan praline. Transfer to a pastry bag fitted with a 3/8-inch (8-mm) plain tip and refrigerate.

FOR THE CARAMEL GLAZE

Soak the gelatin in 1/4 cup (55 g) water to soften. Boil the milk with the cream, glucose, and vanilla seeds and pod. Heat 1½ cups (280 g) of the superfine sugar to 365°F (185°C), then deglaze with the heated cream. Sprinkle in the remaining sugar mixed with the starch and bring to a boil. Let boil for 2 minutes. Cool the mixture to 115°F (45°C), then stir in the gelatin. Use an immersion blender to blend until smooth, then strain though a conical sieve.

FOR ASSEMBLY AND FINISHING

Make four holes in the bottom of each éclair and fill with the caramel Chantilly cream, then a little pecan praline. Reheat the caramel glaze to 80°F (27°C) in a microwave, then coat the éclairs by dipping them in the mixture. Freeze for 5 minutes. Apply another coat of glaze and refrigerate for a few minutes. Make the crispy wafer cookie balls as described on page 319. Add some pieces of pecan inside the balls. Place three crispy wafer cookie balls on each éclair before serving.

1 cup (100 g) walnuts
3 large (110 g) egg whites
¾ cup (90 g) confectioners' sugar
⅓ cup plus 1 tablespoon (50 g) all-purpose flour
3 tablespoons (45 g) unsalted butter
¾ teaspoon (4 g) salt

Preheat the oven to 340°F (170°C). Chop the walnuts. Whisk the egg whites until they begin to form soft peaks. Continue whisking as you add the confectioners' sugar, until the whites are glossy and can form loose peaks. Gently fold in the flour. Bring 2 cups (480 g) water to a boil with the butter and salt, then pour over the first mixture and mix. Spread the batter to a thickness of 1 mm on a nonstick baking sheet. Sprinkle with the walnuts. Bake for 24 minutes, turning the baking sheet halfway through. Cut the wafer into 2½ by 2½-inch (6 by 6-cm) pieces.

PREPARATION TIME: 10 MINUTES

COOKING TIME: 25 MINUTES

SERVES 8

PREPARATION TIME: 2 HOURS 30 MINUTES

SERVES 10

COOKING TIME: 1 HOUR 50 MINUTES

RESTING TIME: 4 HOURS 15 MINUTES

COCONUT PARIS-BREST

FOR THE CHOUX DOUGH

1 quantity (14 ounces/400 g) choux dough (see page 312)

FOR THE COCONUT PRALINE

5 cups (500 g) thick coconut shavings
1¼ cups (250 g) superfine sugar
2½ teaspoons (10 g) fleur de sel

FOR THE COCONUT PASTE

1 cup (100 g) thick coconut shavings
1½ tablespoons (10 g) confectioners' sugar
¼ teaspoon (1 g) fleur de sel

FOR THE COCONUT PRALINE CREAM

2 cups (500 g) pastry cream (see page 314)
1½ cups (400 g) buttercream (see page 314)

FOR THE WHITE CRUMB DOUGH

7 tablespoons (100 g) unsalted butter
¾ cup plus 2 tablespoons (110 g) all-purpose flour
½ cup (125 g) packed light brown sugar
2 teaspoons (10 g) egg white
2½ tablespoons (15 g) shredded coconut

FOR ASSEMBLY AND FINISHING

Confectioners' sugar
Shredded coconut

FOR THE CHOUX DOUGH

Make and pipe the choux dough for Paris-Brest as described on page 312.

FOR THE COCONUT PRALINE

Preheat the oven to 300°F (150°C) and toast the coconut for 15 minutes. In a saucepan, heat the sugar and ⅓ cup (88 g) water until it caramelizes and, while at 360°F (180°C), pour over the coconut. Let cool. Using a food processor, pulse until it forms a paste, then mix with the fleur de sel in an electric stand mixer fitted with a flat beater attachment.

FOR THE COCONUT PASTE

Preheat the oven to 320°F (160°C). Toast the coconut for 15 to 20 minutes. Transfer to a blender, add the confectioners' sugar and fleur de sel, and mix until a smooth paste forms.

FOR THE COCONUT PRALINE CREAM

Make the pastry cream as described on page 314 and refrigerate for 30 minutes. Whisk smooth, then add ¼ cup (65 g) of the coconut praline and 3½ tablespoons (50 g) of the coconut paste. Make the buttercream (see page 314), then in an electric stand mixer fitted with a whisk attachment, whip until smooth. Gently combine with the first mixture. Refrigerate for 3 hours.

FOR THE WHITE CRUMB DOUGH

In an electric stand mixer fitted with a flat beater attachment, beat the butter with the flour and brown sugar. Using a rolling pin, roll to a thickness of ¼ inch (5 mm). Freeze for 15 minutes. Brush the frozen crumb dough with the egg white, then sprinkle with the coconut. Place a sheet of parchment paper over the top and use a rolling pin to press the coconut into the crumb dough. Cut out ten 2½-inch (6-cm)-diameter disks and cut out the centers with a ¾-inch (20-mm) plain tip for individual Paris-Brests. If making one large Paris-Brest, cut a 7¼-inch (18-cm)-diameter disk with a 5-inch (12-cm) opening in the center.

FOR ASSEMBLY AND FINISHING

Preheat the oven to 360°F (180°C). Place the cut crumb pieces over the choux paste. Dust with confectioners' sugar and bake for 40 minutes, then dry in the oven at 320°F (160°C). Cool, then slice the Paris-Brest(s) in half. Flatten the bottom part of the choux pastry and pipe in the coconut praline cream, using a pastry bag with a fluted tip to make little swirls. Pipe six dots of coconut praline on top. Cut the top(s) using a correctly sized cookie cutter so that they are well rounded, then place on top. Sprinkle the cookies with shredded coconut.

COCONUT

FOR THE COCONUT GANACHE

1½ sheets (3.5 g powdered) gelatin
2 cups (500 g) coconut puree
1¾ ounces (50 g) white couverture chocolate, chopped
1 cup (250 g) whipping cream

FOR THE COCONUT SHORTBREAD

Shortbread

2 large (30 g) egg yolks
⅓ cup (65 g) superfine sugar
5½ tablespoons (75 g) unsalted butter, softened
¼ teaspoon (1.5 g) salt
¾ cup (100 g) all-purpose flour
1 tablespoon (7.5 g) baking powder
½ cup (50 g) toasted ground coconut (see page 316)
½ cup (115 g) cocoa butter

FOR THE COCONUT DACQUOISE

1½ cups (185 g) confectioners' sugar
1 cup (115 g) shredded coconut
¾ cup (75 g) ground almonds
1 cup (225 g) egg whites (about 7 large eggs)
⅓ cup (75 g) superfine sugar

FOR THE COCONUT CREAM

1 (4 by 4-inch/10 by 10-cm) piece fresh coconut (2¾ ounces/75 g)
1½ cups (350 g) coconut puree
⅔ cup (150 g) coconut milk
2¼ teaspoons (6 g) xanthan gum
2 tablespoons (30 g) Malibu rum
⅔ cup (150 g) whipping cream
½ cup (100 g) mascarpone cheese

FOR THE WHITE GLAZE

1¼ cups (300 g) white starch glaze (see page 319)

TIP

Be aware that this recipe requires long resting times. Start making it 2 days before serving.

PREPARATION TIME: 3 HOURS

SERVES 8

COOKING TIME: 25 MINUTES

RESTING TIME: 12 HOURS + 7 HOURS + 10 HOURS

COCONUT

FOR THE COCONUT GANACHE

Two days in advance, soak the gelatin in 3 teaspoons (15 g) cold water. Bring the coconut puree to a boil, then pour it over the chocolate. Mix well to melt the chocolate. Add the drained gelatin while the mixture is still warm. Refrigerate for 12 hours.

FOR THE COCONUT SHORTBREAD

The next day, in the morning, preheat the oven to 360°F (180°C). In an electric stand mixer fitted with a whisk attachment, beat the egg yolks with the sugar until pale. Change to a flat beater attachment, then beat in the butter. Add the salt, then the flour sifted together with the baking powder. Continue mixing for a few moments until the mixture becomes smooth, making sure not to give it too much body. Roll the dough out to a thickness of 1/8 inch (3 mm). Bake for 10 minutes. Once cooked, use a food processor to break the shortbread up into small pieces. Mix with the ground coconut, then the cocoa butter. Using an offset spatula, spread this mixture into a 6½-inch (16-cm)-diameter cake ring. Refrigerate for 1 hour.

FOR THE COCONUT DACQUOISE

Preheat the oven to 360°F (180°C). Sift together the confectioners' sugar, coconut, and almonds. Use an electric stand mixer fitted with a whisk attachment to beat the egg whites, then gradually add the superfine sugar and beat until stiff. Add the sifted ingredients, mixing with a silicone spatula. Using a pastry bag fitted with a tip, pipe the mixture into a 6½-inch (16-cm)-diameter cake ring, then bake for 12 minutes. Let cool on a rack.

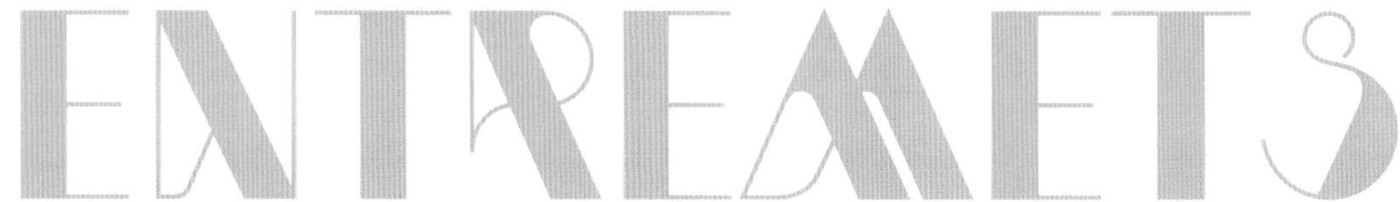

FOR THE COCONUT CREAM

Tap the fresh coconut all over with a rolling pin to detach the pulp from the shell. Break it into pieces, then mix with the coconut puree and coconut milk. Use an immersion blender to mix, sprinkling in the xanthan. Make sure that no coconut pieces are left. Add the rum. In an electric stand mixer fitted with a whisk attachment, lightly whip the cream and mascarpone, then add this mixture to the coconut mixture. Refrigerate for 3 hours. Make the dessert center by pouring the coconut cream over the dacquoise in a 6½-inch (16-cm)-diameter cake ring. Freeze for 3 hours.

FOR ASSEMBLY AND FINISHING

In an electric stand mixer fitted with a whisk attachment, smooth the coconut ganache. Whip the chilled whipping cream with a wire whisk, then combine with the smoothed ganache. Assemble the coconut entremets in a 7¼-inch (18-cm)-diameter cake ring, lined with a Rhodoïd acetate strip. Start with the coconut shortbread, then cover with the whipped ganache. Also use the ganache to fill to the edges of the cake ring. Place the dessert center over the top and press lightly, then cover with the whipped ganache. Smooth with a spatula. Freeze for at least 10 hours before glazing.

FOR THE WHITE GLAZE

The next day, make the white starch glaze as described on page 317. Pour the glaze over the frozen dessert, with the latter placed on a rack over a plate so that it is completely coated.

COCONUT

FOR THE COCONUT DACQUOISE
⅔ cup (75 g) confectioners' sugar
½ cup (50 g) shredded coconut
⅓ cup (30 g) ground almonds
3 large (100 g) egg whites
2½ tablespoons (30 g) superfine sugar

FOR THE PASSION FRUIT-COCONUT CENTERS
1 cup (230 g) passion fruit puree
¾ cup (170 g) coconut puree
1½ teaspoons (4 g) agar powder
¼ cup (48 g) superfine sugar
2 ounces (60 g) passion fruit seeds

FOR THE COCONUT MOUSSE
5 sheets (12.5 g powdered) gelatin
2 cups (500 g) coconut puree
1 tablespoon (15 g) Malibu rum
3 large (90 g) egg whites
½ cup (100 g) superfine sugar
1 cup (250 g) whipping cream

FOR ASSEMBLY AND FINISHING
White coating
¾ cup (200 g) coating mixture (see page 317)
White glaze
¾ cup (200 g) white starch glaze (see page 319)
Coconut chips (see page 316)

FOR THE COCONUT DACQUOISE

Preheat the oven to 375°F (190°C). Sift together the confectioners' sugar, coconut, and almonds. Use an electric stand mixer fitted with the whisk attachment to beat the egg whites, then gradually add the superfine sugar and beat until stiff. Add the sifted ingredients, mixing with a silicone spatula. Spread the mixture ⅝ inch (1.5 cm) thick on a sheet of parchment paper, then bake for 7 to 8 minutes, keeping an eye on it. Let cool on a rack, then cut out ten 1¼-inch (3.5-cm)-diameter circles with a cookie cutter. Freeze for 30 minutes.

FOR THE PASSION FRUIT–COCONUT CENTERS

Heat together half of the passion fruit puree and half of the coconut puree. Add the agar mixed with the superfine sugar, then boil for 2 minutes. Let cool. Use a food processor to mix on low speed, then gradually add the remaining purees. Stir in the passion fruit seeds using a silicone spatula. Pour into 1¼-inch (3-cm)-diameter silicone half-dome molds and freeze for 2 hours. Unmold, then fill the half-dome molds with more of the mixture. Place the frozen domes on top to make spheres. Freeze for 1 hour.

FOR THE COCONUT MOUSSE

Soak the gelatin in ⅓ cup (70 g) cold water to soften. Heat one-third of the coconut puree, then add the drained gelatin. When the mixture starts to thicken, mix in the remaining cold coconut puree and the rum. Use an electric stand mixer fitted with a whisk attachment to beat the egg whites, then gradually add the superfine sugar and beat until stiff. Combine this meringue with the coconut puree mixture. Whip the cream in an electric stand mixer fitted with a whisk attachment, then combine with the previous mixture. The mousse should be "dense" for assembly, so that the centers do not sink. Pipe the mousse into the first section of 1¾-inch (4.5-cm)-diameter sphere molds. Insert a dacquoise circle and a passion fruit–coconut center in each mold. Add the second part of the mold, then fill with the remaining coconut mousse, being careful not to incorporate any air bubbles. Freeze for 3 hours.

FOR ASSEMBLY AND FINISHING

Unmold the frozen spheres and smooth to remove any potential imperfections. Make the white coating mixture as described on page 317, then coat the spheres by dipping them in the coating. Also make the white glaze as described on page 317, then coat the spheres by dipping them. Arrange the coconut chips attractively around each coconut sphere.

PREPARATION TIME: 2 HOURS

SERVES 8

COOKING TIME: 10 MINUTES

RESTING TIME: 6 HOURS 30 MINUTES

PREPARATION TIME: 10 MINUTES

SERVES 8

COOKING TIME: 25 MINUTES

PINE NUT

- 3 large eggs (110 g) egg whites
- ¾ cup (90 g) confectioners' sugar
- ⅓ cup (50 g) all-purpose flour
- 3 tablespoons (44 g) unsalted butter
- 1 teaspoon (4 g) salt
- ¾ cup (100 g) pine nuts (pignoli)

Preheat the oven to 340°F (170°C). Whisk the egg whites with the confectioners' sugar and flour. Bring 2 cups (480 g) water to a boil with the butter and salt, then pour over the first mixture and mix. Spread the mixture to a thickness of 3/8 inch (1 cm) on a nonstick baking sheet. Sprinkle with the pine nuts. Bake for 24 minutes, turning the baking sheet halfway. Cut the wafer into 2½ by 2½-inch (6 by 6-cm) pieces.

PISTACHIO

FOR THE CHOUX PASTE
1 quantity (14 ounces/400 g) choux paste (see page 312)

FOR THE PISTACHIO PRALINE
4 cups (500 g) pistachio nuts
1¼ cups (250 g) superfine sugar
2½ teaspoons (10 g) fleur de sel

FOR THE PISTACHIO PASTE
¾ cup (100 g) pistachio nuts
1 tablespoon (7 g) confectioners' sugar
A few grains (0.2 g) fleur de sel

FOR THE PISTACHIO PRALINE CREAM
2¼ cups (600 g) pastry cream (see page 314)
2 cups (520 g) buttercream (see page 314)

FOR THE GREEN CRUMB DOUGH
7 tablespoons (100 g) unsalted butter
1 cup (125 g) all-purpose flour
½ cup (125 g) packed light brown sugar
¼ teaspoon (1 g) green food coloring
⅛ teaspoon (0.7 g) red food coloring
1 large egg white
⅔ cup (80 g) Sicilian pistachio nuts

FOR THE TOASTED PISTACHIO NUTS
¾ cup (100 g) pistachio nuts

FOR ASSEMBLY
Pistachio skins
Confectioners' sugar

FOR THE CHOUX PASTE
Make and pipe the choux paste for Paris-Brest as described on page 312.

FOR THE PISTACHIO PRALINE
Preheat the oven to 300°F (150°C) and toast the pistachio nuts for 15 minutes. In a saucepan, heat the superfine sugar and 1/3 cup (80 g) water until it caramelizes and, while at 360°F (180°C), pour over the pistachio nuts. Using a food processor, pulse until it forms a paste, then mix with the fleur de sel in an electric stand mixer fitted with a flat beater attachment.

FOR THE PISTACHIO PASTE
Increase the oven temperature to 360°F (180°C). Toast the pistachio nuts for 15 to 20 minutes. Using a powerful blender, blend them with the confectioners' sugar and fleur du sel until a smooth paste forms.

FOR THE PISTACHIO PRALINE CREAM
Make the pastry cream as described on page 314 and refrigerate for 30 minutes. Whisk smooth, then add 1/3 cup (90 g) of the pistachio praline and 1/4 cup (60 g) of the pistachio paste. Make the buttercream as described on page 314 and whip until smooth in an electric stand mixer fitted with a whisk attachment. Gently combine with the first mixture. Refrigerate for 3 hours.

FOR THE GREEN CRUMB DOUGH
In an electric stand mixer fitted with a flat beater attachment, beat the butter with the flour, brown sugar, green food coloring, and red food coloring. Using a rolling pin, roll to a thickness of 1/4 inch (5 mm). Freeze for 30 minutes. Brush the frozen crumb dough with the egg white, then sprinkle with the pistachio nuts. Place a sheet of parchment paper over the top and use a rolling pin to press the pistachios into the crumb dough. Cut out ten 2½-inch (6-cm)-diameter circles and cut out the centers with a ¾-inch (20-mm) plain tip for individual Paris-Brests. If making one large Paris-Brest, cut a 7¼-inch (18-cm)-diameter circle with a 5-inch (12-cm) opening in the center.

FOR THE TOASTED PISTACHIO NUTS
Preheat the oven to 300°F (150°C) and toast the pistachios for about 15 minutes, or until they have an even color.

FOR ASSEMBLY AND FINISHING
Preheat the oven to 360°F (180°C). Place the cut crumb pieces over the choux paste. Dust with confectioners' sugar and bake for 40 minutes, then dry in the oven at 320°F (160°C) for 10 minutes. Cool, then slice the Paris-Brest(s) in half. Flatten the bottom part of the choux pastry, then use a pastry bag with a fluted tip to pipe in the pistachio praline cream, making little swirls. Add the toasted pistachio nuts. Pipe six dots of the pistachio praline on top. Cut the top(s) using a correctly sized cookie cutter so that they are well rounded, then place on top. Sprinkle with toasted pistachios and the pistachio skins and dust with confectioners' sugar.

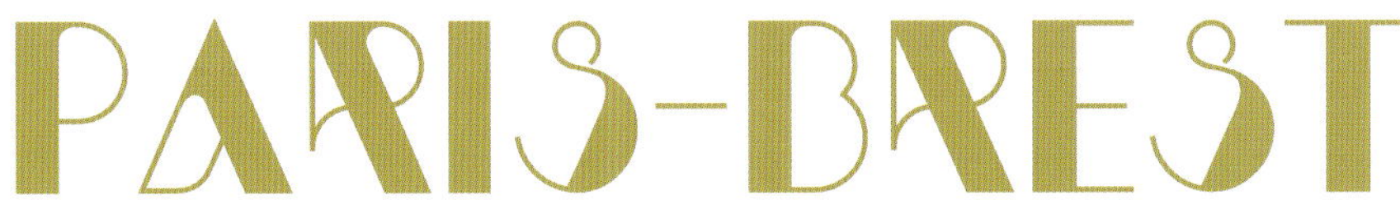

PREPARATION TIME: 2 HOURS 30 MINUTES

SERVES 10

COOKING TIME: 1 HOUR 40 MINUTES

RESTING TIME: 3 HOURS 30 MINUTES

PREPARATION TIME: 20 MINUTES

SERVES 8

COOKING TIME: 10 MINUTES

PISTACHIO

7 tablespoons (100 g) unsalted butter
½ cup (60 g) ground Sicilian pistachio nuts, plus ¾ cup (100 g) Sicilian pistachio nuts, chopped
1 cup (110 g) confectioners' sugar
¼ cup (35 g) cake flour
1 teaspoon (5 g) pistachio paste
3 large (100 g) egg whites, at room temperature
Fleur de sel

Heat the butter until lightly brown and giving off a nutty scent.

Preheat the oven to 360°F (180°C).
Mix the ground pistachio nuts, confectioners' sugar, and flour, then combine with the pistachio paste. Add the egg whites, then combine with the warm browned butter. Let cool.

Pour into 1¾-inch (4.5-cm)-diameter silicone half-dome molds, using ½ ounce (12 g) mixture for each mold. Sprinkle with the chopped pistachios and bake for 6 minutes.

Sprinkle a pinch of fleur de sel on each financier and serve.

FOR THE LEMON, PEANUT, AND PISTACHIO SPONGE CAKES

2¾ cups (260 g) ground almonds
1 cup (225 g) packed light brown sugar
10 large (330g) egg whites
6 large (105 g) egg yolks
2 tablespoons (30 g) coffee paste
¼ cup (60 g) whipping cream
⅓ cup (65 g) superfine sugar
⅛ teaspoon (1 g) salt
1 cup (2 sticks/210 g) unsalted butter
¾ cup (105 g) all-purpose flour
1½ teaspoons (6 g) baking powder
½ cup (60 g) Sicilian pistachio nuts, coarsely chopped
Zest of 4 lemons
⅓ cup (60 g) fresh peanuts, coarsely chopped

FOR THE CENTERS

Lemon cubes (lemon preserves)

¾ cup (180 g) lemon juice
2½ tablespoons (30 g) superfine sugar
2 teaspoons (5 g) agar powder
4 finger limes (2 ounces/55 g), finely chopped
¼ cup (40 g) lemon suprêmes, cut into pieces
1 cup (170 g) candied lemon (store-bought), finely chopped

Pistachio cubes (pistachio praline)

¾ cup (100 g) pistachio nuts
¼ cup (50 g) superfine sugar
½ teaspoon (2 g) fleur de sel

Peanut cubes (peanut praline)

⅔ cup (100 g) peanuts
¼ cup (50 g) superfine sugar
½ teaspoon (2 g) fleur de sel

FOR THE COATINGS

Lemon cubes (lemon-yellow coating)

1¼ cups (300 g) coating mixture (see page 317)
¾ teaspoon (4 g) yellow fat-soluble food coloring

Pistachio cubes (pistachio-green coating)

1¼ cups (300 g) coating mixture (see page 317)
¾ teaspoon (4 g) green fat-soluble food coloring
¼ teaspoon (1 g) yellow fat-soluble food coloring

Peanut cubes (white coating)

1¼ cups (300 g) coating mixture (see page 317)

FOR FINISHING

Lemon cubes (gold leaf)

2 sheets gold leaf per cube

Pistachio cubes (pistachio-green glaze)

1¼ cups (300 g) neutral glaze (see page 317)
2 tablespoons (10 g) edible silver luster dust
⅛ teaspoon (0.5 g) green fat-soluble food coloring
¼ teaspoon (1.5 g) yellow fat-soluble food coloring
½ teaspoon (1.5 g) vanilla powder

Peanut cubes (white glaze)

1¼ cups (300 g) neutral glaze (see page 317)
2½ tablespoons (25 g) cornstarch
¼ cup (20 g) titanium white fat-soluble food coloring

Continued

PREPARATION TIME: 2 HOURS

SERVES 10

COOKING TIME: 30 MINUTES

RESTING TIME: 2 HOURS 30 MINUTES

FOR THE LEMON, PEANUT, AND PISTACHIO SPONGE CAKES

Preheat the oven to 360°F (180°C). Mix the almonds with ¾ cup plus 2 tablespoons (195 g) packed brown sugar, 2 of the egg whites, and the egg yolks, coffee paste, cream, ¼ cup (45 g) of the superfine sugar, and the salt. Melt the butter and keep it warm. In an electric stand mixer fitted with a whisk attachment, whip the remaining egg whites, then add 2½ tablespoons (30 g) superfine sugar and beat until stiff. Mix the warm butter into the almond mixture, then add the flour and baking powder, and, finally, the stiffened egg whites. Divide the mixture among three mixing bowls. To the first bowl, add the pistachio nuts; to the second, add the lemon zest; and to the third, add the peanuts. Pour each mixture into a 12 x 16 inch (30 x 40 cm) baking sheet and cook for 10 minutes, turning the sheet in the oven halfway.

FOR THE LEMON PRESERVES

Heat ½ cup (120 g) water with the lemon juice, then add the superfine sugar mixed with the agar. Boil for 2 minutes, then cool rapidly by pouring into a pan and refrigerating for 30 minutes. When it is cold, use an immersion blender to mix, being careful not to beat in any air. Add the finger limes, lemon suprêmes, and candied lemons.

FOR THE PISTACHIO PRALINE

Preheat the oven to 300°F (150°C). Toast the pistachios for 15 minutes. In a saucepan, heat the superfine sugar and 1 tablespoon (15 g) water until it caramelizes at 360°F (180°C), then pour over the pistachio nuts on a Silpat baking mat. Let cool. Using a food processor, pulse until it forms a smooth paste, then mix with the fleur de sel in an electric stand mixer fitted with a flat beater attachment.

FOR THE PEANUT PRALINE

Preheat the oven to 300°F (150°C). Toast the peanuts for 15 minutes. Heat the superfine sugar and 1 tablespoon (15 g) water until it caramelizes at 360°F (180°C), then pour over the toasted peanuts. Transfer to a Silpat or parchment paper and let cool. Using a food processor, pulse until it forms a smooth paste, then mix with the fleur de sel in an electric stand mixer fitted with a flat beater attachment.

FOR THE CUBE ASSEMBLY

Cut out 27 squares of sponge cakes using 1¼-inch (3-cm) stainless steel square cutters. Pipe the corresponding mixture for each sponge cake on top: lemon preserves for the lemon sponge cake; peanut praline for the peanut sponge cake; and pistachio praline for the pistachio sponge cake. Repeat the process a second time, adding a cake layer and then piping on the filling, completing the cubes with a last sponge cake square on top. Freeze for 2 hours. When the cubes have hardened, unmold them.

FOR THE CUBE COATING

Make the lemon-yellow, pistachio-green, and white coatings as described on page 317, adjusting the quantities and colorings to those specified for each (see ingredients list page 306). Stick a toothpick through each cube and dip it into its corresponding coating, heated to 75°F (25°C): the lemon-yellow one for the lemon cubes, the pistachio-green one for the pistachio cubes; and the white one for the peanut cubes.

FOR THE CUBE FINISHING

Cover each lemon cube completely with two sheets of gold leaf. Make the pistachio-green and the white glazes as described on page 317, adjusting the quantities and colorings to those specified for each (see ingredients list page 306). Dip the pistachio cubes in the pistachio-green glaze and the peanut cubes in the white glaze.

FOR THE RUBIK'S CAKE ASSEMBLY

Place layers of nine cubes on three 4-inch (10-cm)-square stands and pile them up on top of each other. You can adapt this recipe using other flavors and finishings inspired by recipes from the book to create different cubes.

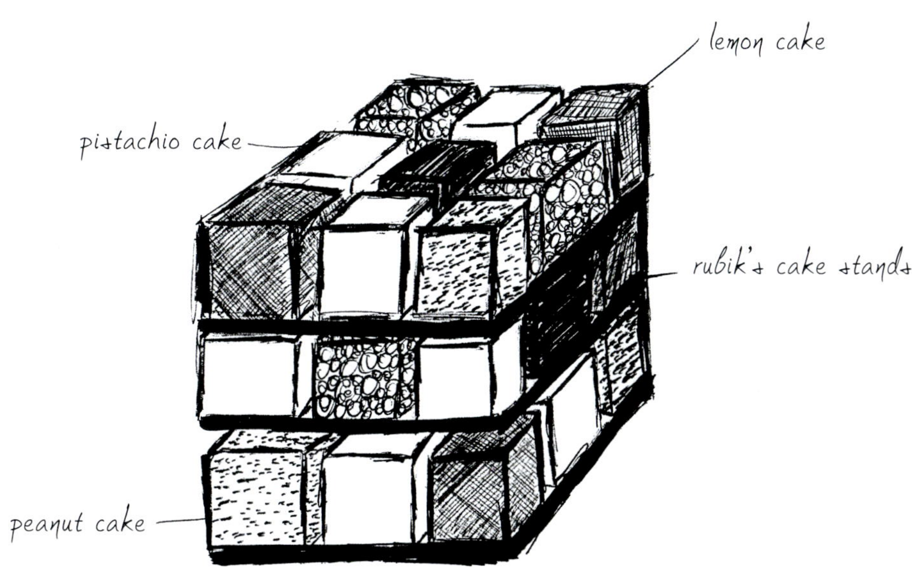

APPE

NDIX

BASIC PASTRIES

SWEET DOUGH

Makes 1¼ pounds (590 g) dough

½ cup plus 3 tablespoons (1⅜ sticks/150 g) unsalted butter
¾ cup (95 g) confectioners' sugar
⅓ cup (30 g) ground almonds
⅛ teaspoon (1 g) Guérande salt
⅜ teaspoon (1 g) vanilla powder
1 extra-large (58 g) egg
2 cups (250 g) all-purpose flour

Using an electric stand mixer fitted with a flat beater attachment, beat the butter with the confectioners' sugar, ground almonds, salt, and vanilla powder. Beat while adding the eggs, then add the flour and mix until smooth. Refrigerate for 4 hours.

For tartlets

Using a rolling pin, roll out to a thickness of ⅛ inch (3 mm), then line ten lightly greased ¾-inch (2-cm)-deep by 2-inch (5-cm)-diameter cake rings. Let dry in the refrigerator for 1 day.

For a tart

Using a rolling pin, roll out to a thickness of ⅛ inch (3 mm), then line a lightly greased ¾-inch (2-cm)-deep by 7¼-inch (18-cm)-diameter cake ring. Let dry in the refrigerator for 1 day.

CHOUX PASTE

Makes 14 ounces (400 g) paste

½ cup (125 g) milk
1 teaspoon (5 g) salt
7 tablespoons (100 g) unsalted butter
1¼ cups (150 g) all-purpose flour
4 large (200 g) eggs

In a saucepan, boil the milk with ½ cup (125 g) water, the salt, and butter. Remove from the heat and add the flour immediately. Return to the heat and, using a silicone spatula, mix briskly to dry out the mixture. Transfer to the bowl of an electric stand mixer fitted with a flat beater attachment and beat the paste, gradually adding the eggs. Let rest for 1 hour at room temperature.

For a Paris-Brest

When the dough is smooth, transfer to a pastry bag fitted with a fluted tip. Pipe out 3¼-inch (8-cm)-diameter circles on a Silpat baking mat for small Paris-Brests or a 6½-inch (16-cm)-diameter circle for one large Paris-Brest.

SAINT-HONORÉ CHOUX PASTE

Makes 14 ounces (400 g) paste

⅓ cup plus 1 tablespoon (100 g) milk
½ teaspoon (2 g) superfine sugar
⅝ teaspoon (4 g) salt
6½ tablespoons (90 g) unsalted butter
¾ cup plus 2 tablespoons (110 g) all-purpose flour, sifted
3½ large (180 g) eggs (¾ cup)
Crumb dough disks (see recipe)

In a saucepan, boil the milk with ⅜ cup (100 g) water, the superfine sugar, salt, and butter. Remove from the heat and add the flour immediately. Return to the heat and, using a silicone spatula, mix briskly to dry out the mixture. Transfer to the bowl of an electric stand mixer fitted with a flat beater attachment and beat the paste, gradually adding the eggs and checking the consistency. Transfer to a pastry bag fitted with a no. 6 plain tip and pipe out small cream puffs on a baking sheet lined with parchment paper or a Silpat baking mat.

CRUMB DOUGH

Makes 12⅜ ounces (350 g) crumb dough

½ cup (100g) unsalted butter
½ cup (125g) packed brown sugar
1 cup (125g) all-purpose flour

Preheat the oven to 340°F (170°C). Mix the butter, brown sugar, flour, and last, depending on the recipe, the food coloring and/or citrus fruit zest, then use a rolling pin to roll the mixture out to a thickness of 1 mm between two sheets of parchment paper. Bake for 7 minutes, then sift the crumbs, keeping any chunks and discarding any powder.

CRISPY WAFER COOKIES

2½ large (85 g) egg whites (⅓ cup)
⅔ cup (72.5 g) confectioners' sugar
¼ cup (36 g) all-purpose flour
1 tablespoon (7 g) starch
2¾ tablespoons (37.5 g) unsalted butter
½ teaspoon (3 g) salt

Preheat the oven to 360°F (180°C). In a mixing bowl, whisk the egg whites, confectioners' sugar, flour, and starch together. Boil 1½ cups (365 g) water with the butter and salt, then pour over the first mixture. To make the balls, put the wafer cookie dough into a pastry bag without a tip, then cut the end of the bag and pipe squares onto a baking sheet. Bake in the top of a deck oven for about 15 minutes, until the wafer turns golden. Remove from the oven, tear into pieces, and scrunch into balls.

PUFF PASTRY DOUGH

For the kneaded butter (beurre manié)

1½ cups (11½ ounces/330 g) unsalted dry butter (84% fat content), at room temperature
1 cup (135 g) pastry flour

For the water dough (détrempe)

2 teaspoons (12 g) salt
½ teaspoon (3 g) distilled white vinegar
7 tablespoons (100 g) unsalted butter, softened
2½ cups (315 g) pastry flour

For the beurre manié

In an electric stand mixer fitted with a flat beater attachment, beat the butter with the flour for about 10 minutes. Using a rolling pin, roll out the beurre manié to make a 16 by 45-inch (40 by 115-cm) rectangle that is ⅜ inch (10 mm) thick.

For the détrempe

In an electric stand mixer fitted with a dough hook, make the détrempe by mixing ½ cup (130 g) water, the salt, vinegar, butter, and flour for about 15 minutes, until a smooth dough forms. Roll out the détrempe to a thickness of ⅜ inch (10 mm), making a 15-inch (38-cm) square.

Place the détrempe in the middle of the beurre manié, then fold each edge over to encase the détrempe. Make the dough with six simple turns: Start by rolling out the dough, then fold it over on itself to make the first turn. Refrigerate for 1 hour. Repeat this process another five times, making sure to refrigerate for 1 hour between each turn.

For a Saint-Hororé

In this case, the dough should be made the previous day. Using a rolling pin, roll it out to 1/16 inch (2 mm) and refrigerate for 24 hours. The next day, bake the dough between two baking sheets for 10 minutes at 360°F (180°C). Cut out 3¼-inch (8.5-cm)-diameter disks for the small Saint-Honorés and a 7¼-inch (18-cm)-diameter disk for a large Saint-Honoré to serve eight people, then place the disks between the two baking sheets. Return to the oven for 15 minutes at 360°F (180°C). Remove the upper baking sheet and dust with confectioners' sugar. Finally, bake for 5 minutes at 360°F (180°C), then brown in a deck or oven at 480°F (250°C).

PASTRY CREAM

Makes 2¼ cups (600 g) pastry cream

2½ teaspoons (7 g) gelatin powder
1¼ cups (300 g) milk
⅓ cup (75 g) whipping cream
1 vanilla bean
⅓ cup (60 g) superfine sugar
3 tablespoon (18 g) custard powder
2½ tablespoons (18 g) all-purpose flour
3½ large (60 g) egg yolks (¼ cup)
1½ tablespoons (20 g) cocoa butter
2½ tablespoons (35 g) unsalted butter
1½ tablespoons (20 g) mascarpone cheese

Soak the gelatin in 2 tablespoons (33 g) cold water to soften. In a saucepan, heat the milk and cream. Halve the vanilla bean lengthwise, scape out the seeds, and add the seeds and pods to the saucepan to infuse for 20 minutes. Meanwhile, whisk the superfine sugar, custard powder, flour, and egg yolks until pale. Pass the hot milk-cream-vanilla mixture through a conical sieve, then pour it over the egg yolk mixture. Return to a clean saucepan and cook over medium heat for 2 minutes, until thick, whisking constantly. Remove from the heat and add the cocoa butter. Also add the gelatin, then the butter, and, finally, the mascarpone. Use an immersion blender to mix, then cool rapidly in the refrigerator for about 30 minutes.

VANILLA WHIPPED CREAM

Makes about 4 cups (517 g) whipped cream

2 cups (500 g) whipping cream (35% fat content)
1½ tablespoons (17.5 g) superfine sugar
2½ vanilla beans

Chill the bowl and whisk attachment of an electric stand mixer in the refrigerator. Boil one-third of the cream and add the superfine sugar. Halve the vanilla beans lengthwise, scrape out the seeds, and add the seeds and pods to the cream mixture. Infuse for 10 minutes, then pass through a conical sieve over the remaining cold cream and let cool. Whip the cream in the chilled bowl of the electric stand mixer until stiff.

ALMOND CREAM

Makes 1¼ cups (300 g) almond cream

5½ tablespoons (75 g) unsalted butter
⅓ cup (75 g) superfine sugar
¾ cup (75 g) ground almonds
1½ large (75 g) eggs (⅓ cup)

In a stand mixer fitted with a flat beater attachment, cream the butter, superfine sugar, and almonds together. Gradually mix in the eggs, then optionally rum, citrus fruit zests, or chopped herbs, depending on the recipe. Transfer to a pastry bag.

BUTTERCREAM

3 tablespoons (45 g) milk
2 large (35 g) egg yolks
½ cup (100 g) superfine sugar
¾ cup plus 2 tablespoons (1¾ sticks/200 g) unsalted butter
1 large (30 g) egg white

In a saucepan, bring the milk to a boil. In a mixing bowl, whisk the egg yolks with ¼ cup (45 g) of the superfine sugar, then pour the boiling milk over the mixture. Return to the saucepan and cook to about 180°F (83°C), until it is thick enough to coat a spoon. Gradually pour this crème anglaise over the butter, while whipping in an electric stand mixer fitted with a whisk attachment. Set aside and clean the electric stand mixer bowl. Put the egg whites in the electric stand mixer bowl and whip to soft peaks using the whisk attachment. Meanwhile, in a saucepan, make a syrup by heating 4 teaspoons (20 g) water with the remaining sugar. When the syrup reaches 250°F (121°C), pour it in a thin stream over the egg whites and continue to whip until it cools and forms an Italian meringue. Combine with the first mixture using a silicone spatula.

MERINGUE

FRENCH MERINGUE

6 large (200g) egg whites
1 cup (200 g) superfine sugar
1⅔ cups (200 g) confectioners' sugar

In an electric stand mixer fitted with a whisk attachment, whip the egg whites until they form soft peaks, then add the superfine sugar and beat until stiff. Using a silicone spatula, gently fold in the confectioners' sugar.

CARAMEL

CREAMY CARAMEL

1⅔ cups (400 g) whipping cream
⅓ cup (100 g) milk
1⅓ cups (310 g) glucose powder
2 vanilla beans, split and scraped
1 teaspoon (4 g) fleur de sel
1 cup (190 g) superfine sugar
½ cup plus 2 tablespoons (1¼ sticks/140 g) unsalted butter

Heat the cream, milk, ½ cup (100 g) of the glucose, the vanilla seeds and pods, and fleur de sel together. Heat the superfine sugar and the remaining glucose to 365°F (185°C), then deglaze with the hot cream mixture. Heat to 220°F (105°C), then pass through a conical sieve. When the caramel cools to 160°F (70°C), add the butter in pieces. Use an immersion blender to blend.

FRESH FRUIT

STRAWBERRY JUICE

6⅔ cups (2¼ pounds/1 kg) frozen strawberries
2½ teaspoons (10 g) superfine sugar

The previous day, put the frozen strawberries and superfine sugar in a heatproof pan and cover with several layers of oven-safe plastic wrap. Bake for 12 hours at 210°F (100°C). The next day, use a colander to strain, covering it with a cloth, and collect only the clear juice.

RASPBERRY JUICE

4 cups (500 g) frozen raspberries
1½ tablespoons (20 g) superfine sugar

The previous day, put the frozen raspberries and superfine sugar in a heatproof pan and cover with several layers of oven-safe plastic wrap. Bake for 12 hours at 210°F (100°C). The next day, use a colander to strain, covering it with a cloth, and collect only the clear juice.

RASPBERRY SEED MIXTURE

Makes about 1¼ cups (400 g) raspberry seed mixture

1 sheet (2.5 g powdered) gelatin
1¾ cups (250 g) frozen raspberries
¾ cup (150 g) superfine sugar
1¾ teaspoons (5 g) pectin NH
2 teaspoons (10 g) lemon juice

Soak the gelatin in cold water to soften. In a saucepan, heat the frozen raspberries with half the superfine sugar. Mix the remaining sugar with the pectin NH, then add to the raspberries. Boil for 1 minute, then add the lemon juice, straining it through a conical sieve over the saucepan. Remove from the heat and add the drained gelatin. Transfer to a vacuum-sealed pastry bag.

APPLE GEL

1 cup plus 2 tablespoons (275 g) apple juice
3 tablespoons (50 g) lemon juice
1½ tablespoons (20 g) superfine sugar
2 teaspoons (6 g) pectin NH

In a saucepan, heat the apple and lemon juices together. Mix the superfine sugar with the pectin, then sprinkle into the saucepan. Boil for at least 2 minutes, then transfer to a pan and refrigerate for 1 hour. Use an immersion blender to mix, beating in as little air as possible.

POACHED CITRUS FRUIT

1 pound 2 ounces (500 g) citrus fruit (Meyer lemons, oranges, Mandarins, etc.)
5 cups (1 kg) superfine sugar

Remove the stems from the citrus fruit, cut them into eight sections, then remove the insides, leaving only ⅛ inch (3 mm) of pulp attached to the peel. Blanch them three times in a large saucepan of boiling water (starting from cold), draining each time. Put 4½ cups (1 kg) water and half the superfine sugar in a saucepan and bring to a boil. Immerse the fruit in this syrup and let simmer, covered, keeping the temperature below 160°F (70°C). Concentrate the syrup by incorporating the remaining sugar in several additions, heating to 160°F (70°C). When the fruit is tender, remove and drain, reserving the cooking syrup. Heat the syrup to 215°F (103°C), then let cool. Return the citrus fruit to this syrup and set aside until required.

SUGAR-COATED RHUBARB

5 stalks rhubarb
1½ cups (300 g) pearl sugar
1 large egg white (30 g)
1½ tablespoons (15 g) superfine sugar
1 teaspoon (5 g) vanilla sugar
1 teaspoon (5 g) honey

The previous day, rinse the rhubarb stalks. Mix the pearl sugar and egg whites. Cover the surface of a plate or pan with the superfine sugar, then place the rhubarb stalks on top. Dust with the vanilla sugar and add a drizzle of honey on each rhubarb stalk. Cover the stalks with the pearl sugar–egg whites mixture until about 3/8 inch (1 cm) above the stalks. Cook in a deck oven at 360°F (180°C) for 45 to 50 minutes, according to the size of the rhubarb stalks. When cooked, transfer the rhubarb stalks to a perforated pan and let drain overnight over a bowl. The next day, retrieve the juice and use the rhubarb pulp.

RHUBARB CHIPS

5 stalks (100 g) rhubarb

Preheat the oven to 160°F (70°C). Using an adjustable-blade slicer or mandoline, cut the rhubarb into thin slices, then bake and dry for 4 hours.

PINEAPPLE CHIPS

¼ pineapple, cored and peeled
(1 cup/150 g)
½ cup (100 g) superfine sugar

Preheat the oven to 140°F (60°C). Using a knife or a mandoline, cut the pineapple into thin slices. Make a syrup by heating ½ cup (126 g) water and the superfine sugar in a saucepan, then immerse the pineapple slices in this mixture. Transfer to a Silpat baking mat and let dry in the oven for 4 hours.

NUTS

COCONUT CHIPS

5 cups (1 kg) superfine sugar
5 fresh coconuts

Make a syrup with 4¼ cups (1 kg) water and the superfine sugar. Using a rolling pin, tap the fresh coconuts all over to detach the pulp from the shell. Break it into pieces, then use a vegetable peeler to make long thin slices. Pour a little syrup over these slices, then roll them up. Transfer to a Silpat baking mat, then let dry in a warm dry place for 24 hours. To keep for longer, store in a container away from moisture.

CHESTNUT CHIPS

½ cup (110 g) superfine sugar
5 cups (500 g) chestnuts

Preheat the oven to 360°F (180°C). Mix the superfine sugar with ⅓ cup (100 g) water in a saucepan and bring to a boil, then let cool to 85°F (30°C) to make a syrup. Cut the chestnuts into thin slices, then dip into the syrup and place on a Silpat baking mat on a baking sheet. Bake and toast for 10 minutes.

TOASTED SHREDDED COCONUT

Shredded coconut

Preheat the oven to 360°F (180°C). Place the shredded coconut on a baking sheet, then toast in the oven for 5 minutes. (For toasted ground coconut, grind in a food processing)

HAZELNUT PRALINE

2¼ cups (300 g) whole unskinned hazelnuts
¾ cup (150 g) superfine sugar
1½ teaspoons (6 g) fleur de sel

Preheat the oven to 300°F (150°C) and toast the hazelnuts for 30 minutes. Heat the superfine sugar and 3 tablespoons (48 g) water to 230°F (110°C), then add the hazelnuts. Caramelize well, then pour onto a Silpat baking mat. Let cool. Using a food processor, pulse to obtain the texture of praline with crunch, then mix with the fleur de sel in an electric stand mixer fitted with a flat beater attachment.

TOASTED HAZELNUTS

Hazelnuts

Preheat the oven to 360°F (180°C). Place the hazelnuts on a pan lined with a Silpat baking mat or a sheet of parchment paper and bake for 15 minutes.

POWDERS

ROSEMARY POWDER

1½ cups (100 g) fresh rosemary

Preheat the oven to 160°F (70°C). Dry the rosemary for 2 hours and pulse in a food processor until a powder forms.

VERBENA POWDER

2 cups (100 g) fresh verbena leaves

Preheat the oven to 160°F (70°C). Dry the verbena leaves for 2 hours and pulse in a food processor until a powder forms.

DECORATION AND FINISHINGS

COATING OR SPRAY MIXTURE

8¾ ounces (250 g)
white couverture chocolate, chopped
1 cup (250 g) cocoa butter
Food coloring

Melt the chocolate and cocoa butter, then use an immersion blender to mix while adding the food coloring(s) specified in the recipe.

CHOCOLATE STEMS

3½ ounces (100 g) chocolate

Pulse the chocolate in a food processor until a paste forms, without letting it melt. Shape it into small stems, adapting the size depending on the fruit.

NEUTRAL GLAZE

3½ teaspoons (10 g) gelatin powder
⅔ cup (140 g) milk
1 cup plus 2½ tablespoons (280 g) whipping cream
2 cups (375 g) superfine sugar
½ cup (100 g) glucose powder
2 teaspoons (10 g) titanium dioxide
or food coloring
3½ tablespoons (26 g) cornstarch

Soak the gelatin in ⅓ cup (70 g) water to hydrate. Boil the milk with the cream, 1½ cups (285 g) of the superfine sugar, the glucose, and coloring for a colored glaze or titanium dioxide for a white glaze. Mix the remaining sugar with the starch and sprinkle over the first mixture. Bring to a boil, then cool in the refrigerator, stirring regularly until the temperature drops to 105°F (40°C). Add the gelatin and mix using an immersion blender. Pass through a conical sieve, then use to frost the dessert.

WHITE OR DARK TEMPERED CHOCOLATE

White couverture chocolate
Dark couverture chocolate

Melt the white couverture chocolate to 113°F (45°C), then let the temperature cool to 79°F (26°C) while working the mixture with an offset spatula and a pastry cutter, directly on the work surface, ideally marble. Once the mixture cools to 79°F (26°C), transfer to a mixing bowl, then heat to 84°F (29°C) in a bain-marie when required.

For dark couverture chocolate, follow the same steps, but use different temperatures first 122°F (50°C), then 82°F (28°C), and last 86 to 88°F (30 to 31°C).

FINELY CHOPPED TOASTED ALMONDS

Almonds

Preheat the oven to 360°F (180°C). Toast the almonds for 10 minutes, then pulse in a food processor until they form fine small pieces.

In this book, you will find several éclair recipes that all follow the same basic steps but are distinguished by their flavors and finishing. Check the page of your chosen éclair recipe to adapt the following recipe.

CHOUX PASTE

Makes 14 ounces (400 g) paste

½ cup (125 g) milk
3½ teaspoons (15 g) trimoline (inverted sugar)
1 teaspoon (5 g) salt
½ cup (1 stick/110 g) unsalted butter
1¼ cups (150 g) all-purpose flour
4 large (200 g) eggs

In a saucepan, boil the milk with ½ cup (125 g) water, the trimoline, salt, and butter. Remove from the heat and add the flour immediately. Return to the heat and, using a silicone spatula, mix briskly to dry the pastry out. Transfer to the bowl of an electric stand mixer fitted with a flat beater attachment and beat the paste, gradually adding the eggs.

When the paste is smooth, let rest for 1 hour at room temperature. Transfer to a pastry bag fitted with a no. 18 fluted tip. Pipe 15-inch (38-cm) lines onto a baking sheet lined with parchment paper, making sure to maintain pressure on the pastry bag so that the lines aren't too thin. Freeze for 30 minutes, then, using a large knife such as a cheese knife, cut out 5-inch (12-cm) éclairs.

CRUMB DOUGH

7 tablespoons (100 g) unsalted butter
1 cup (12 g) all-purpose flour
½ cup (125 g) packed light brown sugar
Food coloring(s) or titanium dioxide

In an electric stand mixer fitted with a flat beater attachment, mix the butter with the flour, brown sugar, and food coloring(s) or titanium dioxide, without giving it too much body. Use a rolling pin to roll to a thickness of 1 mm between two sheets of parchment paper. Freeze for 30 minutes, then cut out ten 1¼ by 5¾-inch (3 by 13-cm) strips and place them on the uncooked éclairs.

STARCH GLAZE

3½ teaspoons (10 g) gelatin powder
⅔ cup (140 g) milk
1 cups plus 2 tablespoons (280 g) whipping cream
2 cups (375 g) superfine sugar
½ cup (100 g) glucose powder
2 teaspoons (10 g) titanium dioxide
or food coloring
3½ tablespoons (26 g) cornstarch

Soak the gelatin in ⅓ cup (70 g) water to hydrate. Boil the milk with the cream, 1½ cups (285 g) of the superfine sugar, the glucose, and food coloring for a colored glaze or titanium dioxide for a white glaze. Mix the remaining sugar with the starch and sprinkle over the first mixture. Bring to a boil, then cool in the refrigerator, stirring regularly until the temperature drops to 105°F (40°C). Add the gelatin and use an immersion blender to mix. Pass the glaze through a conical sieve.

CRISPY WAFER COOKIE MIXTURE

2½ large (85 g) egg whites (⅓ cup)
⅔ cup (72.5 g) confectioners' sugar
¼ cup (36 g) all-purpose flour
1 tablespoon (7 g) cornstarch
2¾ tablespoons (37.5 g) unsalted butter
½ teaspoon (3 g) salt

Preheat the oven to 360°F (180°C). In a mixing bowl, whisk the egg whites, confectioners' sugar, flour, and starch together. Boil 1½ cups (365 g) water with the butter and salt and pour over the first mixture. Put the wafer cookie dough into a pastry bag without a tip, then cut the end of the bag and pipe squares onto a baking sheet. Bake for about 15 minutes, until the wafers turn golden. Remove from the oven, tear into pieces, and scrunch into balls.

RECIPE LIST

CITRUS FRUIT

STONE FRUIT

Continued

BERRIES

WILD FRUIT

NUTS

MULTIPLE FRUITS

INGREDIENTS

AGAR
A natural plant-based setting agent extracted from red algae.

ASCORBIC ACID
A powder used to prevent the oxidization of fruit. Available in specialty stores or online.

BAUMES DES ANGES
A few drops of these natural flavorings add the flavor of the product to the mixture.

BÉTON HONEY
Collected in an urban environment, this honey is renowned for its complex flavor.

COUVERTURE CHOCOLATE
Chocolate with a high cocoa butter content, used in pastry and confectionery making. Available in specialty stores or online.

CUSTARD POWDER
A starch-based powder used as a thickener, particularly to make creams or flans. Available in large grocery stores, specialty stores, or online. It can be replaced with Maïzena cornstarch or flour.

DOLÇ MATARÓ
A sweet red wine with berry and candied fruit aromas.

FAT-SOLUBLE FOOD COLORING
Also known as liposoluble food coloring, powdered food coloring that dissolves in fats, as opposed to water-soluble food coloring, which dissolves in water. Used to decorate chocolate, sweet pastry, or almond paste. PCB is a high-quality brand of food coloring.

GLUCOSE POWDER
Used to improve the texture and preserve ice creams without making them too sugary. Available in specialty stores or online.

ISOMALT
The ideal sugar substitute for making decorations using sugars, such as pulled sugar or angel hair.

KAPPA CARRAGEENAN
A plant-based gelling agent, mainly used to make gelatins and coatings.

LUSTER DUST
A sparking food powder that can be applied using a brush to pastries to make them shine.

NEUTRAL GLAZE
This sugar, water, and glucose syrup mixture is used to cover pastries. It gives them a shine and helps them hold their shape.

PECTIN NH
A natural thickener that can be extracted from different fruits, such as apples or grapes. Available in specialty stores or online.

SARAWAK PEPPER
A black pepper from Malaysia used for its woody and fruity aromas.

STABILIZER
A food additive used to add texture to a food or keep it at a certain consistency.

SUPER NEUTROSE
A stabilizer for use in ice creams and sorbets that absorbs water from their mixtures and gives them body.

TARTARIC ACID
A powder used as an emulsifier, it is used in pastry making to stimulate and stabilize flavors and colors.

TITANIUM DIOXIDE

A chemical element used in pastry making as a food coloring. It is used to whiten mixtures and make them shine. Available in specialty stores or online.

TRIMOLINE (INVERTED SUGAR)

Sugar that comes in a white paste. It adds a moisture and improves preservation. It can be replaced with acacia honey.

VERJUICE

Acidic juice extracted from green grapes.

XANTHAN GUM

Emulsifying powder with strong thickening qualities.

YUZU

An Asian citrus fruit that is commonly used in Japanese cuisine. Available in Asian grocery stores.

TECHNIQUES

BAIN-MARIE (COOK IN A)

A cooking method for cooking foods in a bowl that is placed over a saucepan containing boiling water.

BLANCH AND PEEL

Removing the skin of a product after having scalded it.

BLIND BAKE

Prebake or bake a tart shell covered with parchment paper and filled with dried beans or pie weights to make sure that the shell retains its shape.

BROWN THE BUTTER

When the butter has melted, the whey at the bottom of the saucepan starts to caramelize, giving the butter a subtle nutty smell. Make sure not to let it burn — this will make it bitter.

CHURN

Process an ice cream or sorbet mixture in an ice cream maker or a freezer until it solidifies.

COAT

1. Completely cover a food or mixture with a liquid.
2. Completely cover, or enrobe, an element with a thicker or thinner layer to protect or decorate it.

COAT A SPOON

Cook a mixture until it is thick enough to coat a spoon without running off. If you run your finger through the mixture, the line should remain visible.

COVER WITH PLASTIC WRAP IN CONTACT

Place the plastic wrap directly in contact with a cream or mixture to make sure it isn't in contact with the air. This will prevent condensation and the forming of a film on the surface.

CRIMP

Make small indents around the edges of a pastry crust using your fingers, a pastry pincher, or a knife.

EMULSIFY

Vigorously mix a mixture to incorporate air into it.

HULL

Remove the stem from strawberries.

Continued

KNEAD

Mix different ingredients together to obtain a smooth dough, with or without body, depending on the length of time they have been kneaded.

LINE

Use dough to line a pan, ring, or mold.

MACERATE

Soak fresh, candied, or dried fruit in a liquid for a short or long time so that the fruit becomes permeated with the flavor of the liquid.

PIPE

To squeeze out a mixture through a pastry bag sometimes fitted with a tip.

POACH

Cook a product in hot liquid.

REDUCE

Cook in a saucepan without a lid to reduce the volume of a cooking liquid.

RIBBON CONSISTENCY (WHIP TO)

Whip a mixture until, when the whip or whisk is lifted, the mixture falls like a ribbon, folding over itself.

RISE

Let a dough swell in a warm place.

ROLL OUT

Using a rolling pin or pasta machine to roll out a dough.

RUB-IN

Make a mixture of ingredients crumbly by working it by hand.

SIFT

Filter to remove lumps and obtain a fine, even powder.

SMOOTH

Work a liquid mixture vigorously with a whisk to make it smooth, or using a spatula or silicone spatula, to smooth the surface of a mixture to make it completely flat.

SOFTENED BUTTER

Butter at room temperature that has been worked to make it smooth.

STEW

Cook a mixture gently and slowly until the consistency of a compote is obtained.

TEMPER THE CHOCOLATE

Tempering consists of heating the chocolate to a specific temperature (which varies depending on the chocolate) so that the cocoa butter, cocoa, sugar, and milk powder crystallize together. The aim is to obtain a smooth and shiny texture.

THICKEN

Make a juice, broth, or sauce thicker using an ingredient such as flour, Maïzena cornstarch, another starch, a fat, egg yolks, etc.

THIN

To make a mixture less thick by adding liquid.

TOAST

Dry-cook nuts or seeds to remove all their water content.

WHIP

Whisk an element or mixture to incorporate air and increase the volume.

WHISK/STIR UNTIL PALE

Use a wire whisk or a spatula to vigorously mix an egg yolk and sugar mixture until it turns pale.

UTENSILS

ACETATE SHEET

A sheet of transparent plastic that is used in chocolate work to provide shine.

AIRBRUSH GUN

A kitchen utensil that can be used to cover cakes, chocolate, or sugar with a food coloring or coating.

CHEF'S KITCHEN TORCH

A gas-powered utensil whose flame can be used to caramelize desserts, toast or flambée dishes, or brown meats. It consists of a burner and a gas canister.

CONICAL SIEVE AND FINE CONICAL SIEVE

A metal sieve (or strainer) that can be used to filter and sift ingredients and mixtures.

COOKIE CUTTER

A metal or plastic utensil that can be crimped or plain and is available in many different shapes. It can be used to cut or shape dough.

DRUM SIEVE

A utensil in the shape of a circle fitted with a fine metallic mesh that can be used to pass ingredients through, removing impurities and making the ingredients finer.

IMMERSION BLENDER

A manual blender that can be used to remove lumps from mixtures. It has a long neck and a tip with rotating blades.

MANDOLINE

A utensil with adjustable blades that allows for food to be cut into thin, even slices.

MELON BALLER

A utensil with a hemispherical end piece that can be used to extract balls of pulp from fruit, vegetables, or another food product. Melon ballers are available in different sizes.

MICROPLANE

A grater that is used to obtain very fine zest or to finely grate hard cheeses.

MIXING BOWL

A hemispherical bowl, often made of stainless steel, that is used in cooking and pastry cooking to mix ingredients. The shape facilitates the use of a whip, beaters, or whisk.

OFFSET SPATULA

A utensil with a blade of varying length, it ends in a round or straight end and can be used to fold foods without damaging them or to cover — in other words, to cover a cake with an even coat of a mixture.

PARCHMENT PAPER

Paper coated with a thin layer of silicone that can be used in high temperatures and provides a nonstick surface without using a fat.

PARING KNIFE

A small knife with a short, pointed blade. Its sharp, smooth blade can be used to cut, peel, trim, or carve various foods.

PASTRY BAG

A flexible, waterproof cone-shaped bag at the end of which a tip can be inserted.

RHODOÏD

An acetate strip that is used to line dessert rings for making fruit mousses, charlottes, or bavarois. The smooth, shiny surface of this material provides a clean finish and edge and makes unmolding the dessert easier.

SILICONE SPATULA

A spatula made of silicone that can be used to gently stir mixtures containing, for example, the soft peaks of egg whites. It can also be used to scrape all the mixture out of a bowl.

SILPAT BAKING MAT

A silicone mat used to cook or freeze. Available in specialty stores. Other brands of silicone mat can be used as well.

TIP

The end piece that can be inserted at the end of a pastry bag. There are different types: plain, round, fluted, with or without teeth, etc. They allow for a more precise decoration using many different types of mixtures.

adidas

BRIOCHES, ROLLS, AND PASTRIES

SMALL CAKES AND COOKIES

ÉCLAIRS

TARTLETS

TARTS

CAKES AND ENTREMETS

PLATED DESSERTS

SCULPTED FRUIT/NUTS

INDEX BY

INGREDIENT

CÉDRIC GROLET'S ACKNOWLEDGMENTS

Thank you to Franka Holtmann, manager of Le Meurice Hotel, for her trust;
Thank you to Alain Ducasse for all the precious moments he has given me;
Thank you to Yohann Caron and Thibault Hauchard, my two assistants, for all the work they have put into this project and on a day-to-day basis;
Thank you to my team, without whom this book wouldn't have come into being;
Thank you to Maureen Wathieu for all her invaluable advice;
Thank you to Maison Colom for supplying me with high-quality fruit;
Thank you to Bernadette for all her unique products;
Thank you to Meurice for having given me the opportunity to do this book;
Thank you to Pierre Monetta for understanding my desserts and for having the gift for portraying them in his beautiful photos;
Thank you to Soins graphiques, and particularly to Pierre Tachon for his talent and the incredible work he carried out on the graphic design of this book;
Thank you to Emily Xueref-Poviac for accompanying me through my professional career.

COLLECTION DIRECTOR
Alain Ducasse

MANAGING DIRECTOR
Aurore Charoy

EDITORIAL MANAGER
Alice Gouget

EDITOR
Jessica Rostain

PHOTOGRAPHY
Pierre Monetta

GRAPHIC DESIGN AND ARTISTIC DIRECTION
Soins graphiques
Pierre Tachon, Sophie Brice, and Camille Demaimay

TRANSLATION
Cillero & De Motta

PHOTOENGRAVING
Nord Compo

The publisher warmly thanks Romane Brune for her invaluable help.

The publisher is committed to using paper made from natural, renewable, and recyclable fibers, sourced from wood harvested in forests managed under sustainable practices. In addition, the publisher requires its paper suppliers to adhere to a recognized environmental certification process.

Printed In China by Toppan on certified paper
ISBN: 978-2-84123-988-7
62-4856-1 / 11
Legal deposit 1st quarter 2026

Hachette Livre
58 rue Jean Bleuzen
92170 Vanves, France
contact-lec@hachette-livre.fr